Local Government
and the
States

Local Government
and the
States

Autonomy,
Politics, and Policy

DAVID R. BERMAN

M.E. Sharpe
Armonk, New York
London, England

Library of Congress Cataloging-in-Publication Data

Berman, David R.
    Local governments and the states : autonomy, politics, and policy / by David R. Berman.
        p. cm.
    Includes bibliographical references and index.
    ISBN 0-7656-1085-X (hc : alk. paper) ISBN 0-7656-1086-8 (pbk : alk. paper)
        1. State-local relations—United States. I. Title.

JS348 . B47 2003
320.8'0973—dc21

                                                                    2002030923

Printed in the United States of America

The paper used in this publication meets the minimum requirements of
American National Standard for Information Sciences
Permanence of Paper for Printed Library Materials,
ANSI Z 39.48-1984.

                                    ⊗

            BM (c)   10   9   8   7   6   5   4   3   2   1
            BM (p)   10   9   8   7   6   5   4   3   2

To the Smith Family: Wendy, Scott, and Taylor

Contents

List of Tables

Preface

This work culminates more years than I would like to admit thinking and writing about the relations between local governments and state governments. My chief concern is local governmental autonomy and the goals and activities of local officials as they seek to secure resources, fend off regulations and interventions, and fight for survival as independent units. I look at the intergovernmental struggle from the bottom up, making the central thrust of this work more local-state than state-local. Still, in the process, I examine a variety of political activity at the state level as well as the development and effects of several state policies.

This book consists of a blending and extension of numerous book chapters and articles that I have written as well as some new research efforts of a theoretical, legal, and historical nature. I have also combed through a great deal of historical financial information, much of which is found in two appendices. Overall, I offer a synthesis of my own work and that of a great many others from a variety of disciplines to present an overview of the legal, political, and broad intergovernmental environment in which relations between these units of government take place, the historical roots of the conflicts among them, and an analysis of contemporary problems regarding local authority, local revenues, state interventions and takeovers, and the restructuring of local governments. I find considerable reason to be concerned about the viability and future of meaningful local governments. While complete local autonomy is neither desirable nor feasible, there are good reasons to move more in that direction.

I would like to thank Christine Ulrich, Editorial Director of the *Municipal Year Book* for the International City/County Management Association, for allowing me to draw upon some of the material—including that picked up through surveys of municipal league and county association officials throughout the nation—that I have published in various editions of that publication. I owe a similar debt to John Kincaid, Editor of *Publius: The Journal of Federalism*, for permission to use portions of an article regarding takeovers that I published in that journal. I benefited greatly from discussions with longtime League of Arizona Cities and Towns Director John J. DeBolske and current director Cathy Connelly. I would also like to thank Clive Thomas, University of Alaska Southeast, for supplying me with information about local lobbying, my Junior Fellow assistant Mark Ramirez for some spot research, and my wife Susan for helping me with the editing. A special thanks goes out to Alvin Sokolow, University of California at Davis, for a very valuable critique of an earlier draft of this manuscript.

Local
Government
and the
States

1

Introduction

Relations between local governments and state governments in the United States have been of considerable interest to scholars from a wide variety of disciplines, including law, political science, economics, history, sociology, public administration, and public policy. Many have focused in one way or another on local autonomy, or local home rule. I use these terms interchangeably to refer to the general right of local governments to initiate policies that they deem appropriate and to be protected from outside interference in a sphere of activity reserved solely to them.[1] Local autonomy reflects the principles of local self-determination, local self-government, and local self-sufficiency. Some, too, equate local autonomy with local power, by which is meant the ability of local officials to make meaningful decisions. Scholars differ over how much power local governments actually have in this respect and, indeed, over how much power they should have.

To the student of intergovernmental politics, the term *government power* takes on a different meaning. In this context, it refers to the ability of one unit of government to influence another or, more broadly, to the ability of one type of government to defend or promote its interests in the intergovernmental system. How powerful are localities in this respect? Given their legal status as "creatures of the state," they are at a severe disadvantage in dealing with state governments. The legal status of local units, however, just begins to tell the story about their relationship with the states. Because of what one might call the forces of localism—local officials and their organizations being among them—state-local relations may be said to resemble those between the federal government and the sovereignty-sharing states. Still, though one can speak with considerable admiration of the political clout of the local forces, local officials have had reason to complain about their treatment at the state level, especially in recent years, and there is considerable room for improvement along the lines of local autonomy.

This volume is generally concerned with local governmental autonomy. I use autonomy as a standard by which to measure state policies affecting localities and as a criteria in framing policy options. I also look at how the goals and activities of local officials and the associations that represent them relate to the norms of local autonomy. As a study in intergovernmental politics, the book is additionally concerned with a multitude of questions concerning local influence on state policy. These concerns carry us into an examination of broader intergovernmental factors affecting this relationship, especially the influence of the federal government, the legal and political context in which local-state relations take place, the historical dimension of the conflict between the two units of government, and into issues or problem areas related to local authority and finance, state intervention, and the structure of local government.

This chapter, setting the stage for what follows, takes a broad overview of the philosophical, legal, and political debate over local autonomy and questions concerning local power; of the nature of the intergovernmental political battle, including assumptions about winners and losers; and of some operational theories about how local officials fit into the political process in the states and about how state-local issues arise and are resolved.

Law, Politics, and the Power of Local Governments

There is no doubt about the formal legal status of the approximately 87,000 units of local government in this country: they are at the bottom of the hierarchy of government, at the mercy of the states. To quote from the highly respected nineteenth-century authority on municipal law, Judge John F. Dillon, who did not mince words: "Municipal corporations owe their origin to, and derive their powers and rights wholly from, the legislature. It breathes into them the breath of life, without which they cannot exist. As it creates, so it may destroy. If it may destroy, it may abridge and control. . . . We know of no limitation of this right so far as corporations themselves are concerned. They are, so to phrase it, the mere tenants at will of the legislature."[2] Officially, cities and towns as municipal corporations are no better off than conquered provinces. Counties and other units of local government as quasi-municipal corporations—created by the state for its own purposes—are even worse off in legal status.

Among legal scholars, however, there has been considerable disagreement about the actual significance of this formal legal relationship between state and local governments, and a great debate has developed over just how much power local governments have and, indeed, should have. On one side, for example, Gerald E. Frug contends that legal doctrines, stemming from a deeply imbedded liberal ideology hostile to strong local government, have made American cities virtually powerless, unable to solve the problems that confront them or to control their future development.[3] Frug seeks to strengthen local government power. To him, a strong local government is vital to "public freedom," which he defines as the ability of people to participate in the basic societal decisions that structure their lives. To change things, however, will be no easy task: "The powerlessness of cities has become so basic to our current way of understanding American society that no modest effort to 'revitalize' the cities by decentralizing power can succeed. Real decentralization requires rethinking and, ultimately, restructuring American society itself."[4]

Richard Briffault, on the other hand, contends that the question of local powerlessness turns on how we define "power." According to Briffault, "If power is defined as a legally enforceable right to existence and continuation, to control local resources and regulate local territory and to prevail in conflicts with higher levels of government, then local governments generally lack power. There is no right to local self-government."[5] Yet, "If power refers to the actual arrangements for governance at the local level, then local governments possess considerable power."[6] Briffault, unlike Frug, looks at all municipalities—suburbs as well as cities. He finds that, in practice, most municipalities are far from powerless and that many have considerable autonomy over matters of concern to them. He also finds a strong commitment to localism in the political and legal culture of the country underlying this general autonomy. He does, however, concede that wealthy suburban municipalities are far better off than central cities when it comes to having the power to do what they want to do in light of their needs and priorities.[7] Along with claiming that the extent of local legal power is generally understated, Briffault is also skeptical about the net benefits of so much local power and about the value of extending local autonomy. He argues, for example, that localism reinforces territorial economic and social inequities and thus serves as an obstacle to securing social justice.[8]

While disagreeing about the amount and desirability of more local power, both Frug and Briffault point to the importance of the nation's political culture or belief system in shaping ideas regarding local self-government, and both demonstrate concern about the powerless status of cities. Both scholars reviewed a wide range of literature in making their cases, but neither of them gives much attention to political factors, other than broad cultural or ideological factors, that affect local governmental power or the particular problems of central cities.

How much power do local units have? How much power should they have? On the descriptive level, social scientists have generally agreed with Frug in regard to the absolute powerlessness of cities, although the constraints that they have found are not necessarily legal ones but rather a variety of socioeconomic and political conditions.[9] While there has not been much of an effort to pinpoint the cultural underpinnings for this phenomenon, those who find large cities powerless can point to a strong tradition in American culture that not only extols the virtues of small local governments but also carries a strong anti-big-city bias. Urban scholars, overall, have had very little to say about suburban governments, although one finds in the literature an appreciation of the fact that they are, on the whole, much better off than the older central cities.[10] One study of urban local governments in general suggests that local officials, while under numerous constraints, have at least the potential ability to make important decisions affecting the well-being of their citizens.[11] The related question implied here—about the extent to which local officials actually take advantage of their opportunities to assume authority and make important decisions—is one that we will turn to later.

The normative questions raised by Frug and Briffault concerning the desirability of pursuing local autonomy have long been debated by scholars and practitioners, and they frame the discussions in several of the following chapters. Proponents of shifting authority to local units have been able to draw upon a rich American tradition in which local governments are seen as closer and more responsive to the people and are praised for providing a venue through which people can develop habits of citizenship and a sense of civic responsibility. Self-governing local communities are viewed in this tradition as basic forms of social organization—extensions of the home and family—and as the backbone of democracy. Proponents of local authority also contend that local autonomy produces good public policy because it encourages initiative and experimentation and also places authority in the hands of those best prepared to develop solutions to unique local problems. Those who have a public-choice perspective find the vast number of local governments to be a blessing because it allows people to shop around for the type of community that best suits their needs and desires.[12] On the negative side, however, critics find local governments to be insensitive to the rights of minorities and too parochial, being indifferent to how their decisions affect the welfare of neighboring jurisdictions or the broader area where they are located.

Some observers would join the call for greater local autonomy or home rule if they could alter the size of existing local governmental units, making them either larger or smaller. Some reformers call for a shift toward metropolitan or regional governments to overcome inequities and better address area-wide problems. From the other side comes the contention that some local governments are already too large to effectively serve their citizens. Supporters of this view call for more neighborhood government or for the breaking up of existing municipalities into smaller units. Others want to restrict home rule to those jurisdictions that are capable of standing on their own and providing quality public services, that is, to make governmental performance the criterion for local autonomy. Historically, the battle over local autonomy or home rule in the United States has featured the preceding arguments. Much of the battle, however, has had not so much to do with debates over the inherent value of local government or its proper size as it has with the question of which set of officials, state or local, is the most virtuous or, more negatively, the least corrupt and incompetent.

Looking at the more purely legal and political aspects of state-local relations, many scholars have been struck by the considerable gap between the formal and actual power status of local governments, or, stated differently, between what state governments under prevailing legal theories might do to local governments and what they have actually done. Some observers have suggested that, essentially, political forces have, in effect, altered the legal relationship between states and localities. Political scientist Harvey C. Mansfield, for example, once declared, "The multiplicity of elected local officials, their statewide organizations, the county and city political machines, and the locally oriented legislators make state-local relations usually in fact federal, whatever the theoretical plenitude of state powers."[13]

The suggestion that political forces have, in effect, made the formal legal relationship between the states and local governments irrelevant seems here to be a bit of an overstatement. One still finds considerable discontent over the official legal status of local governments. Home-rule activists continue to find reason to take their case to the voters in an effort to, in effect, get local rights out of the political realm by having them safely tucked away in state constitutions. In another sense, the formal legal status of local officials as creatures and agents of the state continues to be important because it means that the constraints state lawmakers are likely to feel in dealing with localities are those imposed not on their power but on their decision to use their power. In the absence of legal constraints, nearly the only constraints that state officials have had to live with in dealing with localities are essentially political in nature. One might argue that the pressures generated by the political forces of localism—the elected local officials and their groups, the party and constituency ties of legislators and, Briffault would add, the general commitment to "our localism"—while not altering the legal status of local units, nevertheless gives local officials an opportunity to have things their way on some issues at least and to carve out a sphere of independent activity. Local officials, however, face considerable obstacles in exerting political influence on other governments. Moreover, it seems appropriate to conclude that local officials have not exactly zeroed in on local autonomy as an objective, particularly as this involves self-sufficiency. To them, there is good state intervention as well as bad.

Intergovernmental Politics

Given the broader political climate, it is not surprising to find that the disputes between the states and their local governments resemble those between the sovereignty-sharing states and the federal government. Just as states claim "states rights" in trying to fend off what they see as an overextension of federal power, localities rally behind the cry of "home rule" to protect themselves from state actions that they feel are intruding on their sphere of activity. When it comes to money, state and local governments, like state governments and the federal government, fight over access to tax resources and over funding responsibilities. Problems encountered by state and local officials in dealing with the federal government—preemptions, mandates, and the lack of assistance in meeting pressing financial needs—have also characterized state-local relations. Using rhetoric reminiscent of that used by Southern state politicians prior to the Civil War, some cities have even threatened to secede from their states.[14] In the early 1970s, Mayor John V. Lindsay of New York City called on the federal government to charter several "national cities" so that his city, which had a budget larger than that of the state of New York, and other large cities throughout the country could escape the "servitude" imposed by state governments.[15] The spirit of separatism has been kept alive by other New York City politicians serving after Lindsay—most recently by former mayor Rudy Giuliani, who, in the mid-1990s, called for a "new urban agenda" of city independence and self-reliance.

Although relations among the federal, state, and local units of government are often cooperative in nature, tension among these units is built into the intergovernmental system. Part of the problem are attitudes borne out of where individuals sit in the governmental hierarchy. John J. DeBolske, the colorful former executive director of the League of Arizona Cities and Towns, once summarized the situation with three axioms: (1) the level of government I am with is good, (2) any level of government above me is putting it to me, (3) any level of government below mine cannot be trusted and needs watching.[16] In other words, Miles' Law—"Where you stand depends on where you sit"—is fully applicable to intergovernmental relations: where a public official stands on a particular intergovernmental issue may well depend on which level of government he or she represents."[17] State and local officials bring different jurisdiction-serving perspectives to the job, be they members of commissions on intergovernmental relations or of financial control boards overseeing the affairs of some municipality. Tensions among state-local officials are also inevitable because the distribution of authority, finances, and responsibilities among them is often unclear. Given the intricacies of the intergovernmental system, governments regularly bump into each other. "With each bump," political scientist Thomas Anton has noted, "an opportunity is provided to challenge or affirm existing understandings regarding who should do what, on whose budget."[18]

In this country, as elsewhere, local officials have not only decried state intrusions on local authority but, at the same time, also have attempted to extract as much as they can in the form of resources from higher levels of government.[19] Going on the attack from a position of legal inferiority, they have advanced two very un-Dillonist and somewhat inconsistent notions to strengthen their position vis-à-vis the state: (1) local home rule as a means of enhancing local discretion and of protecting local prerogatives and (2) intergovernmental partnerships as a means of enhancing the ability of local governments to extract resources, particularly financial ones, from other governments. The local home-rule movement first gained momentum in the late nineteenth century in response to what many saw as an excessive wave of state intervention in the affairs of large cities. Since then, home-rule advocates have sought to maximize the ability of city officials to initiate action and to preserve a sphere of local activity beyond the reach of the state legislature. Carried to its fullest extent, local home rule creates a state within a state—or a federal relationship in which state and local governments have separate spheres of authority.

One finds evidence of intergovernmental partnerships involving local governments deep in the nation's history, but the partnership idea gained particular strength during the Great Depression of the 1930s. This idea is reflected in many programs in which localities, states, and the federal government assume varying responsibilities in program design, implementation, and funding. Applying the pragmatic-partnership approach, policymakers have made separate decisions about which governmental unit will deliver a service, which unit will set the service level, and which unit will pay for a service.[20]

Groups such as the National League of Cities, the U.S. Conference of Mayors, and the National Association of Counties have generally stressed the interdependency of American governmental units and lobbied for more partnership programs.[21] The local groups have traditionally thought largely in terms of federal-local partnerships that exclude the states. With the reemergence of strong state governments, however, localities have become more insistent on partnerships with that level of government as well.[22]

Local officials, in stressing home rule and partnerships, are, on one level, inconsistent. While home rule calls for governmental separation and competition, the partnership idea places emphasis on the need for cooperation among local, state, and federal governments, each of which is a unit in the same governing system. Combining "partnership" and "home rule" arguments, local officials have, in effect, been telling state legislatures and Congress, "Give us some money and leave us alone." In a general sense, one might argue that local governments have done rather well in both respects. Yet there is considerable tension in state-local relationships, as reflected in the attitudes and behaviors of public officials at each level, and, overall, in recent years things have not always gone the way local officials would prefer. Too often they have heard, "We are not going to leave you alone and we are not going to give you any money." In recent periods of economic stress they have also heard, "and we are going to take back what we've been giving you." More generally, from the state's point of view, the state-local partnership idea has limited appeal. State officials, particularly legislators, have little to gain by being generous in regard to local revenues and authority. Politically speaking, to state lawmakers, the benefits of assertive state action often appear to outweigh whatever costs there are in imposing state authority over local governments.

Winners and Losers

Within the intergovernmental system, we can find winners and losers, as some units expand their activities while others seemingly become less significant. Often, one unit expands its sphere of influence to fill a vacuum created by the failure of another unit to perform properly or to meet its responsibilities. At various times and places, for example, localities have lost powers to the states because they have failed to do the job expected of them. At times, local officials have ducked unpleasant tasks coming their way by claiming that they lacked clear authority—a technique that allows them to happily pass the buck to the state or federal government but also over time works to reduce their significance as governing units.[23]

From the 1930s to the early 1960s, state governments were the units generally being bypassed. Considered by many in and out of active political life to be behind-the-times, unprofessional, rural-dominated entities, states were either pushed aside or voluntarily retreated to the sidelines while cities and the federal government tackled the nation's important problems. As political scientist Charles Press put it, there was a general belief during this period that "the state governments would be left to putter about on unimportant matters."[24] For decades prior to the "one person, one vote" ruling of the U.S. Supreme Court in 1964—a decision that required the states to carve up legislative districts on the basis of population—big-city officials complained about being mistreated by malapportioned state legislatures dominated by "hayseeds" from rural areas. While the extent to which rural legislators were actually the villains is debatable, rural control provided an excuse for big-city governments to bypass the states and forge direct relations with the federal government. With legislative reapportionment, growing professionalism at the state level, changes in federal grants favorable to the states, U.S. Supreme Court rulings protecting states' rights, and a greater emphasis in Washington on devolution, the states came back and, in recent years, have increased their role in matters such as education and landuse planning, which have traditionally been handled at the local level.

In measuring the relative power of federal, state, and local governments, scholars have sometimes examined financial data, looking for shifts in control over revenue resources. We assume that the unit that raises the most revenues is more powerful because it is in a more commanding position in regard to determining policy priorities. For much of the nation's history, local governments raised far more on an annual basis than either the federal government or the state governments. This began to change during the Great Depression years of the 1930s, when the federal government pulled ahead and, since that time, extended its lead. Up to the late 1960s, local governments were still outdoing the state when it came to raising revenues (see Appendix A). In 1962, localities collected 53 percent of the combined state and local revenues. The states, however, began catching up, and by 1967, the two were almost dead even in revenue raising (the actual percentages in that year were 50.2 for local governments and 49.8 for state governments). In 1968, the states overtook local governments, and since the late 1970s have raised 55 to 56 percent of the revenues that state and local governments together have collected. Viewed in terms of their ability to control various functions such as education and land use and to generally control financial resources, local governments may be said to have lost considerable power.

One can, to be sure, come up with a more cheerful conclusion by abandoning the zero-sum approach to measuring power. Under the zero-sum approach, the amount of governmental "power" is a fixed amount (100 percent), and for one unit of government to get more power (a higher percent), it must gain at the expense of another unit. From the zero-sum perspective, if a state pulls ahead in revenue collections, local power must be reduced. Similarly, if we assume that education is a local function, zero-sum reasoning dictates that if any state moves into that field, be it a financial or regulatory move, the result will be a loss of power for localities. Many political activists and scholars look at the power aspects of state-local relations (and, for that matter, federal-state relations) in zero-sum terms.

Looking at power in a zero-sum manner does give but an incomplete view of what has been going on. One can point out, for example, that over time, there has been a tremendous growth in the revenue collections of both state and local governments and, because of this, both can be said in a sense to have become more powerful. Localities may be losing out relative to the states in regard to revenue raising and some other respects, but they are nevertheless collecting more revenues, spending more money, and probably imposing more regulations than ever before. They are, in effect, doing more than they have ever done, although less by themselves. One can also argue that the movement of the states into an area of policy traditionally reserved to localities may well in some cases have the effect of increasing the amount of policy making activity at the local level, making local officials even more significant and, in a sense, more powerful. This appears to have been the case, for example, in regard to the burst of education reform activity in the states during the 1980s. As one study reported, "The busier states became, the busier local districts became; everyone made more policy, and the arena for governance expanded."[25]

For proponents of local autonomy the intergovernmental game is a zero-sum one and, from this perspective, local governments have a great deal to worry about because of the movement of the states into areas where localities once called all or most of the shots and because local units have been losing out to the states when it comes to the raising of revenues. From the partnership perspective held by many local officials, these losses are negligible, especially when measured against increases in their activities. Indeed, local officials have been prominent among those in favor of shifting more of the financial burden to state resources, hoping thereby to reduce local burdens. The loss of local control has been offset, because thanks in part to the pressure of local officials, much of the state-raised money goes back to localities, where the actual spending decisions are made. Still, even those who take the partnership perspective have their own set of complaints against the states. They complain, for example, about state mandates that require them to pick up the costs of expensive programs and about states reneging on shared-revenue agreements.

In considering winners and losers or the extent of local gains and losses, one should keep in mind not only the different assumptions about the nature of the local-state power relationship, but that the relations between the two units are nowhere the result of a consistent, across-the-board application of a well-developed state plan regarding local governments. At any given time, we are apt to find programs in individual states moving in different directions, some showing strong centralizing tendencies, with others giving local governments greater discretion. Inconsistencies exist between and within policy areas. As an example of the latter, education policy in the late 1990s featured both efforts to diminish state control by, for example, abolishing state departments of education, and reforms such as academic bankruptcy laws that increase state control and indeed, the possibility that a state will take over the operation of local schools. In the education field as a whole, however, as noted later, one finds considerably more centralization than decentralization. The same is true of land use planning.

On the other hand, it should be noted that localities have experienced some gains. They, for example, appear to be of growing importance as makers of criminal law under their home-rule and police powers in legislating against public disorder.[26] Welfare in many places has also been an area of increased local activity, as several states have turned over much of the responsibility for administering programs and devising solutions to the work problem to county governments. Thanks to federal legislation, transportation is another area in which localities have increased their input in recent years.

Finally, in considering the balance of power between local governments and local units, one has to give consideration to differences among local units. The galaxy of local governments in the United States includes some 3,000 counties, 19,000 municipalities, 16,000 town or township governments, 13,000 school districts, and 3,000 special districts. The different types of local government vary in regard to their functions and to their relations with state governments. Municipalities and counties are general purpose units of local government, while school districts and most special districts engage in a single function. Compared to counties and other units, municipalities are far more independent from the state in terms of authority and revenues. Major differences, however, also exist among municipalities in regard to their size, wealth, social composition, and thus their status in the governing system. Throughout this work I have taken care to point out these differences when it is appropriate to do so. Much of my discussion concerns the general-purpose governments, particularly municipalities, because the autonomy issues over the years have generally been fought out with these units.

The Players and the Process

In carrying on the political struggle at the state level, a leading role is played by elected local officials, operating on their own or through associations. In describing this role, one has several paradigms from which to draw. They may, for example, be viewed as (1) agents of the state seeking to gain favor or usurp power, (2) representatives of autonomous governments, (3) partners or cogovernors with state officials, or (4) advocates who defend and pursue the special interests of their jurisdictions. These are not mutually exclusive roles and, over time, elected local officials could play all four. Local officials have, as has been noted, placed emphasis on the second and third roles by pursuing both autonomy and partnerships. State legislators, seemingly, have preferred to view local officials somewhat negatively as mere agents of the state or as special interest spokespersons.[27]

I look at local elected officials as sometimes playing the second role as one of the forces of localism, but more consistently, as being a part of an intergovernmental political system in which they, like officials at other levels, seek to promote and defend the interests of the governmental units that they happen to represent.[28] For local governments, these interests are viewed as including survival as an independent entity, securing and maintaining authority and economic resources, and securing a degree of autonomy in operation. Survival is the most basic interest, and local governments are the most vulnerable among all governmental units in this respect—they are the only ones having a real reason to worry about being abolished or consolidated with other units. I see local officials as being more focused on financial well-being than on simple autonomy.[29] The quest for revenues takes them to higher-ups in the federal as well as the state governments, and often brings conflict with neighboring local jurisdictions, for example, over annexation policies. On the other hand, seeing themselves under economic stress or under severe financial constraints, local officials also think in terms of financially rewarding partnerships with just about everyone: officials in the federal government, state government, other local governments, and those in the private sector as well. Working individually or through groups, they have been the prime players in building partnerships, though they have sought at the same time to minimize their loss of control or the degree of interference in their operations that the partnerships may bring.

The basic theme that governmental officials pursue institutional goals—their ideas of what is best for the health and prosperity of the units they represent—in their dealings with other governments has to be tempered with other possible explanations concerning their behavior. We are, for example, looking at elected officials, state and local, whose decisions regarding or touching upon intergovernmental matters may well reflect their electoral ambitions. One might expect to find, for example, elected officials at each level of government attempting to shift the political burden of voting for tax increases to the other level of government.

At times, too, the behavior of state officials toward local officials seems to best reflect the type of feelings that parents might have for their children. Political scientist Alvin Sokolow, for example, has argued that state actions such as coming to the rescue of local governments when they are suddenly faced with a financial emergency are "a natural outcome of the basic paternal relationship between the states and their local creatures."[30] Sokolow does note, however, "paternity does not preclude stinginess at times."[31] Similarly, Thomas C. Desmond, a state legislator from New York, came to this conclusion several years ago: "States view the cities at best as irresponsible, unruly children capable of an amazing amount of mischief; therefore, they must be held to firm standards, if necessary by an occasional fiscal spanking."[32] For their part, local officials commonly complain about being treated by state officials as children. Given their childlike dependency on the state, some have theorized that local officials are likely to be anxious to avoid confrontations with state officials.[33] On the other hand, others have suggested that local officials, like children, have ways of getting what they want. In this connection we might credit local officials with having the behavioral power of children who can exert their will, if in no other way, by causing chaos and disrupting the household.[34] In fact, the formal legal status of local governments has not generally caused local officials to behave as passive underlings, unwilling to confront the states. Every now and then, one even finds local officials engaged in short-term bouts of civil disobedience, for example, refusing to turn over taxes to state authorities and threatening to secede from the state.

Still, on a routine basis, the involvement of local officials with the state takes on more of the flavor of subtle interest-group politics and low visibility dealings than it does of a boisterous family squabble or a grand battle among governments. The problems facing local governments essentially require the cultivation of goodwill or the generation of enough political pressure to force legislators to change their behavior—to make the anticipated costs they would have to pay greater than the anticipated benefits. The success of local officials and the organizations representing them, like other interests, is greatly conditioned by the skills they bring to the job and the political conditions in which they find themselves. Generally, local officials and their organizations bank on and try to cultivate an attachment to the home-rule principle. This principle, as the Illinois Municipal League concluded some years ago, is " a kind of philosophy of government whereby state officials tend to restrain themselves from imposing requirements or restrictions on municipal governments and tend to maximize the freedom of choice granted municipal governments in making policy decisions."[35] Sometimes local officials are on the offensive, trying to secure more authority or revenues, and sometimes they are on the defense, trying to protect what they have.

The large set of issues affecting local governments that reach the state agenda have various sources. Some have their roots in community conflicts, representing, for example, disruptions caused by the efforts of community activists to ban billboards, make firms doing business with the city pay their workers higher wages, or make it more difficult for people to smoke in public places. Often groups go to the state challenging not only what local officials do on such issues but the decisions made directly by the voters on propositions submitted to them. Often a single dispute involving the action of one town in a remote part of a state can lead to a state law or regulation affecting the powers of all local governments in the state. Also, a state legislature, at the prompting of an interest group, might act to discourage other jurisdictions from doing what local governments are doing in other parts of the country, for example, suing gun manufacturers, by preempting such action.

State policymakers, it appears, tackle each policy issue affecting localities one at a time, looking for the best political solution under the particular circumstances rather than for consistency in the treatment of local governments. On many issues such as education reform, moreover, how their decisions impact local governments is likely to be only one of a number of considerations, and, among these, perhaps of only secondary importance or not much more than an afterthought to them. The state may be the aggressor in, for example, requiring localities to pick up the costs of expensive programs out of their own revenues. State intervention, however, usually is initiated not so much as the result of state officials suddenly deciding to impose their will on resisting local officials, but as a response by state officials to demands made by various groups unhappy with local performance, requests from local officials for assistance, or as an attempt on the part of state officials to resolve what are essentially local-local disputes.

Many of the disputes regarding local authority and revenues are either rooted in or heavily influenced by struggles between different regions of the state or different types of settlements (city, suburban, rural) with different economic, social, cultural, and political characteristics for control of state policy. The geopolitical disputes between big cities on one hand and rural areas and suburbs on the other—each trying to use state policy for its own purpose—fall into this category. Conflict in such cases revolves around the distribution of governmental favors. Each area of the state wants its "fair share" of state spending, and no area wants to subsidize spending programs going to other areas. More basically, the divisions often are between those jurisdictions that have money and those that don't. Not only jurisdictions in different parts of a state but also different types of local governments, for example, cities and counties, fight over who should pay for what services and how revenues should be allocated. Similar conflicts take place among local governments of the same type, such as municipalities. State action may also be prompted by conflict between local political leaders and groups of employees, such as police or firefighters, with the latter taking their case directly to the state level after failing to receive what they wanted on the local level. State officials, in many situations, thus function as intervening and sometimes unwilling umpires among feuding local interests and competing local groups. Still, even in this capacity, their decisions to intervene and how they intervene have repercussions for local autonomy and the general well-being of local entities.

Remaining Chapters

The following chapter looks at the broader, federal-state-local intergovernmental context in which local governments function: how they have attempted to influence that environment and their complaints in recent years over the quality of federal-local and state-local relations. Particular emphasis is placed on the development of federal-local relations—including the partnership idea that flowered from the 1930s to "fend for yourself" federalism in the late 1970s and the "devolution" period in the 1980s and 1990s—and how decisions at the federal level have impacted

the ties between the states and local governments. The federal government has, at various times and in various ways, "liberated" localities
from the states but has not always been there when localities need them.
"Liberation from the state," of course, has meant more dependence on
the federal government; still, from the local point of view, it is useful to
have some choice of governmental partners. Chapter 3 presents an overview of an array of political activity on the state level affecting state-
local relations. Much of the attention, however, is centered on the state
legislature, where the local governments have always had ample reason
to concentrate their resources, but even more so in recent years because
of federal spending and devolutionary policies (though the extent of the
latter has been less than might be assumed). From the discussion of
local lobbying in the legislature, we proceed to examine the involvement of governors, administrators, courts, and the voters on issues affecting state-local relations. In Chapter 4, we expanded upon one
dimension of the political struggle: the conflict between state legislatures and the largest cities in the states. This conflict has reflected a
struggle among different types of settlements but, as the chapter dem-
onstrates, has been crucial historically in setting the general tone of state-
local relations. State involvement in local affairs first occurred in large
cities and, in response, the citizens of large cities led the first real effort
for local home rule. In the last several years, local home rule as a means
of fending off state interference has once again become a rallying point
in many of our largest cities.

Chapter 5 focuses more directly on contemporary problems of local
authority. Here we find localities in a constant struggle to maintain local
home rule and to fight off mandates, preemptions, and prohibitions. Local
authority is regularly threatened by interest groups hoping to evade local taxation and regulation by taking their case to the state. Business
interests often successfully petition state legislatures to free them from
a tangle of diverse local regulations by preempting an area of activity.
On the other hand, state mandates requiring localities to pick up expensive programs reflect not so much the play of interest groups but the
force of state budgetary concerns. While local resistance to mandates
has led to several types of mandate reforms, the mandate problem is still
very much alive, and the solution, being fundamentally wrapped up in
the ability or inability of localities to defend themselves through the
political process, is far more elusive. Chapter 6 looks more closely into
what in many respects in the crux of the matter: disputes over money. It

looks at the revenue problems of localities, starting with a discussion of state financial controls, including the citizen-imposed tax and expenditure limitations (TELs) that have been fashionable since the 1970s. From this we go to an exploration of the local revenue base, developments concerning the local property-tax problem, trends and disputes over state aid, shifts in funding responsibilities to the states, and a discussion of what general steps states might take to improve the financial health of localities. In Chapter 7 we turn to the topic of state intervention, focusing on instances in which state governments have suspended local autonomy and taken over local governmental operations. In recent years, takeovers have been particularly common with respect to financially distressed municipalities and to "academically bankrupt" school districts. With the growth of proactive general legislation, such interventions have become commonplace. Yet, there is room to question their propriety, effectiveness, and value.

Chapter 8 takes us into a range of what I call restructuring issues. These revolve around state policies that affect the number of local governments and their survival as legal entities. Issues concerning restructuring have been especially salient in metropolitan areas where observers have been divided over whether we have too many or too few local governments, or whether our local governments are too small or too large. To local officials, state decisions about annexation, incorporation, secession, and consolidation are highly salient. Thanks at least in part to local pressure, state governments have generally not pushed for the elimination or consolidation of many governments or for strong regional entities. They have, however, in various ways, contributed to the proliferation of new local governments and thus created even more pressure to find ways to coordinate policies. The more that localities can do cooperatively, the less need there is for state or federal intervention in local affairs. Still, there are some doubts as to how much can be accomplished simply by relying on cooperative action among local units. Regionalism seems to be very much in the future and may well lead to new entities or more top-down restrictions on existing local units. Chapter 9, the final chapter, offers a summary and some concluding thoughts.

2

Federal, State, and Local Relations

Local governments in the United States are part of a highly complex intergovernmental system that operates on two planes: a vertical plane in which they interact with state governments and the federal government, both of which have the advantage of operating from higher levels of formal authority, and a horizontal plane in which they interact with their fellow local governments.

Our concern in this volume is with the politics of state-local relations. Yet, it is difficult to understand these relations without understanding the other elements and interactions in the broader web of intergovernmental relations. How localities interact with the states depends, in part, on how they interact with the federal government and, as is detailed in later chapters, other localities. In this chapter, we will examine the broad pattern of federal-state-local relations, focusing on the importance of the federal government in the system of vertical federalism and on the development of relations among the three units.

The Federal Connection

The various levels of government—federal, state, and local—are tied together by a variety of factors: money, programs, political parties, and the play of interest groups among them. Interest groups have an important role as vehicles for the movement of policy issues from one level to another. In the American political system, the inability of a particular interest to secure its objectives on one level of government often prompts it to take its case to another level—in effect, to forum shop. For example, in the mid-1990s, with proposals to increase the minimum wage mired in partisan politics in Congress and state legislatures, grassroots groups took the case for an increase to the cities.[1] At about the same time, the National Rifle Association was having trouble stopping gun-control action both in Congress and on the local level and thus looked to the states for support of their cause. Often, the federal government has become involved in an area of activity not so much because of the failure of the states to act, but because individual state action has caused or threatens to cause disparities or so much confusion that the affected groups pressure Congress for help. In the area of business regulation, for example, state laws such as those requiring product labeling have resulted in so much diversity that national companies have called for national uniform action to get away from the "fifty-headed monster." The pressure for uniformity is felt with equal if not even more intensity on the state level, as business concerns regularly petition state legislatures to free them from a hodgepodge of local regulations by preempting an area of activity.

Decisions made by Congress and federal officials are of particular importance in the intergovernmental system. One example of far-reaching federal legislation we refer to in various parts of this book is the federal Telecommunications Act of 1996 which was designed to increase competition in the communications sector. As implemented by the states, the law has had a largely negative effect on local zoning, land use, and right-of-way authority and local control over telecommunications firms, for example, those installing cable services, satellite dishes, or cellular antennas. It has also adversely affected local ability to tax telecommunications operations—depriving local governments of millions in franchise fees. On the other hand, as noted later, it has strengthened the ability of local governments to compete with private firms in the provision of telecommunications services. Another example of federal legislation shaking matters up is the No Child Left Behind Law which went into effect in January 2002. Designed to improve student performance and end chronic gaps in student achievement, the legislation puts pressure on states to take a strong role in designing and implementing standardized testing programs and on local educators to improve achievement across the board or else face a series of consequences ranging from having to pay for private tutoring to being taken over by the states.

Federal policy changes often have a ripple effect on state-local relations—sometimes giving local officials greater independence from the states and sometimes making them more dependent on the states. Local officials also function in an environment in which battles that they have been fighting in state legislatures and courts—for example, those regarding control over the telecommunications industry, the taking of private property, and Internet taxation—could at any moment be rendered moot by preemptive federal action.

The federal government affects state and local relations through decisions regarding grants-in-aid, mandates, preemptions, and policy choices that directly and indirectly stimulate activity on the state and local levels. Cuts or increases in federal aid to local governments make local governments more or less dependent on the state, and the ebb and flow of federal mandates on the states affect the ebb and flow of state mandates on localities and, thereby, the control that local officials have over their budgets and priorities. One important example of a direct federal influence on state-local relations is the Intermodal Surface Transportation Efficiency Act of 1991 (ISTEA), reauthorized by Congress in 1998 as the Transportation Equity Act for the 21st Century (TEA-21). Among other provisions, this legislation requires states to give local officials a greater role in transportation decision making. The federal government sometimes also leads by example. In the early 1990s, for instance, its concern with crime encouraged state and local governments to increase the severity of criminal penalties and the level of law enforcement. State and local authorities sent more people to prison for longer periods of time. Along with the heightened crime-fighting effort came larger state-local expenditures, especially for corrections, and state-local conflicts over which level of government was responsible for these expenditures.[2]

To some extent, both states and localities have become instruments of the federal government in implementing various federal programs. They have also become the beneficiaries of federal programs and, as such, have been anxious to support their continued funding and expansion.[3] State and local officials often also acknowledge that the federal government can come in handy through its regulatory power. During the early 2000s, for example, they were attempting to secure congressional legislation to require vendors to collect sales taxes on Internet or catalog sales.

While state and local governments have many common interests vis-à-vis the federal government, they also compete in trying to influence federal policy. Localities have long sought to cultivate direct ties with the federal government to receive assistance that they could not get at the state level. At various times, the federal government has been more than willing to "liberate" local governments from their states—to bypass the states and directly address problems facing local officials and to bring local officials into the shaping and implementation of policies directed at these problems. At times, too, the federal government has in various ways liberated local governments from state control by giving localities authority to do things that conflict with state law.[4] For example, some time ago, a federal court concluded that the city of Tacoma, Washington, could build a dam under a license from the Federal Power Commission, even though in doing so, the city violated state law. In this case, the construction of the dam could go ahead because the city's federal license preempted state law, in effect, giving a "creature of the state" the ability to defy the will of the state. More recently, some courts have also declared that the federal Telecommunications Act prohibits states from denying localities the right to provide communications services. Federal courts, like federal agencies and Congress, have also been able to empower localities, freeing them from state controls. In 1990, for example, the U.S. Supreme Court upheld the right of a federal district court to authorize school districts attempting to desegregate schools to raise property taxes in excess of the limits contained in a state constitution.[5]

Turning to the federal government for funds makes localities less dependent on the states but more dependent on the federal government. It thus offers little gain, if any, in terms of autonomy or self-sufficiency. From the political perspective, however, securing federal assistance for various programs or projects is more likely to be looked upon in a community as a victory—something sought or longed for—than as an unwelcome intrusion.[6] The same might be said for securing state aid for various purposes. From the local official's point of view, having a choice among potential benefactors is all to the good. From the federal point of view, there are also advantages in keeping localities in the mix and having them compete with the states for federal funds and for control over the implementation of federal programs.[7]

Local officials, particularly those in big cities, have enjoyed associating with the federal government, though the strength of these relationships has varied over the years, from a strong, positive relationship in the early 1930s to a weaker relationship in the 1980s and 1990s. Changes in federal grant and regulatory policies that began in the late 1970s dramatically rearranged the broad pattern of intergovernmental relations. One basic change was the slowing in the growth of federal aid. Another was an increase in the use of federal mandates that required state and local governments to undertake major expenditures. Tension among governments in the early 1990s were made more difficult by tough economic times as the federal and state governments attempted to balance their budgets by shifting costs to local governments, many of which were already finding it hard to make ends meet.

Galloping Intergovernmentalism

Direct federal-local cooperative relations have a long history in the United States but took on an added dimension during the Great Depression of the 1930s.[8] At that time, local officials from all over the country, but especially from large cities, clamored for federal assistance to meet the problems of unemployment, relief, housing, public works, and slum clearance. The federal government stepped in when it became clear that the states were not going to be of much help in providing relief or administering programs. It was during the Depression years, some have argued, that localities "began to emerge as partners in a system of cooperative federalism instead of being viewed as the bottom layer of governments in a three-tier federal system."[9] Officials of the United States Conference of Mayors, which was organized in this period as a big-city lobbying group, were happy to declare in 1936 that "for the first time in American history, cities are the recipients of direct Federal benefits without the necessity of having the Federal moneys funneled to them through the state governments."[10] Direct national-city relations were founded on a mutual dependence: the cities' need for national finances and the national government's need for local administrative support and leadership in swiftly implementing the emergency programs. The political nexus between the administration of Franklin Roosevelt and the Democratic party organizations in large cities strengthened these ties.[11]

Although the partnership between the federal government and municipalities was on the surface a voluntary one during this period, the local governments were, in fact, in no position revenue-wise to refuse the grants or the various strings attached to them that allowed the federal government to interfere in municipal operations, for example, to dictate how various projects were to be built or financed.[12] Still, mayors dismissed the idea that they were on the verge of becoming "puppets, whose strings will be managed by swivel-chair autocrats in some Federal bureau."[13] Rather, cities had simply entered "a new plane of Federal-city cooperation in the complicated business of governing."[14]

Cities were liberated from the state in the sense of being able to deal directly with the federal government. As a matter of policy, however, Congress did not ask or encourage municipalities with which it dealt to violate state constitutions or laws. Rather, it asked the states to make such changes in state laws as were necessary to enable municipalities to qualify for federal grants, for example, to permit municipal bond issues. States were generally willing to go along with these requests.[15] States also went along with federal programs in areas such as welfare, health, and education, which actually encouraged greater state supervision of local personnel.[16]

Groups representing local officials—principally the American Municipal Association (which later became the National League of Cities) and the United States Conference of Mayors—helped spur the rapid expansion of the federal role in domestic policy during the Depression years. From the 1930s into the 1950s, these local government groups also helped produce direct federal-local programs in such areas as housing and urban development and water and air pollution control that called for only minimal involvement of state governments. School districts, counties, and other units of local government also enjoyed relatively free access to federal funds. Although state legislatures provided a large portion of local revenues, they had only fragmentary information as to how much money was coming to local units from federal sources and how that money was being spent. Big-city officials argued that because of malapportioned state legislatures, the interests of their citizens were not adequately reflected at the state level and that they, as agents of their citizens, had no alternative but to appeal to the federal government. They also contended that federal-local ties should be direct, excluding the states, because the states had nothing to add to the provision of particular programs.

The broad theme articulated by prominent local officials and their groups during this period, however, was one of partnership or cooperative federalism, with its emphasis on interdependence, the sharing of functions, and a pragmatic focus on what has to be done rather on which level of government should do what. They attempted to steer talk away from "levels of government," which, as the executive secretary of the National Association of County Officials wrote in 1954, only led to conflict and confusion, causing federal, state, and local officials to act "as if we were independent governments rather than separate arms of the same general system of government." He concluded, "We are the same people motivated by the same ultimate desires and purposes, whether we exert our self-control through the city halls, the county courthouses, the State capitals or the National Government."[17] Nine years later, Vice President Lyndon B. Johnson sounded a similar theme, telling a gathering of municipal officials, "Whether we work as public servants in the City Hall or in the halls of Congress, whether we are at the state houses or the White House, we are all part of the same system—the system of government, the oldest unchanged system of government on earth.[18] Continuing, Johnson contended, "What much of the world has still to learn and we must not forget is that levels of government must function interdependently if any are to succeed independently. Ours is a system of interdependence."[19]

From the 1960s to the late 1970s, the nation experienced what one observer described as the "galloping intergovernmentalization" of nearly all governmental functions.[20] In reflection of the increased federal role, between 1960 and 1980 the number of federal aid programs rose from 132 to over 540, and the dollars involved grew from $7 billion to over $80 billion. A robust economy that swelled federal revenues made this explosive growth in federal aid possible. Spearheading the push were individual entrepreneurial members of Congress who, governors complained, were too inclined to leave the states out of the process. Many appeared to agree with this comment of Daniel J. Evans, governor of Washington from 1965 to 1977: "I think that if given a choice, the Congress would just like to ignore the states, go about their business, and handle all the problems of the country."[21] Governors criticized the new federal grant programs, especially those that appeared to empower localities.[22]

Organizations representing local officials helped produce the flurry of federal activity in the 1960s and 1970s. Although local officials were not completely happy about the initial results—they complained about meddlesome conditions attached to federal programs—they continued to press for more programs. As Harland Cleveland, dean of the Maxwell Graduate School at Syracuse University, noted before a gathering of municipal officials in 1960, "I have heard the annual convention of the American Municipal Association described as the occasion on which the nation's mayors get together to complain about federal intervention in municipal affairs—and demand more of it.[23] Working with others, the local groups reduced this intervention by successfully pushing for general revenue sharing and a shift in federal funding from categorical grants to less-restrictive block grants. General revenue sharing and block grants were popular with elected local officials because they gave them greater control over spending; the alternative form of aid, the categorical grants, sent funds directly to administrative agencies. The virtually no-strings general-revenue-sharing program, adopted in 1972, provided considerable relief to some 38,000 localities; some general-purpose local governments used it to cover 10 percent or more of their expenditures. Revenue sharing was especially beneficial to small local governments, which had not enjoyed much federal aid previously.

The expansion of federal aid and the addition of revenue sharing in the 1970s led to a large growth in the percentage of federal aid money bypassing the states and going directly to local governments. This percentage had climbed in the New Deal period, reaching higher than 29 percent in 1940, but it fell thereafter and was often under 10 percent until the early 1970s. From 1974 to 1984, localities received more than 20 percent of the federal monies, with the high point coming at 27 percent in 1979 (see Appendix A).

Some governors in the late 1970s were concerned about growing amounts of federal money going directly to local governments, but others supported direct federal-city programs. Martin J. Schreiber, governor of Wisconsin from 1977 to 1979, for example, argued that while there may be some governors "who are so thin-skinned and self-centered and egotistical that they just can't stand anything coming into their state without having their stamp of approval on it," that position was "nonsense."[24] Schreiber continued, "If the cities can mount a strong lobbying effort and get moneys into their communities that will help them do the job, God bless their souls and more power to them. I'll stand behind them. And I am not about to get into a fight with Congress that might diminish the impact of federal funds going to help people in our cities based on who or who's not in control."[25] In the governor's opinion, federal aid to the cities was in the state's interest: if the mayor of Milwaukee, "can get the federal government to help him out in the city of Milwaukee, that helps me out."[26]

Fend-for-Yourself Federalism

As the federal government's fiscal strength began to wane in the 1970s, Congress, with the enthusiastic support of President Reagan, took another look at federal aid for state and local governments and began to scale down the assistance programs. In 1979, federal aid constituted approximately 22 percent of state-local general revenues. By 1989, that figure that had fallen to 16 percent (see Appendix A). Termination of general revenue sharing in 1986 accounted for some of this decline. During the 1980s and early 1990s, federal dollars for municipal programs—including low-income housing, wastewater treatment, public transit, and job training—were also particularly hard hit. The 1980s brought further reductions in the percentage of federal aid bypassing the states to localities, from 24 percent at the beginning of the decade to 8 percent at the end. The Reagan administration was unusually hostile to federal grant programs in general and, in particular, to the idea of federal-local partnerships. Democrat Michael Dukakis, governor of Massachusetts, labeled Reagan's "New Federalism" as "New Feudalism" and contended that Richard Nixon was much more the true new federalist in attempting to put more flexibility into the system, while Reagan just wanted to cut the federal budget. According to Dukakis, Reagan's message was, "See you later. We're walking away from this. Good luck."[27] Unlike his predecessors, dating back to Franklin Roosevelt, Reagan challenged the notion that federal grants to state and local governments, in general, were necessary and useful.[28]

In the mid-1970s, the federal government began to compound the financial woes of state and local governments by using regulatory mandates rather than subsidies to encourage states and localities to take various courses of action. Congress proceeded to impose costly mandates in several policy areas, including air and water quality, solid waste, hazardous waste, transportation standards, labor management, health care, the courts, and corrections. Examples of congressional legislation creating unfunded mandates included the Americans with Disabilities Act, the Safe Drinking Water Act, and the National Voter Registration Act. Congress claimed credit for passing these programs and, by shifting much of the burden for paying for them to state and local governments, reduced the pressures on the federal budget. As a National Governors' Association official put it, "The idea is that they get the credit, we get the bills."[29]

Along with the slow-down in federal aid and the growth in costly federal mandates, increased citizen demands for services and a taxpayers' rebellion that led to more restrictions on local ability to raise revenues further compounded the financial problems of local governments in the late 1970s and early 1980s. The states responded to the financial woes of localities by assuming some of the costs that localities had been handling and by giving localities greater revenue authority. When it came to aid, the state response was spotty and, as the economic stress increased, unreliable. Although the states generally responded with increases in state aid, this response was less impressive on inspection than it first appeared. Total state aid to local governments jumped from around $83 billion in 1980 to close to $130 billion in 1986 and to $175 billion in 1990 (see Appendix B). Studies show, however, that this growth in state aid lagged behind the growth in state economies during the same years.[30] Moreover, as states experienced trouble balancing their budgets in the late 1980s and early 1990s, the percentage increases in state aid began to shrink. From 1985 to 1991, increases in state aid lagged behind increases in state and local spending.[31] With good reason, local officials showed little confidence in the states' willingness to provide adequate funding for the programs that local governments administered.[32]

To make matters even worse, when faced with budgetary problems brought on by hard times and reductions in federal assistance, state officials began to look with more favor on the idea of imposing costly mandates on local governments. In addition to passing along federal mandates to local officials, state governments imposed more than a few of their own. Local governments, being at the end of the path of "one-way federalism"—or what some call "shift-and-shaft federalism"—wound up paying many of the costs of government.[33] One estimate made in the mid-1980s was that localities dedicated over 40 percent of their expenditures to implementing federal and state mandates.[34]

The local lobby generally fell out of the loop in Washington in the 1980s and early 1990s as the federal government largely abandoned its role as an intergovernmental partner. Rather than uniquely constituted co-governors or partners, local officials and their organizations acquired the image of one among many special pleaders for special causes, and with a particularly large appetite. In the Reagan White House, cutting back aid programs was seen to be a matter of "defunding the left."[35] In the mid-1980s, Henry Cisneros, mayor of San Antonio and president of the National League of Cities, condemned the "disastrous dismantling of the federal-local partnership" and told an audience of municipal officials, "We must be determined to stand up for what is right in the face of what I can only call disrespect: a disrespect for our cities, disrespect for people who govern them, and disrespect for the people who live in them."[36]

In 1991, Sidney J. Barthelemy, mayor of New Orleans and president of the National League of Cities, criticized a "go it alone" approach to governance and suggested, "It is time for our federal and state governments to join us in examining the assignment of functions and the allocation of costs."[37] The same year, an angrier-sounding county official, D. Michael Stewart, chairman of the Salt Lake County Commission and president of the National Association of Counties, called for "a federal attitude that would view local government as a partner in an intergovernmental system, not as a special interest."[38] Three years later, Michael Pappas, president of the New Jersey Association of Counties, told the New Jersey state legislature, "Your pressures are no different than ours. We share a common bond. Your taxpayers are our taxpayers. . . . If there is no state money available for programs initiated by the Legislature, then the implementation of these programs by counties and municipalities should be optional and not mandatory."[39]

Local officials throughout the 1990s and into the twenty-first century commonly voiced concern about the quality of federal-local and state-local relations.[40] They worried about the loss of local governmental authority, the lack of sufficient discretion to generate revenues, the lack of support of federal and state agencies, and, perhaps most of all, the growth of unfunded mandates. Complaints came from everywhere, from general-purpose cities, towns, and counties to school boards and special districts, from appointed as well as elected officials, and from local officials in all parts of the country. Local officials did more than complain. On the mandate front, for example, they waged extensive lobbying campaigns, put together comprehensive catalogs with assessments of the financial impacts of mandates, took their complaints directly to the public through media campaigns and by attaching notices to tax and utility bills blaming mandates for increased taxes, initiated and campaigned for antimandate ballot measures, and brought court suits challenging the validity of mandates. During much of the 1990s, local officials were on the defensive, trying to fend off costly mandates and protect what funds they had from further cuts. Yet the most striking aspect of intergovernmental politics in the early 1990s was the increased willingness of local officials to fight challenges to their authority and financial well-being at both the state level—where, as discussed later, they succeeded in obtaining several mandate-related reforms—and at the federal level.

In 1995, Congress took a step through the Unfunded Mandates Reform Act to make federal mandating more difficult. This came, in part, as a result of an intensive lobbying effort by state and local officials and their organizations, which peaked on October 27, 1993, on what the local officials declared to be "National Unfunded Mandate Day." It was also greatly facilitated by the election of a Republican Congress. Mandate reform had been part of the House Republicans' "Contract with America." The legislation makes it more difficult for the federal government to adopt future unfunded mandates; however, it does not apply to mandates in effect before the law was passed. The law also exempts large categories of legislation from coverage, for example, civil rights mandates and mandates associated with major entitlement programs. Even where the act does apply, Congress is empowered to waive the requirement for full federal funding by a majority vote of the Senate or House.[41]

The Unfunded Mandate Reform Act has improved both the quantity and quality of information provided to Congress about mandates and has caused Congress to give greater attention to the costs of mandates.[42] There has been some dispute, however, about how to identify mandates. The federal Office of Management and Budget has determined that many federal regulations that look like mandates to state and local officials are exempt from the law's requirements. Practical problems also exist when it comes to estimating costs.[43] More importantly, thus far, the law has had only a modest impact on Congress's proclivity to enact mandates.[44] Given the history of similar legislation in the states, some authorities doubt that the federal mandate law will be very effective in that regard.[45]

Local officials also appear to have little to look forward to in regard to federal aid. While federal aid has increased in terms of total dollars since the late 1970s, it has generally declined since that time as a percentage of total state and local general revenues—meaning that state and local governments have been raising more of the revenues that they spend. Over the years, as has been noted, there has also been a shift toward funneling more of the federal aid directly to the states rather than to local governments. Of the some $324 billion in federal aid in fiscal year 2001, over 40 percent went to the Medicaid health services program (the federal government shares the costs with the states), and much of the remainder was distributed among highway, housing, welfare, and education programs.[46]

Since the mid-1990s, the federal level has devolved or returned some responsibilities to the states. States, in turn, have passed some of their new authority along to local governments. Under the Welfare Reform Act of 1996, for instance, states assumed the leading role in regard to welfare policies and several proceeded to give counties greater control over welfare programs. State-to-county devolution has been particularly noticeable in states that already had state-supervised, county-administered welfare systems, such as California, Colorado, Maryland, New York, North Carolina, Ohio, and Wisconsin. Legislatures in these states generally set basic policies regarding eligibility and benefits standards, for example, but give counties considerable discretion in designing plans to meet federal work requirements.[47] In many states, on the other hand, the shift of authority to the states—be it for welfare, environmental protection, or another function—has forced local officials to readjust to a new set of state supervisors and state controls. This has produced some local frustration and caused some local officials to complain: "We get treated worse by our state government than we ever did by the federal government."[48] For many more local administrators, however, devolution may not have brought much important change at all. Survey information from chief administrative officers in municipalities with populations over 100,000 in the late 1990s suggested, for example, that devolution had not really been a "big deal"—few of those surveyed reported any significant overall reduction in federal or state rules, regulations, or mandates affecting their work.[49] Among the few changes that seem to have mattered to local officials in being given a meaningful input in policymaking was the ISTEA legislation mentioned earlier.

Local officials continue to make use of national organizations such as the National Association of Counties, the National League of Cities, and the United States Conference of Mayors. Such organizations commonly describe themselves as "public interest groups" and collectively are known as the "intergovernmental lobby." These groups provide structures through which local officials can network, exchange ideas and information, and both shape and respond to changes in public policy. They also help educate people in Washington about the roles and activities of local governments in the federal system, define problems affecting local governments, and help shape the federal policy agenda. Local government groups continue to stress the interdependency of American governmental units and lobby for a greater federal role as partners in various programs. They have not altogether given up on the idea of a restored federal-local partnership. Yet they have little reason to expect a return to the generous policies of the 1960s and 1970s.

Another sign of changing times was the closure of the Advisory Commission on Intergovernmental Relations (ACIR) in 1996. This bipartisan body, created by Congress in 1959, brought federal, state, and local officials together to monitor the operation of the federal system, conduct studies, and recommend improvements. It was the federal government's only forum for addressing broad intergovernmental issues. Members of Congress, feeling that the agency had become irrelevant to the issues facing them, made some major cuts in ACIR's budget in the late 1980s and early 1990s before closing it down.[50]

Developments in the States

Disputes between state and local governments—often complicated by actions of the federal government—are nothing new. Over much of this nation's history, local governments have been in combat with their states—demanding more authority and greater financial resources, and complaining about expensive state mandates.[51] Some of the earliest disputes over such matters developed in the mid-nineteenth century between state legislatures and the largest cities within their boundaries—a topic that will be explored in Chapter 4. States backed off somewhat from intervening in affairs of large cities in the early 1900s; with the growth of federal-city relations, the states moved farther to the sidelines as far as the big-city problems were concerned in the 1930s and stayed there for several decades. From the mid-1920s to the early 1940s, however, one can point to certain centralizing trends in the states, particularly at the expense of county governments in such areas as welfare (in part because of federal laws), public health, and highway construction and maintenance. State police departments also expanded rapidly during this period, providing the bulk of law-enforcement activity in rural areas.[52]

Local officials have always been concerned about their ability to influence state policy. Still, basic changes in the intergovernmental system over the past several years—including a slowing in the growth of federal aid relative to local spending and the transfer of more authority to state officials—have made this concern, if anything, more pronounced. The movement toward devolution at the federal level has, as mentioned above, encouraged states to devolve some additional authority to the local level. While this may be all to the good, change under the banner of devolution also carries the risk that additional responsibilities will be placed on local units that lack the financial and technical resources to handle them. With good reason, many local officials fear that the states will use devolution as an opportunity to saddle local governments with yet more costs. Local officials have argued that (1) if devolution is to occur, localities should play an active role in program design, and (2) the states should not transfer additional responsibilities to local units without also transferring the necessary resources. Devolution raises questions not only about the proper allocation of governmental authority, but also about state and local government financial and managerial capabilities and the willingness of each level to assume responsibilities.

One does find some instances of devolution in state-local relations. However, one finds more signs of centralization as the state level, particularly as the states, with some prodding from the federal government, have moved into areas that have traditionally been dealt with on the local level, such as education and land-use planning. Localities have been losing control over education, in part, because of unhappiness with local property taxes. To get away from reliance on property taxes, many states have shifted the burden of financing education to state taxes. Increased state funding has been accompanied by greater state meddling in the details of policy. While school officials may be busier than ever before, the end product of these developments has been an undercutting of the overall control of local officials, particularly at the district level. If the unpopularity of property taxes were all that was involved, the drift toward state centralization could be reversed by shifting the funding of education to less controversial local taxes or to a more diversified set of local taxes. Yet, more is involved. For the courts, the central problem is the wide variation in the tax bases or resources of various jurisdictions— a problem that surfaces whatever local taxes are used—that permits one area to spend far more on education of children than can another area. Issues feeding the growth of the state role, moreover, have been as much about the quality of the educational product produced at the local level as they have been about local finance. Since the early 1990s a drive to make schools and school districts accountable for the performance of their students (or lack thereof) as measured by testing has been a central feature of state and national politics.

Difficult questions also have been raised concerning whether local governments are up to the task of regulating land use, in part because they are tied to developers as part of local "growth machines," but also because the nature of the growth-control problem is so vast and complex that it cannot be done through a go-it-alone, piecemeal, city-by-city approach. In this policy area, local officials have historically set off on their own, with little regard for the effects of their actions on neighboring communities or the region as a whole. Although local officials have stoutly resisted sharing authority with regional or state entities, continuing problems of sprawl and related transportation and pollution problems seem destined to lessen the amount of local control. Still, as noted later (Chapter 8), some types of possible state action are less intrusive than others.

Although local home rule remains an important legal concept, local governments still worry constantly about threats to their authority in the form of mandates and preemptions. For the past decade, states and localities have waged a major battle over mandates, with local officials staunchly resisting state efforts to require localities to undertake various activities and absorb the costs. Many costly mandates originated at a time when state governments were experiencing economic problems; by shifting costs to local governments through mandates, state officials could help balance their own budgets. State mandates, however, continue to be a problem even in states that enjoy healthy economies and budget surpluses. Local units, moreover, have had to battle to retain authority over such matters as the regulation of handguns and tobacco products.

State financial assistance to local governments—another perennial matter of dispute—comes and goes with changes in the general economy. With improved economies that bring both more revenues and a decline in pressures for Medicare and cash-assistance expenditures, states are better prepared to increase aid to local governments. At any given time, however, aid to general-purpose local governments (cities, towns, and counties) has to compete with demands for tax relief as well as with increased demands for spending in various areas such as education, health care, and corrections. Some state leaders, as a matter of ideology or philosophy, moreover, are simply not inclined to support state aid to localities. In recent years, some state-aid programs, especially those that share revenues with local governments for unrestricted purposes, seem particularly endangered.

After the turn of the century, we also find a renewed interest on the state level in sorting out responsibilities between state and local governments and among local governments. State officials seem more aware of the fact that the system of local government is largely what they choose it to be. State laws and regulations determine the number and types of local units, and their relative powers and duties. Whether intentionally or unintentionally, they also influence the strategies that local units follow when it comes to such basic functions as raising revenues and controlling land use—strategies that frequently bring them into conflict with other local units. States have the ultimate responsibility for umpiring disputes among types of governments or different local governments of the same type and for modeling the local governing system as a whole. States too, as problem solvers, are increasingly concerned with how to grapple with problems such as land use that spill over local boundaries and still retain some vestige of local control.

Local officials, for their part, can hardly ignore the intergovernmental environment: dealing with other governments is an essential aspect, and an increasingly important one, of the job of representing the people of a county, municipality, or school district. For local officials, however, there is no more important government than the state government.

3

Localities in State Politics

Former National Association of Counties executive director John Thomas noted in the early 1990s, "County governments live and die at the state legislature. What Congress does to us is irrelevant in many ways."[1] Thomas's comments could be echoed by representatives of municipalities, school districts, and other governments that, like officials representing particular types of local governments and particular occupational groups such as teachers and police officers, have to keep track not only of what the legislature is doing but also of a wide array of other activities at the state level involving governors, administrators, judges, and, increasingly so, voters.

Local Interests and the Legislature

Given the importance of decisions made by state legislatures to their well-being, it comes as no surprise to find that elected officials representing particular local jurisdictions regularly take their case to state lawmakers. Many cities and counties have full-time staff members who specialize in lobbying. Some have permanent, in-house lobbyists stationed at the state capitol. More than a few hire high-priced, well-connected private lobbyists with many clients to represent local interests at the legislature. One observer of this development in Texas has noted, "Clearly, the cities believe that if they are going to be able to compete in the legislative process then they are going to have to have hired guns."[2]

Local governments in some states are among the highest-spending lobbying groups. In California, where this is the case, individual local governments have been particularly active since the adoption of local property tax limitations in the late 1970s. These limits made local officials more dependent on state assistance, and local officials found that state funds did not come automatically: if they did not go after them, the money went somewhere else.[3] In California and elsewhere, local officials have no choice but to lobby. They have to go to the state capitol for defensive purposes if for no other. As an Arizona local governmental lobbyist once observed, "The organization that doesn't lobby the Legislature is the one that they do the bad things to."[4] Similarly, Dallas mayor Ron Kirk told reporters not long ago that he had nothing but sympathy for the cities that weren't paying attention to what was happening in the Texas legislature: "If someone isn't there to speak for the voice of those cities and present the other side, some very bad things can happen to cities and the people they represent."[5] For many localities, but particularly for those municipalities with local home-rule powers, the legislative task is primarily a defensive one of trying to ward off threats to their authority.[6]

Local officials from particular cities or counties may have considerable input through their state representatives in shaping state policies affecting their affairs and the welfare of the geographical areas they serve. This is so because state legislators tend to think locally; that is, they try to please those in their home districts if for no other reason than to build up support for the next election. Indeed, from time to time state legislators have been criticized, as they were in 1788 by James Madison in "Federalist Paper Number 46," for sacrificing "the comprehensive and permanent interests of the State, to the particular and separate views of the counties or districts in which they reside."[7] In the late nineteenth century, commentators such as James Bryce also found that the spirit of localism was dominating state legislatures and were particularly critical of the tendency of legislators to try to get the most they could for their constituents out of the state treasury.[8]

State legislators have been in a position to "do good" for individuals, organizations, and businesses as well as local governments in the areas that they represent because the common practice of legislative courtesy gives the leaders of a county or city delegation in the legislature considerable control over legislative matters affecting the jurisdictions that they represent, particularly if the legislators are in the partisan group that controls the legislature. Because of legislative courtesy, what passes as the will of the legislature is often, in reality, the will of a particular member or group of legislators from the area most directly affected by a piece of legislation.

Although state legislators may be presumed to be generally attentive to demands coming from their districts, on any given issue, this might not work to the advantage of elected leaders from a particular local government. What legislators hear in their districts from elected

local officials from a particular municipality may be effectively countered by what they hear from elected officials from another part of the
legislative district, from associations representing public employees such
as police officers who frequently make end runs to the legislature for
pension and other benefits, and from a variety of nongovernmental groups
within—or for that matter outside of—their districts. Legislators may
also seek to further the interests of a political party that is out of power
on the local level or pursue a more personal motive by working on behalf of some group or local faction whose goals are inconsistent with
those of local elected officials. Ideological factors may also separate
elected local officials from their state delegations.

The overall usefulness of the legislative delegation to local government officials further depends on the size, cohesion, and political composition of the delegation. In some cases, the delegation representing a
city may be too small or too weak—because, for example, members are
divided by infighting, or most if not all of the members are in the minority political party in the legislature—to do elected local officials much
good even if they were anxious to do so. Localities in these circumstances find it more profitable to rely on hired lobbyists. Local officials
may also be able to increase their strength in the legislature by forming
coalitions, for example, along regional lines, with other local governments. To be safe, cities are best off taking the advice of Hartford, Connecticut, mayor Carrie Saxon Perry: "We (cities) have few resources
and we're always hat-in-hand, so it behooves us to build a really good
relationship with state legislators—not only those from our city but
throughout the state."[9]

Most counties and municipalities leverage their lobbying through associations that focus on general bread-and-butter issues affecting the
welfare of their particular type of local government. These associations
are unique types of interest groups: those through which dues-paying
local governments attempt to influence policy at the state level. Local
officials working through local governmental organizations such as state
leagues of cities or municipal leagues are concerned about several issues, but none appear to be more important to them than state actions
that affect local financial capacity.[10] They want more revenue, more
authority, more state aid, more discretion in spending funds, and fewer
expensive mandates. From their point of view, however, state governments also need adequate revenue sources, because if the state revenue
systems fail, so too do state aid programs and whatever inhibitions there

are against shifting the costs for state programs to local taxes. As Suzette Denslow, executive director of the Tennessee Municipal League once noted: "If the state doesn't have a way of fixing its tax system, we know our money is at stake. . . . If they don't have a new revenue source, they'll have to look at where to cut spending—we're one of the places."[11] Often, local groups are on the defensive, trying to protect what state funds they have from being cut or to fend off costly mandates and unnecessary regulations. Local officials and lobbyists often succeed in securing a change or preventing some unwanted action, though, in the latter case, they sometimes have to depend on a gubernatorial veto. Historically, municipal leagues have focused simply on trying to explain their position to legislators, and, by some accounts, they have been more successful when opposing bills rather than pushing for change.[12]

Municipal leagues are prohibited, as are their member municipalities, from making campaign contributions and engaging in other forms of electioneering. For them, the key to success may well be in getting their members engaged, especially lining up mayors or other top elected officials to make vital, politician-to-politician contacts with state legislators. Pursuing their objectives, local lobbyists working for associations of local officials cultivate ties with legislators, meeting with them individually between as well as during legislative sessions to discuss their concerns and to inform them about local issues. Sometimes they work with business groups and others to magnify their influence in the legislature.

For local officials and their organizations, an essential goal is timely involvement in state decision making, that is, having the opportunity to express the local point of view before decisions are made rather than trying to reverse a decision: "It is a question of having the municipal point of view brought up before they make the decision, instead of having to go back and try to get them to reverse it. You don't get decisions reversed very easily. You want to get in there ahead of time."[13] To ensure timely action, state leagues encourage their members to charge someone with the responsibility of keeping in touch with the league lobbyists during legislative sessions and initiating a quick response to sudden developments by the mayor and other officials.[14] Along with "staying informed," league members are reminded "to thank legislators *regularly* and *publicly* for their work, their support, their votes." This can be done though such means as presentations of certificates or letters to editors praising helpful legislators. On the flip side, member cities are warned not to publicly criticize a legislator's actions, as this may result in the loss of a vote needed in the future.[15]

State municipal leagues and leagues of cities are among the oldest government lobbying groups in the country—dating back to the 1890s. They are known for relatively mild, straightforward, information-based lobbying, generally shunning media and public relations campaigns.[16] There have, of course, been some exceptions, such as the sharp and sometimes combative Herbert Bingham, executive secretary of the Tennessee Municipal League from the 1940s into the 1980s.[17] Bingham faulted state legislators for opposing centralization at the federal level while favoring it at the state level. In Bingham's view, municipalities "must fight at every session of the legislature the efforts of the state bureaucrats and the big special interests to curb and limit local powers and to centralize the control of various municipal functions in the state bureaucracies—either control them by law or control them by bureaucratic administrative controls."[18]

While leagues have usually shunned the spotlight, going public has been more common in recent years in campaigns against mandates or to save revenue-sharing programs. Among the more aggressive leagues in recent years has been the League of California Cities, which, feeling a loss of clout in the legislature, has set out to form a political action committee through which local officials can raise funds from various sources, including companies doing business with cities, to better enable the association to speak out on issues. Speaking of the need for the political action committee, one league official, noted, "Money talks in Sacramento. . . . We don't have any."[19] Member municipalities have also increased dues to create field offices around the state to create "grassroots networks" to draw support from local service clubs, chambers of commerce, and other organizations in lobbying legislators.[20]

Locally elected officials may have an advantage in gaining access to state lawmakers because the lawmakers view them as having a legitimate right to speak on behalf of their constituents.[21] Local officials, appointed as well as elected, also may be listened to because legislators regard them as experts possessing inside information that state officials need to know in order to make informed decisions and because their cooperation will be needed to implement a program. Some research suggests that state legislators with backgrounds in municipal or county government are particularly inclined to be sympathetic to the viewpoints of local officials and particularly skeptical about the value of state intervention in local affairs.[22]

As Anthony M. Masiello, who spent thirteen years in the state legislature before becoming mayor of Buffalo, New York, has noted, "I came out of the state system. . . . If I had been mayor first, I wouldn't have voted for half of that stuff." By "stuff," the mayor was referring to a host of mandates and restrictions on city governments in the state.[23] One of the positive but unintended consequences of term-limit legislation at the local and state legislative levels may be an increase in the number of state legislators who have had experience in local government.

Most legislators may think locally in the sense that they are inclined to represent the interests of individuals, groups, or governmental jurisdictions within their districts. This does not mean, however, that they have a natural inclination to think in terms of preserving or promoting a system of strong local government. Indeed, legislators may be reluctant to go in this direction because local governments are, in many respects, rival institutions. Legislators, moreover, have little to gain in an electoral sense by giving away authority to local governments, by improving the general level of state aid to localities, or by avoiding mandates on local officials. The election-based desires to personally do what they can for people in their districts—to be at the center of things as far as their constituents are concerned—makes state legislators less than favorable to the idea of transferring authority to local officials because this diminishes their opportunity to provide local services. Giving money away to local officials is likewise objectionable because it diminishes the resource base that legislators can use to build a political record. Mandates on local governments, on the other hand, are valuable to state lawmakers in an electoral sense because they save money for other purposes and allow them to claim credit for providing programs and services while avoiding the negative feedback that comes from levying taxes to support them. Given the stakes that politically ambitious lawmakers have in such matters, it is no wonder that the political resources of local units often fall short when seeking more general authority or more financial relief.

Whatever their actual level of success, city and county officials do not believe that they enjoy a privileged position with the legislators. Indeed, many feel that legislators regard them as a special interest seeking special favors, rather than as partners in the governing system.[24] Surveys suggest that representatives of county organizations often find that while state legislators are often open and friendly, this behavior does not necessarily translate into favorable legislative action. As one county association official has noted, "Legislators are fine in the coffee shop back home, but when they get to the capitol, they clearly work for the state."[25] Several association directors interviewed in one study felt that legislators treated counties no differently than from a tavern association or a tobacco lobby.[26] Indeed, at times, state legislators have dismissed local lobbyists not only as special interests but also as irritating poor-mouthers—people who claim that they don't have anything, can't get anything, and have no hope for the future.[27] The underlying problem may be, as a former League of California Cities lobbyist remarked not long ago, that "Legislators find out very quickly they can stiff cities with impunity. . . . There are no political consequences . . . . If they stiff teachers or prison guards, they die."[28] Similarly, another lobbyist for the league noted in regard to the lack of municipal influence in the legislature, "It gets down to priorities and we're not a priority because there is no political downside to hurting us or cutting local (city) services."[29]

When it comes to the influence of the local lobby, one does have to distinguish among groups. Political scientist Deil Wright concluded some years ago, for example, that county officials have had considerable leverage with state officials on important policy matters such as health, highways, and welfare. In several states, Wright noted that "county officials have greater access and impact at the state level than do city officials."[30] The local education lobby may, on the other hand, have the most going for it, considering the amount of state aid (over 60 percent of the total in the typical state) that is spent on that activity. In the competition for state aid, education funding has long taken priority over funding for other local spending needs. Not surprisingly, educators prefer to go it alone in dealing with the legislature. For lobbyists representing cities or counties that do not have responsibilities for education, the claim that education has on state budgets puts them in a bind. Writing in 1994, for example, a Minnesota League of Cities official noted, "Education is one of the responsibilities of the state identified in the constitution. Likewise, quality education is part of the culture of Minnesota and one reason the state has been so successful. But education is extremely costly and becoming even more so. Coupled with the political clout of the teachers' unions, education funding is perhaps always going to be a priority before cities. And even though we may not be able to change that, we need a strategy to deal with it."[31]

The education lobby may have slipped in recent years, because governors and legislators have wrestled control over the education reform agenda from people in the profession. Driving this shift has been public discontent over the cost and quality of education and the demands made by business leaders for a better-educated workforce. Local education officials appear to have shied away from the political struggle. Writing in the mid-1990s, for example, the director of the Center on National Education Policy in Washington, D.C., contended, "Based on my nearly 100,000 miles of travel over the last 18 months to talk to educators, parents, and legislators, I believe the reason for the lack of response is that educators are turning inward as a result of overly negative criticism of the public schools. They are more inclined to grouse among themselves about the unfairness of the criticisms, while all but giving up on any effort to convince elected officials that the schools need and deserve support. That attitude has deadly ramifications for public education."[32]

Nevertheless, the prominence of the education lobby in state government is attested to by several observers.[33] One recurring survey has regularly ranked this lobby among the top, if not at the top, in terms of influence.[34] The same source, based on the observations of informed observers in each state, has ranked general local government associations for cities and counties as sixth or seventh in terms of influence in recent years (behind a variety of business groups), while individual cities and towns have been ranked much farther down the list. In 1998, the survey ranked general local government organizations as being very effective or somewhat effective in thirty-eight states.

Over the years, associations representing local governments have encountered a set of legal problems not encountered by more purely private groups. At one time, courts commonly ruled that municipal and county governments could not use taxpayer money to lobby the state legislatures on matters affecting local interests.[35] Most of these decisions came down in the late nineteenth and early twentieth centuries—a time when corruption in municipal politics was a widespread and serious problem—and judges feared that allowing local government lobbying at the state level would only encourage corrupt activity. By the 1940s, courts were more permissive, though the fear of spreading corruption persisted, and some courts allowed local lobbying, only if the lobbyists did not exert "personal, private, or sinister influence on legislators."[36] Eventually, however, courts upheld local lobbying without qualification, and some courts even acknowledged that such lobbying had considerable value as a means of facilitating cooperation between state and local governments and of making better state policy. Along similar lines, state leagues officials have argued, that "Legislators need to hear from municipal officials. Otherwise, they are forced to make decisions on important local issues without knowing the impact on municipalities in their districts."[37] While courts have accepted the value of articulating the local government view through lobbying, without being totally consistent, they have been less generous when it comes to allowing local governments to engage in electoral activity. Courts have not taken it upon themselves to clarify the distinction between the two types of activity.[38]

Governors and Administrators

From time to time, governors have expressed concern over the quality of state-local relations. In 1949, for example, the always-eloquent Adlai E. Stevenson, at that time governor of Illinois, told the state legislature, "The people are impatient with bickering between the state and local governments over the division of duties and revenues. They look only for efficient and responsible government by whatever agency is best fitted."[39] At the time, the state government had a large financial surplus, but state lawmakers were in no mood to share it with local officials, even though the latter were in great need. Noting this, Stevenson declared, "There is no justification for preserving the frills and extravagances of one government when the functions of other governments within the boundaries of the same state have been reduced beyond the minimums of common welfare. The citizens of the towns and school districts of this state are also citizens of the state. We want no feast within our borders when there is also famine."[40]

Governors set the agenda for taxing and spending programs that generally impact localities and are often able to influence the fate of legislation directly affecting local governments. Several in recent years have taken a leadership role in education reform, calling for increased standards for students and even for state or municipal takeovers of poorly performing schools. Other governors, such as Nelson Rockefeller of New York in the 1960s, have led the effort in their states to address pressing urban problems that had long been neglected by state legislatures. Governors have had more of an incentive to address broader urban issues than have legislative leaders because, unlike them, they have a statewide constituency.[41] Some governors have immersed themselves in the day-to-day affairs of particular cities, in effect becoming an integral part of local governing coalitions. This has occurred, for example, in Hartford, Connecticut, where the governor has joined local leaders in an effort to bring about the city's economic recovery.[42] By leading the way in education reform and in urban economic development, governors hope to improve their states' ability to maintain and attract businesses. This gets them into local affairs, though not always in an unwelcome way. Some governors, such as Tommy Thompson of Wisconsin in the 1990s, have stimulated more concern from local officials by calling for comprehensive studies of state-local relations with the goal of adjusting funding and service responsibilities. On an everyday level, communication between local officials and the governor is enhanced by having an intergovernmental unit or officer in the governor's office to serve as a contact point and to help develop and implement intergovernmental policies.[43]

Much of state governments' day-to-day involvement in local affairs occurs through administrative supervision. Faced with ever-increasing and complicated urban problems, legislatures began in the early decades of the twentieth century to follow the lead of several European nations by delegating broad authority to administrative agencies to supervise local affairs. By turning to administrative supervision as an alternative to the then-common practice of direct legislative supervision, reformers hoped to bring increased flexibility in dealing with complex problems and a supervisory system characterized by greater expertise and professionalism and less partisanship. The emergence of state administrative agencies also represented an effort to establish minimum statewide standards in regard to finance, road building, health, education, welfare, and other functions.

Early on, state agencies employed devices such as reports and inspections to implement state standards. Cooperation, however, was the dominant theme of the early state boards and, indeed, those few who attempted to dictate policies to local governments found themselves in a world of political trouble.[44] The preferred and much safer route in dealing with localities was one of seeking local voluntary compliance with state suggestions.[45] State authorities did their work quietly and "usually showed singular tact in the credit they gave to local officials."[46] Still, early students of developing state agencies warned that administrative control may prove to be every bit as objectionable as legislative control.[47]

State administrative supervision began on a function-by-function basis; for example, a state department of education assumed the authority to implement legislative directives regarding education on the local level and a state department of welfare was charged with ensuring that county or municipal welfare officials were implementing state policy. State agencies with more general responsibilities in regard to local governments came later. Nearly every state now has an office of community or local affairs that functions as a clearinghouse for information and, on request from local governments, a provider of technical assistance on matters such as local finance and planning. Such services particularly benefit the smaller municipalities that lack well-developed professional staffs. Though the responsibilities of some of these agencies have broadened a bit, most have stayed true to the original notion that they should be as unobtrusive as possible and "blushingly provide assistance and information on technical matters to local governments, all the while being careful to imply no lack of competence on the part of sensitive local functionaries."[48] In addition to providing information and technical services, community and local affairs agencies serve as a communications link between state and local governments. One study has suggested that officials in these agencies "usually consider themselves as intermediaries between state and local governments, the advocates of the state point of view in dealing with local officials, and the advocates of the local point of view in dealing with state officials."[49]

Other state officials attempt to promote interlocal cooperation, coordinate state and federal grants to localities, and, in a far more intrusive fashion, to ensure that local units obey state laws, particularly in regard to budgetary and financial matters. States, from time to time, have established little advisory commissions on intergovernmental relations (ACIRs) or comparable organizations that provide a forum for state and local officials to discuss intergovernmental issues. Such bodies may also conduct research, analyze problems, and make recommendations to the legislature and governor. The range of their activities depends on the size of their budgets and staffs. Unfortunately, the budgets and staffs have generally been minimal and their reports and recommendations appear to have had only modest exposure and impact. The underlying problem may be political. As one observer noted, "An important problem for most state ACIRs and similar bodies is that they are not tied closely enough to powerful political figures. Lacking such support they exist in a sort of twilight zone of limited clout."[50]

Financial controls, as is detailed in Chapter 6, have long been a central feature of state policy regarding local governments, and in this area, one finds state agencies deeply immersed in monitoring the activities of local governments. One also finds relatively obtrusive state agencies in the area of local planning. States commonly require local governments to prepare plans for land, transportation, and housing development. Implementation of these planning mandates by administrative agencies, however, is highly variable, depending in part on the level of local government resistance. Administrative agencies wind up requiring what they find is practical and politically feasible in a given situation. As a consequence, the amount of actual planning by local jurisdictions is apt to vary widely.[51] In some cases, differences with local officials have existed over ends, for example, the need to control low-density development rather than the means of getting to an end. In the latter case, states can avoid conflict with localities by allowing them considerable discretion in reaching the shared goals. Differences over ends are much more difficult to resolve (see Chapter 8).

Historically, there has been much emphasis on the control and regulatory aspects of state-local relations—relations in which state agencies ride herd on local officials, monitoring their performance and threatening various types of action. Often, however, local officials are part of the clientele of a state agency; they receive the types of benefits that they want from an agency and, in return, help the agency establish a power base and preserve its resources and administrative autonomy. Such a relationship exists, for example, between local political leaders representing various local businesses and other interests, and state departments of transportation. Local leaders are as much a part of the constituency of state departments of transportation as are paving contractors and automobile clubs, who make up the traditional "highway lobby."[52]

State administrators in transportation and other areas often seek out the cooperation of local officials in securing support for programs in the legislature and in implementing programs. For their part, local officials do not hesitate to contact state administrators about issues in which they have a common interest.[53] Often, local officials or groups representing them are involved in the formation of state regulations affecting localities. Cooperation is facilitated because state and local administrators have a common, vested interest in keeping programs alive. Administrators at the state and local levels in various areas such as education and transportation are also tied together by common professional values and experiences.

The Courts

Courts, particularly those on the state level, have considerable influence on local governments. They regularly review local governmental powers, serve as a means through which various groups can challenge those powers, and condition the ability of local governments to challenge state legislative limitations on their authority. Historically, courts have encouraged lawsuits challenging local powers by taking a narrow view of local governmental powers and by making it relatively easy for citizens to bring lawsuits against local authorities. During the last half of the nineteenth century, several state legislatures sought to protect citizens against incompetent or corrupt local officials by giving them standing as taxpayers to challenge municipal ordinances in state courts. The courts followed up by showing a willingness to entertain taxpayer suits against local legislation, even when the amount of money involved was trivial, on the grounds that taxpayers had a general interest in good government.[54] Local governments remain relatively easy to sue and, as a consequence, local officials have to constantly worry about the possibility of expensive liability and other suits.

Over the years, state courts have built up an enormous body of case law specifying what local governments can and cannot do. They regard local governments as subordinate agencies of the state, which cannot act contrary to state policy. State judges play a major role in determining the extent of home rule (or general discretionary authority) on the local level. How they have performed in this regard, as was suggested in Chapter 1, is a matter of some disagreement. While some criticize the courts for being too restrictive of local authority, others see the courts as supportive of strong local government. Few would disagree, however, that state courts have had an important impact on local taxing, spending, and regulatory powers in general as well as in several policy areas, including education, environmental protection, land-use planning, and housing. Courts have been conscious of the fact that localism brings inequities in regard to education and housing and employment opportunities.[55] State courts in some places have prodded state and local units into addressing these problems. New Jersey courts, for example, have led the way in requiring each municipality in the state to assume its share of responsibility for providing low-income housing.[56]

Some of the most important recent state court rulings affecting local governments have involved the application of "the new judicial federalism"—that is, the growing practice of protecting basic rights on the basis of state law, particularly state constitutions. Following the retreat of the federal courts in civil rights and liberties cases during the 1980s, lawyers representing various groups began taking such cases into state courts using state constitutions to base their claims. Former U.S. Supreme Court Justice William Brennan was among the first to urge state courts to actively "step into the breach" left by the departure of the federal courts, and several state courts chose to do so.[57] A particularly salient application of the new judicial federalism has been in the area of school finance. Courts in several states have relied on the respective provision of state constitutions to invalidate local property-tax-based funding systems.

Traditionally, state courts have made it difficult for municipalities and counties to challenge state governments in court. Over the past several years, however, state courts have become more inclined to regard local governments as "judicial persons" with standing to sue their "parent" state governments on a number of matters—such as the state's failure to meet constitutional funding obligations.[58] In addition, state courts have become more willing to examine basic legal questions, such as whether state actions violate state constitutional bans on special or local laws.[59] Still, as noted later, courts have been of little help on the mandate question. On another dimension, state courts have been important to local governments as a means of directly pursuing specific policy objectives. Some localities, for example, have brought suits against the gun industry. In this particular policy area, however, some state legislatures have frustrated local action by cutting off local government access to courts.

The Voters

Initiative and referendum elections commonly feature measures of vital importance to local officials. Some of these originate with local government associations. Frustrated by their failure to get what they want through the legislature, they have sometimes taken their case for reform directly to the voters. Legislators are not likely to think highly of groups that do this—they are apt to be even angrier when groups go to the electorate directly without even trying the legislature—and those who take this route risk some political payback. Municipal leagues first turned to the initiative in the 1940s when the Arizona League of Cities and Towns used the ballot to secure a share of state sales tax collections for municipalities—the payback for this was a lawsuit that almost destroyed the league.[60]

Voters in recent years have frequently had a direct say on matters involving local authority and finance placed on the ballot by a variety of groups. With respect to mandates, citizens have often taken the side of local officials and approved measures requiring states to reimburse localities for state-mandated expenditures. On the other hand, voters have often favored proposals that force localities to reduce taxes and spending. Much of their antitax wrath has been directed toward the property tax. California voters set the pace in 1978 when they approved Proposition 13, which capped local property tax rates and limited increases in assessed property values except when the property is sold. As a result of voter adoption of a series of propositions since 1978, California now requires that virtually all local revenue-raising actions (taxes, fees, and charges) be approved by two-thirds or more of the voters.

Changes in the pattern of state-local financial relations in Oregon have also been underway since November 1990, when voters adopted initiative Measure Number 5. This severe property tax limitation measure restricts the amount that can be raised by cities, counties, and special districts, and forced several communities to make dramatic cutbacks in their services.[61] Measure 47, sponsored by an Oregon property taxpayers' group and approved by voters in 1996, further limited property taxes, though some of the force of the measure was modified by a subsequent vote. Overall, state officials in Oregon since 1990 have found it increasingly difficult to budget within the restrictions mandated by popular initiatives. In particular, they have had to grapple to come up with sufficient funds for education.[62]

Under the Taxpayers Bill of Rights (TABOR) constitutional amendment, approved by Colorado voters in 1992, both state and local governments voters must approve (1) any new state or local tax or increase in an existing tax and (2) any state or local spending increases that exceed a certain limit. Under the amendment, revenues that exceed the amount that state or local governments can spend must be refunded to taxpayers unless voters decided otherwise. The law also limits state government spending to changes in inflation plus population and restricts local government spending to population and property value changes.

Not long after the adoption of the amendment, one observer noted that "Colorado now has budgeting by popular ballot" through the "committee of the whole state" which operates "without deliberation, without priorities and without consideration of the relationships among expenditures items or between revenues and expenditures."[63] Along the same lines, the city manager of Greeley, Colorado, in 1998 denounced

TABOR as "an arbitrary, unnecessary intrusion on local governance" and one "effectively reducing the ability of elected representatives to make decisions based on local factors and needs."[64] Since 1993, Colorado voters have rejected the state's four major tax initiatives. About half of the requested local tax increases have passed, often after a difficult struggle. In the large majority of cases, however, voters have allowed local governments to exceed revenue and spending limits. While somewhat reluctant to increase tax rates, voters have been generally willing to allow local governments to spend money already collected.[65]

Throughout the nation, local officials have frequently lined up in opposition not only to proposals that directly limit local funding and financial flexibility, but also to proposals that limit state governments' ability to raise and spend revenues. Local officials fear that limitations on state taxing and spending will have two undesirable effects: first, states will be forced to pass on more of the costs for various programs to local governments—shifts that will bring either greater property taxes or reductions in service; and second, a successful campaign to limit state taxing and spending is likely to be followed by an equally successful campaign to limit local taxing and spending. Often, local officials also have much to lose directly with the adoption of proposals limiting state income or sales taxes because they share revenues from these sources with the state.

In addition to approving measures limiting local finances, voters have often favored measures that strip local governments of control over various matters. In several cases, interest groups have succeeded in circumventing local authority by putting proposals on statewide ballots that are designed to negate ordinances enacted by a few municipalities. Thus, even though residents of particular localities have shown their support for certain local actions (for example, controlling rents and extending legal protection to homosexuals), their decisions have been reversed by the wishes of voters in the rest of the state.[66] In recent years, voters also have played an active role in regard to land-use policies. In November 2000, for example, initiatives by the Sierra Club were on the ballot in Colorado and Arizona that would have forced most municipalities to create growth boundaries that ban development beyond a certain point. Both measures were opposed by developers and failed at the polls. Proposition matters, as the above discussion suggests, may be of enormous significance to local officials. Yet, they and their associations have encountered political and legal trouble when they have attempted to use public funds to influence voter sentiment regarding measures on the ballot. From time to time, legislators have proposed laws that would limit the electoral activities of organizations such as municipal leagues and county associations that are partially supported by public funds. In 1997, for example, the Washington state legislature passed a bill that would have prohibited an association from participating in statewide ballot issues if it received more than 25 percent of its income from public funds. This measure failed because of a gubernatorial veto. In 1999, however, a Washington state court of appeals put a chill on the ability of associations of local governments to participate in electoral politics by holding that associations representing counties were the functional equivalent of public agencies and, as such, could not take an advocacy position on ballot measures.[67]

All-in-all, from where they sit, local officials and their organizations have several individuals, groups, and bodies to worry about when it comes to promoting or defending their cause in the states. They have to shift their attention from venue to venue and have to react to developments on several fronts, often on very short notice. The legislative phase is important, but not necessarily decisive—one can still go to the governor, the courts, or the voters. Still, there is considerable uncertainty throughout the governing process, and local governmental associations, while far from powerless, have some distinct disadvantages when it comes to money and their ability to engage in electoral activity. Other problems relate to how local officials are perceived by legislators— sometimes as representatives of an inferior unit of government that they are free to handle in a paternalistic way and sometimes as just another set of special-interest advocates—and to the legislators' calculations as to what they have to win or lose by giving local officials what they want. Problems caused by these perceptions and political calculations may also sour local officials' relations with the governors. On the administrative end, we find a variety of relationships, depending in part on the mission of the agency, and, as anticipated by reformers, a more professional tone to the interactions—yet not always cautious and deferential. Mixed messages have also been characteristic of the courts and the voters when it comes to the local agenda.

4

Cities and the States:
The Historical Perspective

One of the most persistent themes in state-local relations has been the conflict between state legislatures and the largest cities in the states. This conflict has particular historical significance because the drive for local home rule originated in the struggle of large cities to free themselves from state legislative interference. The struggle first surfaced when state legislatures began to exert themselves in the middle of the nineteenth century—sometimes with good reason, sometimes out of corrupt or base political motives, sometimes invited, sometimes uninvited—into the affairs of their largest cities. Intervention produced a local home-rule movement intended to give cities greater freedom to take action without first securing legislative approval and to erect a barrier against legislative intervention in local matters. Partially because of the movement, cities enjoyed a large measure of independence for several years. By the 1930s, however, dislocations caused by the Great Depression prompted big-city officials to think not in terms of independence but of securing help to meet emergency conditions. They received little support from the states. Putting much of the blame on unfriendly rural legislators who held power, they turned to the federal government for assistance and were considerably successful in that endeavor. In recent years, however, ties with the federal government have weakened, and large cities have also had considerable difficulty exerting influence on state legislatures either to secure assistance or to secure protection against unwanted intervention.

The Growth of State Intervention

Many early cities came into being as the result of charters granted by proprietors or colonial governors. These took on the character of binding contracts that could not be altered or revoked without the consent of

53

city officials and thus constituted formidable barriers against the intervention of colonial legislatures in local affairs. Following the American Revolution, however, control over local governments shifted to state legislatures, and this was to make local home rule far less secure. Legislatures, with the eventual approval of the courts, abandoned the notion that municipal charters were inviolable contracts and came to regard them as nothing much more than statutes that they could make or amend as they saw fit.

A strong force behind this changed attitude was the desire of legislators to democratize local charters granted in the colonial era in such places as New York, Philadelphia, Newport, and Norfolk, which had, in effect, created closed corporations, thereby putting control of local government in the hands of self-perpetuating economic oligarchies. Charters in these cities limited both suffrage and office holding to merchants and other individuals who had a significant stake in the local economy, and the elite took full advantage of its power to impose a host of regulations on commercial operations.[1] Responding to popular unhappiness over the dominance of entrenched economic interests in the charter cities, state legislatures democratized the charters by, for example, extending participation in local elections to all those who could participate in state elections. State action represented a victory for democratic forces, but it also served to bolster state authority over local government and, as one authority has noted, to transform the municipal charter into "an instrument of the central authorities, subject to their changing policies and demands."[2]

Soon after gaining independence, state legislatures began granting municipal charters through special acts tailored for particular communities. They also retained control over any subsequent charter amendments changing the structure or powers of specific municipalities. Up to the middle of the nineteenth century, however, legislatures were generally reluctant to reach out in an uninvited way to interfere in the operation of specific cities, even though there was little doubt about their legal ability to do so. Cities were protected somewhat against state intervention by a tradition of local self-government. Many cities had been operating as units of government before state governments were organized. There was, moreover, little reason for the states to get involved: cities were largely self-sufficient units willing and able to take responsibility for their local affairs, while the states could focus on statewide matters.

Cities, however, were about to change in terms of size, composition, and problems. In 1790, cities of any size were few and far between. Philadelphia, with some 42,000 people, and New York, with around 33,000, were the largest. By 1830, the order had reversed, though both cities had swelled in population: New York to 202,000 and Philadelphia to 161,000. Urban dwellers in the United States increased from 5 to nearly 20 percent of the population from 1790 to 1860 and from 20 percent to around 46 percent from 1860 to 1910. Most of the growth occurred in what were already the nation's largest cities. Much of the growth of these cities came from the migration of Americans from farm areas, but foreign immigration, largely from Europe, also contributed a substantial amount.[3]

To some extent, state intervention in the affairs of large cities came as what we might consider a natural or understandable response to their growth. As they grew, cities lost their status as relatively isolated and self-contained units. Intense urbanization broke down their insularity: they became a part of a larger whole, the state, and their decisions on streets, education, sanitation, health protection, and a host of other matters became of concern to nonresidents as well as to residents.[4] Because of this, the distinction between a local responsibility and a state responsibility became increasingly blurred. At the same time, it became increasingly clear to many that local officials in big cities were unable to handle a burgeoning array of serious urban problems. Local officials were suddenly faced with the need to provide useable streets, sanitation facilities, an adequate water supply, and competent fire and police services. Doubts about the ability of cities to do these things or to head off impending crises, such as a cholera epidemic, often provided the incentive to form state commissions to perform various functions. Such commissions, legislators believed, would be able to act with far greater effectiveness than city departments could.

Along with doubts about the ability of officials in large cities to handle the magnitude of problems that they suddenly faced, many observers in the mid-nineteenth century, inside and outside of government, had doubts about the ability of urban citizens, particularly the many recently arrived immigrants, to govern themselves. Behind the condemnation of large cities, one found anti-immigrant, anti-Catholic, and anti-alcohol sentiments, particularly on the part of people in rural areas and state legislators from those areas. The rural-urban split in state politics often paralleled divisions between Republicans and Democrats, the former in the country, the latter in the city, and divisions between social and cultural groups, such as native-born Protestants in the country versus foreign-born Catholics and, later on, the "New Europeans" from southern and eastern Europe in the cities. Rural state legislators sometimes demonstrated a dislike of urban ways and were more than willing to use the state to crack down on illegal and immoral activities in the cities, especially drinking. Efforts to mold the character of people in the big cities brought state-imposed prohibition and blue laws regulating activities on Sunday. Rural concern about the honesty of urban elections increased with the rapid growth of foreign-born residents and led to state voter-registration requirements—for example, the creation of a list of registered voters—that were sometimes imposed only in the cities. Corruption in local elections affected not only local contests but also, and more important from the state legislators' point of view, contests for state and federal offices.[5]

Those wishing to intervene in the affairs of large cities in the 1850s could draw upon an already well-established tradition of anticity sentiment to justify intervention. In 1800, Thomas Jefferson expressed the bias felt at the time when he wrote, "I view great cities as pestilential to the morals, the health, and liberties of man."[6] Alexis De Tocqueville, reflecting on his travels to America in the early 1830s, also expressed concern about the urban rabble that he came across and of the danger large cities presented to the future of the republic.[7] Such sentiments were common in the popular literature of first half of the nineteenth century.[8] During the mid- and late 1800s, reformers commonly identified big-city corruption with the local branches of the major political parties—the "machines" headed by "party bosses"—that, with the help of immigrant votes, flourished in many cities. The machines performed necessary welfare services. These, however, were financed by bribes, kickbacks on contracts, and assessments on pay. Politicians regarded city hall as a prize, and to the victor belonged the spoils of power. Local bosses not only controlled city elections but often were able to influence the course of county, state, and national elections, which, in the era of the political machine, were commonly held at the same time as local elections. Vote fraud was a way of political life in the cities, as was collusion between the political machine and local businesspeople in the granting of charters to transit companies, in the procurement of city equipment and supplies, and in contracting for municipal public works.

Individuals and businesspeople could get just about anything they wanted by bribing a city official.

State legislature-city relations changed dramatically in the middle of the nineteenth century as state legislatures began the practice of passing large volumes of special legislation for particular municipalities. Much of this activity was invited, as local officials, faced with numerous problems caused by population growth, often pressed for legislation enabling them to take action and, indeed, were disappointed when their requests were denied. Demands for state action also came from local "good government" citizen groups who tired of trying directly to "throw the rascals out" of local government and to change local practices or policies. Alarmed by the corruption of political machines and by the low quality of city services, "good government" groups of leading citizens appealed to the state for assistance. Often, they were successful in having the state assume responsibility for particular functions such as police and fire protection.

In other cases, ambitious state politicians intervened in local affairs without much prompting in anticipation that sponsoring local bills would be a useful way of building up a following in the vote-rich big cities. The practice of legislative courtesy gave the leaders of the city delegation considerable control over legislative matters affecting their districts. State legislators from big cities often chose to further the interests of a political party out of power on the local level or, pursuing a private profit objective, to work on behalf of business interests in return for various favors. Many profited financially, for example, by receiving a kickback from a company that they had granted a monopoly on some urban service. Urban legislators enjoyed the benefits, both political and economic, of controlling city hiring decisions and the awarding of franchises and contracts. This type of corrupt activity grew in the 1870s as city governments increased their spending to keep up with population growth and to undertake projects that were deferred because of the Civil War.

State intervention in the 1870s also reflected strategic decisions on behalf of party leaders as to which policies would best promote their party's interests. In New York State, for example, Radical Republicans who came into power in 1864 on the basis of national issues soon began looking around for a way to sustain if not strengthen their position in a politically competitive environment.[9] Realizing that they probably could not rely on their chief vote-getting issue of opposition to the Confederacy in many future elections, they sought a program based on state issues. They found what they thought they were looking for in a host of problems in New York City. By focusing in on the heavily Democratic city, they hoped to cut into the strength of their well-organized opposition and to pick up electoral support. The Radical Republicans felt they had much to gain by exposing the corruption of city government and through "a new departure" of reforming the city from the state level. As a result of this reform effort, New York City lost control of the health and fire departments as these functions were transferred to metropolitan agencies whose boards were appointed by the governor. The state also became directly involved in the provision of education and housing services. The reform activity, however, did little to help the Radical Republicans gather in votes, and when the Democrats came back to power at the state level, they returned many of the services that the state had taken over back to city officials.

Throughout the 1860s and 1870s, the partisan aspects of state legislature and big-city conflict were often the norm as Chicago, Boston, New York, St. Paul, St. Louis, and many other large cities were controlled by one party while the state was controlled by another. Depending on the partisan split, governors and legislatures sometimes worked in conjunction with the political organizations that dominated big cities, for example, by channeling state patronage to the local organizations and sometimes setting out to destroy them.[10] Changes in the partisan composition of state legislatures often brought retaliatory measures. For example, Republicans coming into control of the New Jersey legislature in 1871 got back at the previous Democratic legislature for putting the police department in Republican Newark under state control by putting control of all public functions in Democratic Jersey City in the hands of state officials. The experiment was tarnished when the state-appointed city treasurer absconded to Mexico with the city's funds.[11]

During the last half of the nineteenth century, several states took over big-city police departments, putting them under the control of a state commission or board. State officials had a blank check: they were free to spend what they felt was necessary on law enforcement, and the cities had to pick up the cost of whatever police services the state officials decided upon. Not surprisingly, the per capita costs of police protection under state control were much higher than for those under city control.[12] Like other examples of state intervention, several factors motivated the legislators. Legislators in some states were prompted to take action after sensational disclosures of corruption in local police departments. Other takeovers reflected legislative disappointment over the failure of the police to enforce laws, particularly those regarding liquor. On the positive side, state legislators commonly expressed the belief that state-administered systems, being remote from local political influences, were likely to be more honest, efficient, and effective than city police systems. On the more material side, state legislators were attracted by the fact that police departments were large employers and thus valuable sources of patronage and party workers during campaigns. Takeovers with such practical political ends in mind were especially likely when the politicians running the state governments were of a different political party or a different political faction of the same party from those running the cities.

While the reasons behind state intervention varied, there was no doubt as to its devastating effects on local self-government. State legislatures, in effect, became "spasmodic city councils."[13] They regularly took away local powers, altered local structures and procedures, and, quite often, directly substituted local decisions with decisions made by the state law-makers. Legislatures felt free to create new local offices, abolish old ones, and take over municipal functions by transferring them to boards controlled by the governor and/or legislature. At times, legislatures voted to grant an exclusive franchise to a particular company that wished to operate a street railway or sell water and gas in a particular city. State intervention sometimes also meant legislation requiring a city to purchase out of its own funds a high-priced piece of private property for a city park or other public purpose—the sale being made not because the city wanted the property but because the owner wanted to sell it and, with friends in the legislature, could do so at an inflated price.

Legislatures further used their powers to pass "ripper legislation" that gave them the right to both appoint and remove municipal officials and to dictate how much cities had to pay them. Personnel changes might result from the legislature's discovery that officials had to be replaced for misfeasance, malfeasance, or nonfeasance in office or simply because they belonged to a political party different from that of the majority of the legislators. Salaries could go up or down, depending on how local officials stood with the state legislative majority. Legislators would prolong the term of a favored local official who appeared headed for defeat, shorten the term of a local official who was in the wrong party, or simply remove someone from office and name his or her successor. While legislators often justified state intervention as necessary to protect citizens from corrupt local officials, more than a few legislators seemed envious of the corruption they saw at the local level and hoped to get their share of the action.

Reflecting on his term of office as mayor of Brooklyn from 1882 to 1886, Seth Low noted that state interference in city affairs had become almost second nature and "not the least important of his duties, as mayor, was to protect the city from unwise and adverse legislation on the part of the State."[14] As mayor, he regularly went to Albany to fight off proposals to legislate local officials out of office, create new and useless local offices, and increase the pay of police and fire personnel. Taking stock around the turn of the twentieth century, New York City Democratic ward boss George Washington Plunkitt found that his city was ruled entirely by hayseed legislators at Albany. To the boss, it was bad enough that the legislators were hayseeds, but worse still that they were Republicans who looked at the city as a pie or "a nice big fat goose" that they could hardly wait to carve up and dole out in slices. Plunkitt complained that when it came to home rule, New Yorkers were worse off than the "downtrodden people of Ireland and the Russian peasants and the sufferin' Boers"; they had little or no control over their public facilities, were forced to live with Sunday closing laws and other state regulations on their behavior, and, to top everything off, were required to send in tax money to the state so the hayseeds could spend it on the farmers. As for the legislature, Plunkitt had this to say: "Did you ever go up to Albany from this city with a delegation that wanted anything from the Legislature? No? Well, don't. The hayseeds who run all the committees will look at you as if your were a child that didn't know what it wanted, and will tell you in so many words to go home and be good and the legislature will give you whatever it thinks is good for you. . . . And if you try to argue with them, they'll smile in a pityin' sort of way as if they were humorin' a spoiled child."[15]

By the last decades of the nineteenth century, rural legislators in many parts of the country, while in a position to intervene or not intervene, as they wished, had a problem: The rapid growth of cities was threatening their control. The surge in the population of Chicago—which nearly tripled its percentage of the state population from 1870 to 1890—so frightened the rural legislators that they refused to do any legislative redistricting at all in 1901 and, indeed, did not do so until 1955, even though the state constitution required equitable representation based on population and redistricting every ten years.[16] Around the country, state legislatures, by adopting apportionment plans that gave disproportionate representation to rural areas or by accomplishing the same result by refusing to recognize population shifts, severely reduced big-city influence in state politics.

Reform Activity

Looking back on the tangle of special legislation at the turn of the twentieth century, one scholar concluded, "Whatever the motive for state interference with municipal affairs, the result was almost invariably bad. State legislators soon proved that they were as inefficient and corrupt as city councilmen, and far less familiar with city needs."[17] Local protest over state intervention in the 1870s centered not so much on the question of whether the states could lawfully dominate cities, but rather on the wisdom or fairness of the state actions. Citizens complained that state mandates unfairly forced an escalation in local taxes. Many were bothered that state legislators took payment in return for granting favors to businessmen and others through special legislation. To be sure, local officials were also up to taking bribes and kickbacks for favors rendered when the opportunity presented itself, but, while local citizens hated to see their local officials behave badly, the offenses seemed to them to be even more outrageous when committed by state legislators, a set of "outsiders."[18]

By the 1890s, it had become clear in many parts of the country that state intervention had done little to cure the problems of the cities. Academics and citizen reformers began to think in terms of making strong city governments, that is, strengthening the powers of city government and the ability of cities to manage their own affairs.[19] Pioneering political scientist Frank J. Goodnow was among those who saw greater local autonomy as necessary to spur citizens into meaningful civic action. In 1895, he called for "the grant to municipalities of such a degree of local autonomy or home rule as will cause all municipal citizens to feel a healthy sense of responsibility for the evils from which they suffer, as well as an assured conviction that they have it in their power to work a sensible improvement in their condition."[20] Progressive reformers in the early twentieth century argued that municipalities needed to eliminate corrupting influences within their own boundaries and, in the exercise of purely local functions, free themselves from state legislatures no matter how "benevolent and well-intentioned that interference may be."[21]

By the late nineteenth century, urban reformers linked together through associations such as the National Municipal League set off in quest of local home rule and a form of local government insulated from state government that would enable cities to cope with the pressures of industrialization and urbanization. Some reformers came up with the businesslike council-manager form of government as the model for operating cities. Others suggested reforms such as the use of nonpartisan elections and holding local elections separately from state and local elections to isolate and protect the local political process from partisan influences.

Municipal officials also were organizing by the late 1890s as many began to join state municipal leagues or leagues of cities in the hope of bringing change. Local officials felt that they had a special insight as to what had to be done—that they were, as the founders of the National League of Cities were to later put it, "on the inside looking out" while others were "on the outside looking in."[22] Similarly, mayors calling for a general organization in 1897 contended that "true municipal reform must necessarily come from the work of those actually engaged in the duties of municipal administration, from a discussion of municipal problems by the men who are actually in the work and know its conditions."[23] Municipal officials in the 1890s saw their principal challenge to be one of securing greater powers, for example, to make structural changes that would improve city administration and gain greater independence from reluctant rural legislatures.[24] As time went by, big cities, acting on their own or through leagues, increasingly depicted malapportioned state legislatures that kept the rural interests in control as a major problem to be overcome.

The central thrust of the municipal reform movement that worked its way through the states in the late nineteenth and early twentieth centuries—a movement associated with the broader progressive movement—was toward lessening state legislative interference in the affairs of municipal governments, particularly the larger cities. Toward this end, reformers put limits on special or local legislation, gave municipal governments—particularly the largest ones—home-rule powers, and set out to replace legislative supervision over localities with a system of state administrative supervision. States adopted bans on the ability of legislatures to take specific actions, such as granting public utility franchises and, more broadly, passing special or local legislation affecting individual localities. The bans were intended to reduce the possibility that private interest or local political cliques would circumvent the local political process and secure what they wanted by directly working through state legislatures.

Yet, while reformers appeared to believe that special legislation was wrong in that it improperly interfered with local decision making and could result in discriminatory treatment, they also appeared to believe that when it came to legislation, one size did not fit all—that different types of local jurisdictions had different problems and that what was appropriate state action for one municipality might not be appropriate for another. To retain some of the flexibility offered by special legislation, reformers allowed states to pass general legislation affecting various classifications of municipalities based, for example, on the value of the property within a jurisdiction or on its population size. The problem was that a state's largest city often fell into a classification by itself. Because of this, the ban on special legislation as far as big cities were concerned was meaningless. Reformers, moreover, left municipalities of all sizes vulnerable to whatever "general" legislation the states chose to pass. The turn to state administrators was not intended to liberate cities at all but rather to make state supervision more professional and flexible but less political (partisan) than when conducted by legislators.

Local home rule, which provides the greatest local flexibility, discretion, and immunity from state action, made its first major breakthrough not in the East, where the problem of state intervention was often most severe, but in the Midwest and West. Action first came in Missouri in 1875 when delegates to the state constitutional convention, hoping to generate voter support in St. Louis for the constitution they were preparing, agreed to include a provision in that document giving charter-making powers to all municipalities with populations over 100,000—St. Louis being the only one in the category at that time. After Missouri, local home rule spread to California, Washington, and Minnesota by the end of the nineteenth century and to several other midwestern and western states shortly thereafter. The chief thing going for home rule, one legal commentator later noted, seemed "to lie in the absence of plausible arguments against it."[25] How, indeed, could anyone oppose local self-government or self-determination?

Although the states advanced slowly toward some type of local home-rule authorization, this movement did little to change or even challenge fundamental assumptions about the legal status of municipal or other local governments. Some jurists followed the lead of Judge Thomas M. Cooley, who, in the spirit of the Progressive movement, declared in 1871 that localities had an inherent right of self-government that the state could not take away.[26] Most jurists, however, agreed with Judge Dillon's view that local governments were nothing more than legal creatures of the state, totally subject to state control. To some extent, both Cooley and Dillon can be looked upon as engaging in "political forum-shifting arguments"; that is, arguments shifting power away from the level of government one fears the most. Cooley and Dillon wrote in the 1870s, at a time when governments at both levels were caught up in a panic caused by their issuance of railroad bonds. In Cooley's view, there was more to fear by vesting power in the state government, while Dillon felt that it was far more important to limit local power.[27]

Although Dillon won out, in the early 1900s local self-government in the nation's largest cities was generally healthy—the force of the home-rule movement had prompted state legislatures to back off somewhat from intervening in city affairs, state administrative supervision was in its infancy and largely cooperative in nature, and cities, with all the money they needed generated by property taxes, were able and willing to both expand their traditional activities and move into new ones.[28] Also by the early 1900s, states were returning control of police departments and other functions to the cities and were generally allowing the larger cities to go it alone in coping with major problems such as road building, heath protection, and sewage disposal. To deal with such problems, large cities both recruited and developed highly trained administrators who had little need for state assistance and, indeed, little tolerance of supervision by state administrators, whom they commonly viewed as unskilled paper shufflers and record keepers. The states, in turn, adopted the practice of isolating big-city bureaucracies from state programs.[29]

The Changed Environment

With the 1930s Great Depression, the self-confidence and self-reliance that large cities had been demonstrating over three decades rapidly diminished. The Depression cut into municipal treasuries—causing both a decrease in assessed values and an increase in welfare costs—and sent municipal officials and their organizations off to the state capitols in search of a share in more stable state-collected taxes such as those on sales, income, and gasoline. State aid was often slow in coming, particularly as it affected big cities—rural interests in the legislature were reluctant to support tax increases to meet crisis situations in urban areas—and when the states did act, the aid fell far short of what was needed. With the states unwilling or unable to help, local governments turned to the federal government for assistance. City officials spoke less and less of home rule—using it selectively to challenge unwanted state intrusions—and, as has been noted, more in terms of partnerships, particularly with the federal government.

While ties with the federal government grew with the addition of federal aid programs going directly to city governments—making city governments, in effect, agents of the federal government—relations between city governments and state legislatures steadily deteriorated in the 1930s, 1940s, and 1950s. Some observers blamed the big cities for staking out a go-it-alone policy as far as the states were concerned and for not trying hard enough to get along with rural legislators.[30] A more popular view was that rural legislators, who unfairly dominated state legislatures because of malapportionment, were largely indifferent to the problems of the cities and refused to either help the cities or allow the cities to do much on their own. Still another view was that the large cities suffered not because of the hostility of rural legislators, but because of the shortcomings of big-city delegations and/or the failure of legislators from urban areas—the big cities and suburbs—to pull together.

In the late 1930s, the author of a federal study looking into the problems of urban government, Harold B. Smith, found that the historic struggles of the cities with rural legislatures had, if anything, become worse.[31] Part of the problem, Smith contended, was that the rural legislators had had "little opportunity to sense the struggles of cities to meet the new responsibilities of government thrust upon them by thousands of new inhabitants."[32] Smith, on the other hand, was also critical of the practice of legislative courtesy and of how urban representatives had taken advantage of this practice for their own political advancement. In the early 1950s, reformer Richard Childs also blamed both rural forces and big-city delegations for the poor treatment given cities by state legislatures.[33] Joining the discussion in the mid-1950s, Thomas C. Desmond, a New York state legislator since the 1930s, claimed that the short-changing of cities by states had little to do with rural representatives, as they were "by and large disinterested and [did] not mix in city affairs," and put most of the blame on legislators from the cities.[34]

Many city officials in the 1960s also refused to view rural legislators as the main cause of their problem with state legislatures. Some, such as

Cincinnati councilman Charles P. Taft and Milwaukee mayor Henry W. Maier, saw suburban representatives as being far less sympathetic than rural legislators to the needs of large cities. Taft noted in 1962, "Our own representatives, state representatives from Hamilton County, go to the capitol usually with no municipal government experience or contract, and often they come from the suburban areas where the concern of the population is not quite the same as ours—about relief or about the core area, or about a number of other things. These representatives often have no real contact and acquire no real understanding of city problems. In my own experience, I have found intelligent rural members quite reasonable about many, if not most, of the city problems."[35] Maier told his colleagues, "It seems to me that it is an oversimplification to say that the basic conflict in states is between urban and rural areas. . . . My own experience in the state senate has indicated to me that the greatest pressures against legislation favoring the central city do not come so often from the rural areas as they come from the suburban municipalities. This is not always the case, but it is often the case."[36]

In fact, rural squires were not always unresponsive to metropolitan needs.[37] In many places, big cities probably had more determined enemies among suburban legislators. Still, whatever the precise political obstacles, big cities had reason to complain about the treatment they received from state legislatures. During the 1930s, 1940s, 1950s, and early 1960s, conservative rural legislators commonly joined with conservatives from urban areas, particularly from the suburbs, and much of the business community to check the liberal-labor coalition and the "radical" voting power of the masses found in big cities. In the end, city residents paid a disproportionately high percent of the taxes and received a disproportionately low percent of the services. While programs in education, welfare, slum removal, and urban development were neglected, there was plenty of money for road building, particularly for "farm to market" roads.[38] Business groups, along with organized farming and mining interests, found state legislatures easy pickings when it came to escaping local taxes and regulations and the demands of organized labor.

Several cities during the 1960s intensified their efforts to get a fairer apportionment of state legislatures, that is, one in which representation better reflected population. Following a speaking tour of the country, for example, Mayor Ben West of Nashville, Tennessee, reported to his colleagues in 1962, "I told as many people as would listen to me that our cities and towns were voiceless in their state governments; that the calculated, systematic disfranchisement of the urban citizen was the biggest, the greatest, political embezzlement of our times for the fact was his vote had been taken away from him and given to the pigs in the pens and the cows in the pastures. I cited figures to prove that the pigs and cows of a rural county in my state had three times more representation in the hallowed Halls of the General Assembly in Tennessee than the citizens of my county."[39] The efforts eventually led to the U.S. Supreme Courts' one person, one vote, 1964 decision in *Reynolds v. Sims.*[40] This victory, however, did little to help large cities in much of the country.

By the mid-1960s, when reapportionment of state legislatures finally began to take place, large cities in much of the country were losing out in the competition for population to suburban areas and, as a consequence, gained very little in representation because of the new population standard. Indeed, in many places they would have eventually benefited in terms of representation if reapportionment had not taken place. At any rate, by the 1970s, some big-city mayors had begun to think twice about "the bad old days" of domination by rural squires. "'At least you could buy the rural legislators!' Chicago Mayor Richard J. Daley reportedly complained after a difficult day of trying to negotiate with the new suburban leadership in the Illinois legislature."[41]

Big cities in many states have had a weakened position in state politics in recent years because their populations have been relatively stagnant, if not shrinking, thus causing them a loss in legislative representation, and because they have remained Democratic strongholds while voters, statewide, have leaned Republican, often giving their states Republican governors and Republican-dominated legislative bodies. In the mid-1990s, such shifts had made life much more difficult for Chicago, Cleveland, Detroit, New York, and Philadelphia. City leaders in these and other places found Republican legislatures inclined to take a more conservative path when it came to state aid for cities.[42] Although Republicans did not seem to be interested in humiliating the big cities just for the fun of it, they did try to gain control of patronage and revenue-rich city facilities such as airports, stadiums, and waterworks. In Illinois, for example, this meant stripping power away from various boards and districts in Democratic Chicago and shifting it to the state or to agencies in the suburbs under Republican control. During one skirmish in 1995, Mayor Richard M. Daley (the son of long-time Chicago Mayor Richard J. Daley) short-circuited a legislative plan to turn control over the city's airports to suburban Republicans by entering into an interstate compact with Gary, Indiana, to form a new airport authority. The legal maneuver surprised and outraged the GOP-controlled Illinois legislature, which, in retaliation, passed legislation repealing pay raises that the Chicago city council had recently voted for council members and the mayor. Republican Governor Jim Edgar, however, opposed this effort and vetoed the measure. Edgar told reporters, "Despite the repeated assertions of the proponents, this legislation is widely perceived to be retaliatory and would increase tensions between leadership in the city of Chicago and those who champion suburban interests. . . . We need to ease—not escalate—those tensions."[43]

In Michigan, a series of confrontations in 2000 between the Republican legislature and the Democratic-voting city of Detroit—involving the legislature's attempt to remove residency requirements for employees, change the method in which city council members were selected, and take control over the city's water and sewer department—fed into an intense but unsuccessful effort for more local home rule. At about the same time, similar disruptions occurred in Pennsylvania as the Republican legislature took over the Philadelphia Parking Authority, long prized for its patronage appointments, and eliminated residency requirements for teachers that were on the books in Philadelphia and Pittsburgh. Said the Democratic House minority leader about the Republicans, "They campaign . . . proclaiming their allegiance to smaller government and local control and then they arrive in Harrisburg breathlessly anxious for the state to cudgel the big cities into immediate submission."[44] Complaints have also come from Democratic mayors of big cities in Ohio in recent years over how they have been treated by legislatures dominated by suburban-area Republicans. In complaining about the legislature in 2002, the mayor of Akron noted: "We (cities) are almost looked at as a liability. We want them to look at us not as enemies but as partners."[45]

In the long run, local home rule, like the "reapportionment revolution" of the 1960s, has wound up to be something of a loss to big cities. In a sense, home rule came at the wrong time. It emerged when what were purely local problems had become too much for the cities to handle on their own and when they were too extensive for the states to properly ignore. By the 1930s, big cities had all but abandoned the goal of home rule insofar as that meant revenue self-sufficiency and had come to favor the establishment of an intergovernmental arrangement in which they were partners with other governments in the broader governing system—an arrangement that recognized interdependence rather than independence of governments. While home rule continued to have utility as an argument for fending off unwanted state intervention—though often failing in that purpose—it also worked against the cities by becoming a legislative excuse for denying requests for aid and ignoring urban problems.[46]

For proponents of local government reform, home rule also became something of a headache in that it became the rallying cry of small local governments fearful of being consolidated with other local governments or of being gobbled up entirely into a new metropolitan government. As one observer put it in the early 1960s, home rule had "been distorted not only to protect the right of the people of a city or other local unit to govern themselves in local matters, but to continue the existence of such a body politic until doomsday."[47] With population shifts outward from their boundaries, home rule came to mean less and less to big cities but more and more to satellite communities that feared being absorbed by the cities. Big cities also became torn between critics who contended that they were too small and ought to be reunited with their suburbs in a metropolitan government and those who said they were too large and should be decentralized down to the neighborhood level.

5

The Authority Problem

Politically, the dispute over local autonomy has shifted over the years from when the major issue was whether large, central cities should separate themselves from the state, especially the legislature, to one of whether suburban and small-town governments should be allowed to enjoy the benefits of independence, regardless of the consequences. Home rule offered by state statutes or constitutional provisions to certain categories of municipalities, be they central city or suburb, large or small, and to certain counties, however, has meant at best only modest gains in terms of the ability of local officials to initiate action and to be protected from state interference in their operations. Home-rule jurisdictions have little of the protections against arbitrary state action that private corporations, also chartered by the states, commonly enjoy. Legally, the basic rules remain the same: local governments are the legal creatures of the state, subject to state control. Local officials have had to worry about their authority to take action and have been kept busy trying to fight off expensive mandates and state limitations on their authority through various types of preemptions and prohibitions.

Home Rule

While judges at various times and places have claimed that there is an inherent right of local self-government, the dominant legal view has been that cities, counties, and other local units are the legal creatures of their states. Consistent with this, courts have also commonly applied Dillon's Rule of strict construction, named after nineteenth-century Iowa jurist John F. Dillon, to limit the power of local governments. Said Dillon, "It is a general and undisputed proposition of law that a municipal corporation possesses and can exercise the following powers, and no others: First, those granted in express words; second, those necessarily or fairly implied in or incident to the powers expressly granted; third, those

70

essential to the accomplishment of declared objects and purposes of the corporation—not simply convenient, but indispensable. Any fair, reasonable doubt concerning the existence of power is resolved by courts against the corporation, and the power is denied."[1]

According to Dillon's Rule, local governments must obtain specific legislative authority for virtually everything they wish to do. Legislators in Dillon's Rule states are busy passing bills affecting one or a few local governments and are immersed in minor local matters at the expense of policy issues of statewide interest. Localities in such situations can and sometimes do take advantage of their apparent helplessness. In Alabama, for example, the dominance of the state has given municipal officials the opportunity to deflect citizen complaints over services by asserting that they have no authority to do anything about whatever problem citizens happen to be complaining about.[2] Usually, however, most localities in Dillon's Rule states bristle at their lack of authority to initiate action or to prevent state interference in local affairs.

Nationwide, Dillon's Rule has been somewhat eroded by judicial rejection of the rule and by state constitutional or statutory requirements that courts give a broad interpretation to the powers of local governments. An example of the latter is Article VII, Section 34 of the Michigan Constitution which reads: "The provisions of this constitution and law regarding counties, townships, cities and villages shall be liberally construed in their favor." Courts, however, have been known to be slow in changing their approach to construction even when encouraged by the legislature to do so. In North Carolina, for example, courts have found it difficult to abandon the application of Dillon's Rule, even though the legislature in 1971 adopted a rule of broad construction for the scope of local governmental authority.[3]

To circumvent Dillon's Rule, several states have also given home-rule authority to local governments. The traditional and most common form of home rule gives local governments that qualify under state constitutional or statutory provisions—for example, a municipality with a certain population size—the right to make decisions without specific grants of authority on local matters and limits the power of the state to intervene in local matters. The goal of this approach to home rule is to create an *imperium im imperio* for municipalities by making them a state within a state and to construct a strict division between state and local powers comparable to the notion of dual federalism. In practice, however, courts have found it difficult to distinguish between what is a local affair and what is of statewide concern and have usually resolved uncertainties in favor of the states. In some other states where home rule exists, Alaska being an example, state statutes or constitutions avoid the problem of distinguishing between state and local concerns by taking a devolution-of-powers approach, that is, by authorizing local units to carry out any function or exercise any power not expressly forbidden or preempted by the state—in essence, a reversal of Dillon's Rule. The National League of Cities (then known as the American Municipal Association) promoted this approach in 1953 in an effort to strengthen the ability of municipalities to initiate policy. Courts, however, even in these states, have tended to interpret the law to limit municipal action to a small sphere of local affairs.[4]

As noted in Chapter 4, most states have constitutional prohibitions on special or local legislation, that is, acts affecting only a particular local jurisdiction such as a county, city, or town. To avoid such legislation, states commonly classify municipalities and counties by a criterion such as population size or the value of the property within their jurisdictions and require that the legislature treat all cities in the same category equally. The problem is that legislatures may design the classification schemes so that only one jurisdiction (often a large city) falls into a classification—a move that gives state legislatures nearly as much freedom in dealing with their large cities as they would have under a system that allowed special legislation.

In practical terms, the amount of actual home rule depends not only on state constitutions or laws, but also on how judges have interpreted these laws and, perhaps most fundamentally, on how legislatures have chosen to live up to the spirit as well as the letter of the law. The scope of local authority in every state is highly influenced by judicial decisions. Even when essentially the same home-rule law is involved, state court interpretations of local authority vary widely. Wyoming's experience provides an example of this phenomenon. In the hope that Wyoming courts would interpret the law as liberally as Kansas courts had, Wyoming patterned its home-rule provision on the one used in Kansas. Wyoming courts, however, did not follow the precedent set by Kansas courts, choosing instead to keep Dillon's Rule alive in the state.[5]

Although many of the questions concerning local authority end up in court, state legislatures settle many more of them and, not surprisingly, usually on the side of the state. Regardless of their constituencies, ideologies, or party identification, state legislators are generally reluctant to relinquish control over local governments. From where they sit, local officials usually see more local autonomy as being a good thing. From where they sit, state legislators—regardless of party, ideology, or type of constituency they represent—tend to see more local autonomy as a potential problem.[6] As an Alabama state senator said of county governments, "I oppose any Home Rule. We exist for checks and balances to keep county commissioners from doing anything unreasonable. Those good old boys back home can cook up things that might not be palatable to the local public."[7] In some states, particularly in the South, there is a long tradition of giving state legislators a great deal of control over legislation affecting the localities they represent, and the legislature routinely passes whatever local legislation the local delegations propose. This practice effectively compels local elected officials to constantly go back to the legislative delegation for additional authority. State legislators may like the arrangement, but local officials sometimes tire of playing Mother, May I."

Various groups also worry about local government discretion. Business groups, for example, often oppose local home rule in the belief that local governments will or might use their newfound authority to impose more business taxes and regulations or take other steps that will adversely affect profits. When it comes to regulations, they find it easier to deal with a single state legislative body and a single set of standards than with a multitude of local government authorities imposing a variety of regulations. Builders, for example, have called on state legislatures to adopt statewide building codes in place of a system in which building requirements vary from city to city. Merchants who sell tobacco products also commonly favor statewide standards over local regulations. Likewise, those in the wireless communications industry, anxious to avoid a patchwork of municipal and county ordinances, have pressed for uniform statewide laws regarding the use of cell phones. In all these situations, local officials counter that important differences in local needs and conditions make varying regulations necessary.

In practice, the amount of local discretion varies by region, by the type of local government unit, and by the type of function performed.[8] The tradition of local self-government is, for example, stronger in New England than in the South, where prohibitions against special legislation never caught on and local bills are common. Throughout the nation, municipalities generally enjoy more discretionary authority and a greater measure of legal protection from state interference than do counties or other units of local government.[9] Local governments of all types generally have more discretion with respect to structure and functions than with respect to raising and spending revenues. Research suggests that demographic pressures—such as increases in urbanization, level of educational levels, and income—may encourage state officials to give localities more discretion in regard to structure. However, changes in discretionary authority about other matters—for example, which functions are to be performed—are linked to slower-changing cultural conditions and managerial factors.[10]

Over the years, the view that local governments should have home rule or greater discretionary authority has gained ground: some degree of home rule is available for municipalities in 48 states, and county governments have such powers in 37 of these 48 states with viable county governments.[11] State extension of home rule to counties has sometimes faced the opposition of municipal officials who fear that giving counties a charter will upset the local balance of power.[12] The fact that home rule is available, however, does not mean that local governments—municipalities or counties—will apply for it, or indeed, if they receive it, that they will exercise the authority that home rule gives them. In some places, municipalities have not sought home-rule status because the legislature has given them the discretion to do many of the specific things that they want to do and has thus made it seem less necessary to secure charters. By allowing municipalities the right to elect rather than appoint a mayor, for example, the Arizona legislature appears to have eliminated a particularly strong incentive to secure a home-rule charter. In some states, there is doubt about whether home-rule municipalities actually have much more or any more power than non-home-rule cities.[13] Even in Dillon's Rule states, the incentive to go after a charter may be lacking because the legislature has adopted a large number of statutes that collectively allow discretion on a broad range of matters.

Nationwide, only one out of every ten counties eligible to adopt a home-rule charter has done so. In some cases, voters have rejected charters, municipal as well as county, because they saw them as being linked to the elimination of elective offices, were uncertain of what changes would occur under the new arrangements in regard to taxes, or, simply, were in no mood for change.[14] Often, it appears, adoption rests on the existence of a special set of problems that local officials and citizens feel could best be handled under home rule, for example, the ability to tax certain types of businesses currently escaping taxation.[15] Particularly—but not exclusively—in jurisdictions that have recently attained home rule, both county and municipal officials are often uncertain about how much authority they have, and therefore they feel more comfortable receiving specific grants of authority from the legislature. In such instances, home rule has little effect on local authority or the workload of state legislatures.

In sum, although some progress has been made in achieving greater local discretion, many local officials are still caught up in a routine of constantly returning to the legislature for authority or to head off interference in their operations. The battle for home rule continues, though often with disappointing results. In 2000, for example, the Vermont Municipal League tried, without much success, to give cities and towns greater authority to adopt and amend their charters without securing legislative approval. This effort was in reaction to the Vermont legislature's practice of altering charter amendments passed by voters in various localities in a manner contrary to the actions of the voters. In other cases, locally approved changes had failed to go into effect simply because the legislature did not get around to voting on them.

Also in 2000, a similar set of grievances sparked a movement in New Hampshire, a Dillon's Rule state, for a constitutional amendment giving municipalities the authority to pass their own laws in areas where the state has not acted. The New Hampshire Municipal Association and several local officials led the fight for the amendment, contending that the cities and towns had to constantly secure state legislative approval for routine decisions—such as whether they could impose a user fee for trash removal, post warning signs on frozen ponds, or allow their citizens to pay municipal bills with credit cards. Business groups were prominent in the opposition, contending that local home rule would lead to more regulations and a crazy quilt of conflicting local laws. Similar arguments had helped defeat earlier efforts to obtain home rule in 1974 and 1984. In November 2000, the effort once again went down to defeat, failing to win even a simple majority (a two-thirds majority was required). In Michigan, meanwhile, conflicts between the state legislature and the city of Detroit over a host of matters—and a growing perception that the legislature was eager to impose its will on all local governments—powered a drive to place on the November 2000 ballot a constitutional amendment that would require a two-thirds vote of the legislature (rather than a simple majority, as under current law) to eliminate or preempt local ordinances or charter provisions. As in other states, the issue found local officials and their organizations on one side and business groups, such as state and local chambers of commerce, on the other. Voters rejected the proposal by a large margin.

All in all, there are few practical barriers to state intervention into what one might consider local affairs. On the average, about one-fifth of the hundreds of measures introduced yearly in state legislatures significantly affect local governments. State laws extend to several aspects of local governmental operations. Some determine the general level of local authority and the types of governmental structures that local governments can adopt. Other types of state laws concern incorporation, annexation, consolidation, and intergovernmental service agreements. In recent years, states have also passed a great deal of legislation relating to local governments' finances and personnel management. State laws often set debt limits, mandate public budget hearings, require a referendum for bond issues, and outline property-assessment methods. Most local governments must abide by state laws requiring employee training and workers' compensation.[16] Among the most common types of regulations affecting local governments are open-records and open-meeting requirements. The latter have been particularly controversial, leading to charges that particular laws hamstring local officials and their staffs in doing their work and create unreasonable criminal offenses.[17]

State legislators have long felt the need to intervene in local affairs to protect citizens from dishonest or incompetent local officials. They have also acknowledged a duty to address problems that spill over local boundary lines and to ensure fair treatment for all people within their borders in regard to educational and other services. In extreme cases, state governments have felt justified in suspending local autonomy and taking over local governmental operations (see Chapter 7). More frequently, in nearly every session, state legislators tinker with laws that they think will improve local governmental operations or service delivery. Such efforts sometimes represent a genuine desire to make local government more accountable, effective, and efficient. In the case of mandates, however, the motivation may simply be to shift program costs to local governments. In the case of prohibitions and preemptions, legislative action is often a matter of acceding to the demands of private groups eager to avoid local taxes or regulations. Because of local governments' inferior legal status, states have virtually unlimited ability to intervene in local affairs: they require localities to follow certain rules and procedures and to perform certain functions, and prohibit local governments from taking certain types of action.[18]

The Mandate Problem

Late in the 1990s, Sam Mamet of the Colorado Municipal League complained, "One week we have legislators pretending to be planning directors; the next week they're pretending to be police chiefs. I have no idea what local control means anymore."[19] Mamet was complaining about mandates. Apparently he had good reason, as one Colorado legislator freely admitted: "We are real good as legislators at picking or choosing our mandates. . . . Sometimes we'll trample all over local control if it suits our objectives."[20]

State mandates come in the form of statutes, executive orders, and administrative regulations and often create unfunded costs for local governments by requiring that localities adopt new programs or meet higher performance standards. Individual states impose many more mandates on their local governments than does the federal government—though some of the most expensive mandates are federal mandates that states have passed on to localities. At times, local officials have taken out their anger about the federal mandates on state officials. In Indiana, a state environmental manager noted in the mid-1990s, "We have all these environmental mandates coming down, and we have all these cities and counties asking, 'Why are you doing this to us?'"[21]

Mandates address matters ranging from the important to the inconsequential. A study of Kansas, for example, suggests that the state has a compelling interest in the adoption and enforcement of only about 100 of the 941 mandates it imposes on local governments. About 300 of the mandates are obsolete and widely ignored (for example, one mandate—more than a century old—requires counties to pay the burial expenses of civil war veterans and limits the payment to $20 per headstone). The remaining mandates are examples of excessive intervention, prescribing in detail what has to be done and how it is to be done, or both. One mandate, for instance, requires that county stationery be of uniform design; others describe how local officials are to get rid of noxious weeds, build sidewalks, or construct culverts. In Kansas, state intervention through mandates has not been deterred by home rule but has actually increased since municipalities (1960) and counties (1974) were granted this protection.[22]

State mandates commonly reflect the recognition of the need for minimum standards of service levels. Often, such intervention has valuable results. One example has been state standards for local jails.[23] Local officials have little objection to the goals of many mandates; they may even welcome the political "cover" that mandates provide for the implementation of programs that are unpopular with segments of their communities (the creation of low-income housing, for example).[24] Moreover, local officials themselves are sometimes responsible for mandates. In 1997, for example, county executives and county commissioners asked the Tennessee legislature to require that counties adopt certain personnel policies. From the local point of view, these did not impose extra burdens and were necessary to ensure that all county officials comply with existing state and federal laws. Mandates may also reflect the efforts of municipal officials to make county officials assume particular responsibilities or the efforts of county officials to try to shift some costs to municipal governments.[25]

Finally, some mandates are the products of "end runs" by local government employees, who succeed through state legislation in securing benefits that they could not obtain through collective bargaining; for example, some states require local governments to pay police officers and firefighters what some observers consider overly generous pension benefits. In 1999, for example, at the prompting of organizations representing police officers and firefighters, the Florida legislature enacted an unfunded mandate for over 100 cities that increased municipal police and fire pension benefits at an estimated cost of at least $55 million per year. A year later, local elected officials in California were equally upset by a measure that requires cities and counties to use binding arbitration when they fail to reach an agreement on salary and benefits with firefighter and police unions. Critics of binding arbitration, a goal often sought by police officers and firefighters, contend that elected officials—rather than an appointed arbitrator—should decide the salaries and benefits of police and fire personnel—and that if they are not allowed to do so, they lose control over a large part of their budgets.

Even when local officials are in sympathy with the goals of state mandates, they are nevertheless aware that all mandates distort local priorities, restrict local managerial flexibility, and impose costs that have to be paid through local revenues. The extent of the unfunded mandate problem varies from state to state. For example, a study in Ohio estimated that about one in twelve laws passed in that state in recent years imposed an unfunded mandate on local governments.[26] A similar study in Tennessee put about one in four laws into this category.[27] The costs of mandates are likely to be substantial. Another study in Connecticut found that some 700 statutory state mandates and a host of additional administrative regulations accounted for half of all municipal expenditures.[28] On the basis of several studies, localities appear to devote from 20 to 90 percent of their expenditures to the implementation of federal and state mandates. Each year, local officials must guard against legislation burdening their jurisdictions with expensive or inefficient state programs. Although some of the shifts cost relatively little money, their aggregate effects can be staggering, and big-ticket items—in areas such as health care, education, and environmental protection—can overwhelm local governmental budgets.

Local officials have been somewhat handicapped in opposing state mandates. They do not wish to alienate the legislators who impose the mandates, because they are also financially dependent on these legislators.[29] Nevertheless, as we have noted, local officials have been anything but passive when it comes to mandates. They have had only limited success in challenging state mandates in the courts because the courts have been inclined to defer to the judgment of the legislatures in such matters and to make it difficult for localities to bring suit.[30] However, as noted earlier, local officials have had some success in securing voter support for measures intended to reduce the number of mandates or that require the states to pick up the costs of their implementation. Voters appear to view such measures as a means of reducing local property taxes and preserving local control over spending priorities.[31]

Local officials and their lobbying organizations constantly seek state support to cover the costs of new mandates. Sometimes they are successful. At other times, legislatures give local governments more authority to raise the revenues needed to meet the costs of new mandates—a less desirable outcome, because complying with the mandates means that local officials run the risk of incurring the wrath of their taxpayers for programs demanded by the state.

Other strategies for coping with mandates focus on the mandate process. Over forty states have fiscal note requirements that require state agencies (in some places, commissions on intergovernmental relations) to estimate the costs that state laws or regulations will impose on localities. Several states combine fiscal notes with a requirement that the state reimburse localities for the expense of undertaking the mandated activity. Other states use fiscal notes simply to call attention to the costs incurred by local governments.

Whether the requirements are for estimates only or for reimbursement as well, several problems impair the usefulness of fiscal notes. To begin with, the lack of staff, time, and expertise makes it difficult to secure timely and reliable cost estimates. Second, the problem of accuracy is exacerbated by efforts on the part of competing groups to push for the use of their own estimates of a mandate's costs, purposely either underestimating or overestimating them. Finally, political parties may differ over a mandate's costs or even over its very existence. The result is that many measures with a potential financial impact on local government may not even be identified, or, if they are identified, the costs attributed to them may be wide of the mark. In an effort to improve the process, some states involve local officials in cost estimation.[32] This practice has worked with considerable success in Connecticut and Nevada. Since 1997, Minnesota also has been experimenting with a process in which committees made up of municipal and county officials work with the state's department of finance to estimate the impact of local expenditures for bills and proposed rules. When employed alone (that is, without a reimbursement requirement), fiscal notes appear to have only a limited effect on legislative behavior. Even if legislators are made more aware of the financial burden that they are passing on to local governments, they do not necessarily refuse to impose the costs—which are, after all, assumed not by the state but by local governments. As an antimandate strategy, the primary value of fiscal notes seems to be in providing local governments with lobbying ammunition.[33]

Several states have statutory or constitutional provisions limiting the ability of states to impose mandates on local governments. Some laws call for full or partial state reimbursement of the costs of new mandates. In some places, the state must either pick up the costs for mandated programs or give localities the authority to raise taxes to finance them. Most laws, however, have a "safety valve" allowing the legislature to pass an unfunded mandated through a supermajority (two-thirds or three-fourths) vote.

As a deterrent to unfunded mandates, a statutory or constitutional requirement for reimbursement appears to be more effective than a requirement for cost estimates. Reimbursement requirements added to the constitution with the backing of the voters may be initially more effective in influencing legislative behavior than those created by statute. Over time, however, the deterrent effect brought about by the expression of public opinion may diminish. Also over time, decisions made by the legislature in implementing constitutional mandate requirements can prove to be troublesome. Legislatures in some states have made the reimbursement procedures that localities must follow so cumbersome and costly that they have discouraged localities from seeking reimbursements. In some states, the legislature has control over the agency that it has charged with making decisions as to what is a mandate and what is the proper level of reimbursement; if they are unhappy with these decisions, localities have no real input or recourse but to sue in court.[34] Extensive funding for mandates does not appear to be the major effect of reimbursement provisions; instead, the provisions seem more likely to deter mandates or to cause them to be modified so that they are less expensive.[35] When it comes to determent, perhaps the most effective remedy is to require a two-thirds vote to impose a mandate.[36]

In several states, such as Florida, Maine, New Hampshire, and North Carolina, antimandate laws appear to have helped reduce the total number of mandates. The same seems to be true in Oregon, where voters in November of 2000 overwhelmingly favored retaining an antimandate provision in the state constitution. In recent years, moreover, mandate commissions created by state laws have made some significant rulings. For example, in 2000, the New Jersey Council on Local Mandates, created through a 1995 amendment to the state constitution, declared that a change that the legislature had made in the rules governing local school districts' funding of charter schools was an unconstitutional unfunded mandate that had to be paid for by state funds rather than local property taxes. In 1998, the California Commission on State Mandates came down on the side of school districts complaining about the costs imposed on them by state mandates regarding special education. After lengthy grappling with the decision of what to do next, in 2000, the commission voted to let the state's school districts begin filing claims with an estimated total value of at least $1.6 billion. School districts in Michigan have also received considerable relief by virtue of a 1997 state supreme court decision that the legislature's refusal to fund mandated programs for school lunches, special education, driver education, and bilingual education programs violated the Headlee Amendment, added to the state constitution in 1978, which places limitations on taxing and spending increases.[37]

Legislatures in some states, however, have simply ignored reimbursement requirements (there is no penalty for doing so) or have gotten around them by earmarking as mandate reimbursement a part of the funding already allocated for state aid to localities—in effect, deducting mandate reimbursement costs from local aid programs.[38] In Colorado, a provision of the TABOR law allows a local government with the exception of a school to "reduce or end its subsidy to any program delegated to it by the general assembly for administration." This section was billed as a mandate-relief provision but has been limited by subsequent legislative action and court decisions. The state also imposes constitutional and statutory limitations on legislative ability to impose mandates on local governments, and it has executive order on regulatory mandates. Whether any of these approaches are in fact working is unclear.[39]

The mandate problem gained prominence during the 1980s and early 1990s when the federal government began addressing its own economic difficulties by shifting program costs to state governments, and state governments, in turn, shifted program costs to local governments. From the mid-1990s to the early 2000s, the overall number of new state mandates appeared to decrease presumably because of antimandate laws, the publicity given to the mandate problem, and the improvement in state revenues. Legislatures in several states also eliminated specific mandates as unnecessary or outdated. A decline in state revenues in 2001, however, created pressure to return to a policy of shifting the cost of programs to localities. Mandates have by no means disappeared, and regardless of reforms on the national and state levels, local officials continue to worry about them and to blame them for much of their trouble.[40] At the beginning of 1999, a National League of Cities survey found that nearly half (47 percent) of city officials surveyed felt that the unfunded mandate problem had worsened over the past year, and 8 percent said that the situation had improved.[41]

Legislators continue to have a considerable incentive to impose costly mandates and, especially in difficult economic circumstances, may be expected to do so.[42] As one expert has warned, "Despite the stringency of the anti-mandate legislation, when a state legislature has a will to pass an unfunded mandate, a way will ultimately present itself."[43] The major underlying problem is of increasing the ability of local governments to participate in and influence decisions made on the state level affecting them.[44] Moreover, the mandate problem is something of a no-win situation for localities: even if a state decides to relinquish a long-standing requirement that localities provide a particular service, municipalities or counties may have no choice but to fund and provide the service anyway because their citizens want it continued.

Prohibitions and Preemptions

Along with demands that they do certain things, local governments are regularly bombarded by the states with a range of "thou shalt not" directives. Legislative acts prohibiting local governments from taking certain actions often reflect a particular group's desire to minimize—if not completely avoid—government taxation or regulation. Local officials must be continuously on guard against state legislation that would, for example, exempt certain businesses from local sales taxes or completely preempt local sales tax authority. State legislators are attracted to certain proposals—such as granting sales tax exemptions—because they are both politically popular and carry no costs to the state. Tax-exemption bills, however, can significantly reduce the flow of funds into local treasuries and can be as financially devastating as the mandates that make them assume the cost of various programs.[45]

Local officials must also guard against attempts to preempt their ability to undertake a wide variety of regulatory activities. As the result of landlords' efforts, for example, thirty-three states now prohibit local governments from adopting rent-control measures.[46] Some, such as California, have loosened local restrictions by allowing landlords to increase rents when tenants leave. Massachusetts ended rent control by a statewide vote in 1994—even though the only communities with rent control voted to keep it. This was a clear case of statewide norms prevailing over local norms. This action came after landlords had unsuccessfully challenged rent controls in the courts and failed as well to get the state legislature to overturn or restrict the enabling statute.[47]

Tobacco companies meanwhile have encouraged the move away from municipal and county nonsmoking ordinances in favor of state legislation on the subject. Commonly, states have preempted local action through the passage of statewide clean-indoor-air bills. Because of industry pressure and the lobbying activities of groups such as restaurant associations, statewide regulations are often less demanding than the local ordinances that they replaced. Legislation in about a dozen states prevents localities from passing antismoking measures that are more restrictive than state standards. The tobacco industry has preferred to direct its efforts to the state level, finding it easier and less expensive than going from locality to locality, while antismoking coalitions have enjoyed more success at the local level.[48] When the tobacco companies win through preemption, they are able to prevent local jurisdictions from adopting a level of regulation or protection that many of them would prefer. The relation between statewide and local antismoking regulations, however, is complex. In New York, for example, the existence of strong local ordinances in 60 percent of the state did not lead to a successful preemptive effort at the state level that lowered standards but, to the contrary, strengthened the effort to impose strong regulations throughout the state. As one of the players in the process put it: "The experience in those areas covered by local laws was positive. The restaurant industry did not collapse, plants did not close, smokers did not get carted off to jail."[49] Lawmakers thus felt comfortable imposing high standards in places constituting only a minority of the population, where localities had not yet adopted them.

Around the nation, tobacco industry groups have also challenged proposed local bans on cigarette vending machines, arguing that any regulation of this business is reserved for state authority.[50] Local action is clearly preempted in those states where there are state laws specifically addressing the existence or placement of cigarette vending machines. Courts, however, also have voided local regulations on the grounds that state preemption of the field is implied by related state laws. In 1993, for example, the Maryland Court of Appeals rejected the effort of a city to restrict the placement of cigarette vending machines to locations not accessible by minors, holding that the state, by its adoption of a licensing scheme for cigarette vending machines, had acted with such force that "an intent by the State to occupy the entire field" regarding the sale of cigarettes through vending machines was implied. The Connecticut Supreme Court in 2001, however, in a 5–2 decision, upheld ordinances banning cigarette vending machines, giving a broad interpretation to municipal powers.

Thanks in large part to the National Rifle Association, forty states prohibit local gun-control ordinances, and a majority of the states deny local authority to regulate who can carry concealed weapons. Some states prevent local jurisdictions from imposing firearm ordinances that are more restrictive than state laws. Other states have rescinded local ordinances to ensure uniform firearms laws statewide. In five states, preemption has come through judicial rulings rather than by statute. In the late 1990s, several cities and counties—inspired by the success of lawsuits against the tobacco companies by state attorneys general—sued gun makers and dealers to recover the cost of gun-related violence. This prompted the NRA to lobby state legislators to prohibit local governments from taking such actions. Thus far, the NRA has been successful in thirteen states, including those where suits had been initiated and those where localities had not even contemplated suing gun makers. The laws, some of which are based on a model prepared by the NRA, generally prohibit any municipality or county from filing product-liability suits against the firearms industry (manufacturers, trade associations, or dealers), reserving that right to the state. In Florida, a 1999 legislative proposal that was later withdrawn would have gone so far as to make it a felony for any local official to sue the gun industry. In both Louisiana and Georgia, laws prohibiting suits were passed after cities (New Orleans and Atlanta) had already filed suit but were written to ban these pending actions as well as future actions. Courts have generally upheld such legislation, thus allowing the states to prevent, even retroactively, local governments from making their arguments in judicial proceedings.[51]

One is not hard-pressed to find several examples of state-imposed limitations on the ability of localities to regulate economic activity. In some places, for example, business groups have successfully targeted local laws that contractors doing business with a local government pay their employees a living wage above that required by the state or federal government. Such measures, backed by a coalition of labor and religious groups in an effort to reduce poverty rates for the working poor, have often been adopted by the voters only to be banned by legislative activity or invalidated by the courts on the grounds that they conflict with an area of activity reserved to the states. In 2002, the Louisiana Supreme Court, responding to a suit brought by the local chamber of commerce and restaurant association among other business groups, invalidated a voter-approved charter amendment for all workers in the city, not simply for workers employed by contractors doing business with the city. The court found the measure an illegal encroachment on state power and in conflict with a state law banning localities from adopting minimum-wage laws. The legislature had passed the state ban in 1997 in response to the initiation of the petition drive in New Orleans to put the local minimum-wage reform on the local ballot. Along with direct bans, opponents to local living-wage measures have sought state legislation that takes away state revenue-sharing dollars from communities that adopt such reforms.

A development in various parts of the country in recent years has been state preemption of local regulations regarding the use of cell phones while driving. Industry members have pushed for state action in the interest of uniformity, but those outside the industry worry that state regulations might be much friendlier to the wireless carriers and therefore be relatively ineffective in promoting safety. The state of New York was the first to ban the use of hand-held phones while driving and, in doing so, superseded existing county and municipal laws in the state. Nationwide, a score of local governments have laws affecting cell-phone use. Another hot regulatory preemption issue in recent years concerns local governments' ability to regulate large livestock operations. County governments, in response to citizens' complaints about odors and pollution from large hog farms and similar operations, have attempted to control the location of such operations and to make them subject to health regulations and ordinances regarding air and water quality. Some courts, for example, in Iowa and North Carolina, however, have ruled that such regulations are preempted by state laws.[52]

Beyond the financial and regulatory areas, prohibitions and preemptions have been aimed at everyday local government decisions about personnel and other internal matters. Of importance in several states in recent years have been efforts, sometimes supported by groups of local employees such as police, firefighters, and teachers, to eliminate local residency requirements for city workers. Supporters of state action ending residency requirements argue that the state has an interest in safeguarding their employees' freedom of movement. Supporters also argue that ending residency requirements will help cities attract teachers, police personnel, and other needed workers. Opponents counter that making public employees part of the community they serve increases their commitment to the community and their job performance. This, in turn, facilitates the building of positive community attitudes. Those in favor of residency requirements also see them having a positive effect in keeping relatively well-paid, middle-class people in cities. As far as police and other public-safety personnel are concerned, residency requirements have the additional virtue of helping to reduce response times during emergencies. More generally, state prohibitions are criticized on the grounds that decisions regarding residency requirements, whatever their merits, should be made not by the state, but by the local governments involved. One legislator dissenting from the decision of the Pennsylvania legislature in 2001 to prohibit Philadelphia and Pittsburgh from setting residency requirements for teachers declared to his colleagues, "If we want to abolish local government, let's come right out and say we want to abolish local government. Let's not patronize them and strip them of their authority to make meaningful decisions."[53]

Most would agree that allowing localities to make meaningful decisions is key to their good health, whether these have to do with taxation, regulation, hiring, or social welfare policy. In this spirit, some contend that municipalities should be allowed to get into profit-making ventures, "clearly shattering the image of the city as a receptacle solely for industries that lose money (mass transit, hospital emergency rooms) rather than those that could make money to serve community ends."[54] Local government–marketplace issues are now being hammered out in regard to right of communities to build and operate their own communications infrastructures. Some states have attempted to limit such activities or to entirely prevent municipalities and municipally owned utilities from providing, directly or indirectly, certain telecommunications services that compete with privately owned companies. Some federal courts have found, however, that such state acts are in conflict with the federal Telecommunications Act of 1996, which, as we have noted, was designed to increase competition in the communications sector. Throughout the country several hundred municipalities and counties have already chosen to compete with the private sector in the investment-intensive telecommunications industry, playing an entrepreneurial, risk-taking role, and many more appear willing to do so because of dissatisfaction with existing service.

Proponents of this movement say that the local government action makes up for the market failure, gives consumers more choice, and increases citizen access to telecommunications services. They also see it as a way of increasing the revenues of municipal power companies (the profits of which are threatened by energy deregulation) and keeping localities competitive with other jurisdictions in the race for business and investment. Opponents of local entry into the market complain that local government competition is unfair because localities have several advantages over private businesses—for example, being exempt from taxes, being able to secure low interest rates through municipal bonds, and having some direct power over their private competitors through the fees and regulations that they may impose on them.

In some states, localities also now have the opportunity under energy deregulation laws to act as an aggregator and enter into an agreement with other local governments for the purchase of energy for their own use and for the use of their citizens. By aggregating their loads, local governments may achieve considerable savings in their energy bills. In 1999, 148 of Connecticut's 169 cities and towns formed a massive buying pool for purchasing electricity and natural gas. A similar pool of over 130 cities has been formed in Ohio. While local governments commonly can aggregate, if and when they may do this depends on state law. In 1999, for example, electric deregulation legislation passed in Maryland included a provision that forbids local governments from acting as aggregators for their citizens or businesses unless it has been determined that no competition exists in that jurisdiction. In New Jersey, meanwhile, despite the efforts of organizations representing local officials, the legislature chose to force municipalities and counties to go through a complicated and costly process to form strong buying groups among themselves and with their residential, commercial, and industrial energy users. Unlike Ohio, where municipalities are automatically included in the pool until they opt out, in New Jersey they are out of the pool until they opt in.

Over the years, one might conclude, local governments have made considerable progress in regard to formal local home-rule authority. It is also clear, however, that these gains have been offset by increased mandates and preemptions of local authority. Localities have often been restricted from making meaningful decisions or undertaking important service activities. In some states, the legislatures have whittled down the value of county and municipal home rule and made it difficult for local governments to function effectively. For example, one legal expert has concluded that in New York, "Local governments have relatively limited autonomy, limited fiscal resources, and precious little protection from state interference or state impositions. Nor is there any assurance that local governments have the resources necessary to discharge their state-delegated duties."[55] The financial limitations on local government, as detailed in the following chapter, are of particular importance.

6

The Revenue Problem

Several years ago, the mayor of a medium-sized American city identified his three major problems as "money, finances, and revenues."[1] He,
like other local officials in the United States, however, has had only
limited control over his city's financial problems. Local officials rely on
whatever sources of income the states are willing to let them tap into
and on whatever financial assistance the states or the federal government are willing to give them. They also face the constant prospect that
other governments, especially when confronted with revenue difficulties of their own, will both cut local aid and shift as many of their costs
as possible to local governments. In a broad sense, state and local governments are in the same boat when it comes to gathering revenues:
both are subject to the ups and downs in the general economy and to
shifting public attitudes regarding taxing and spending. Still, there is
much the states could do to give localities greater revenue stability.

Financial Controls

State governments have long imposed various types of control on local finances. Regulations on local taxation, accounts, budgets, and indebtedness first came in the early 1800s.[2] More restrictions grew out
of the Great Depression of the 1930s, which caused local financial
operations to collapse throughout the nation. Several states in this period placed cities facing financial emergencies in receivership. To head
off future problems, state legislatures in the 1930s placed controls on
nearly all aspects of local financial management: assessment, taxation,
indebtedness, budgeting, accounting, auditing, and fiscal reporting.[3] The
Depression also gave rise to the idea of giving a state agency complete
control over the financial management of all municipalities, though this
occurred in only a few states, where municipal default problems had
been extensive. Among the powers given to state agencies in these places,

New Jersey being one example, were those of reviewing local budgets before their adoption and, if necessary, ordering changes to avoid a deficit.[4] The 1970s brought another wave of reform as citizen pressure on legislators and direct action at the polls produced measures throughout the country limiting the ability of local officials to raise revenues, especially through property taxes, and limiting overall local spending.

States currently impose many constitutional and statutory limitations on the ability of local governments to raise and spend revenues. State constitutions and statutes prohibit certain types of local taxes (for example, sales tax or graduated income tax) and limit the raising of tax rates (such as the property-tax rate) and property assessments beyond certain levels. In a half-dozen states, the amount of total revenue that can be raised is tied to such measures as the growth of personal income, inflation, or population, and funds raised over the limit have to be refunded to the taxpayers. Total expenditures in some states are also limited by being tied to a growth index. Many states make tax increases and spending increases above a certain level dependent on voter approval.

Several of the more recent tax and expenditure limitations (TELs) on state and local finances are the product of efforts by citizen groups that have used the initiative process. Tax protesters such as Howard Jarvis in California during the 1970s and 1980s and, more recently, Bill Sizemore in Oregon and Douglas Bruce in Colorado, have been able to tap a groundswell of antitax sentiment in their states and lead successful initiative campaigns to limit taxing or spending. A majority of the TELs adopted since the late 1970s, however, have come through the state legislative process as legislators have moved to preempt the protest movement and to shape the nature of reform.[5]

The immediate effect of these efforts over the last three decades has been a loss of local revenues. In some jurisdictions, these losses have affected the ability of local governments to attract intergovernmental aid because local officials have found it more difficult to meet matching requirements for state and federal grants. Often, however, local officials have succeeded in reducing their losses through targeted revenue increases, for example, new or increased fees, and through productivity improvements. Because of such steps, TELs appear to have had little effect on total spending. They have, however, affected the composition of local revenues; specifically, they have decreased local governments' reliance on the property tax and increased their reliance on state aid and on locally collected fees and sales taxes. Overall, TELs appear to have encouraged (1) centralization of authority at the state level, a shift that has accompanied the switch to greater reliance on state-collected taxes, and (2) local dependence on more regressive revenue sources such as sales taxes and fees.[6]

Other state-imposed limitations on local finances have to do with borrowing. Many of these date from the post–Civil War period, when cities sought to keep up with sudden growth and the subsequent demands for schools, streets, and water supply systems by going on a great borrowing splurge. This ended in near bankruptcy for many of them in the depression years of the 1870s. As an outcome of this experience, "The state legislatures were made painfully aware that local governments may be, and often are, financially irresponsible."[7] The 1930s Depression, with investment bankers in anguish over the number of municipal bonds in default, did little to dispel the notion that local governments were more irresponsible in financial matters than state governments. Writing during this period, economist William J. Shultz argued, "It is not enough to require that proposed local bond issues, like proposed state issues, be submitted to popular referendum. Counties, cities, and other local units occasionally fall into the grip of political 'rings' strong enough to carry any project, no matter how lacking in merit, through a popular vote. Control of some sort must be imposed from an outside force."[8]

Following up on this advice, state constitutions and laws relating to the borrowing power of local governments currently include not only requirements that public referenda be held to permit the issuance of bonds, but also restrictions on the purposes for which localities may borrow and, most important, maximum limits on the amount of debt that localities can incur. Debt limits most often apply to borrowing through general obligation bonds and are often expressed as a percentage (from 15 to 25 percent) of the value of the property within the jurisdiction, but they may also be stated in specific dollar amounts. One effect of these restrictions has been to encourage state and local governments to turn to more costly revenue bonds, which are supported only from the revenues derived from the project for which the money is borrowed. Borrowing restrictions have also encouraged localities to create special districts, authorities, and various other kinds of financial arrangements to bypass the limits.[9]

The Revenue Base

Local governments in the United States raise around 61 percent of their own general revenues. Most of the outside revenue, about 35 percent of the total, comes from the states, while the federal government contributes the remaining 4 percent (Table 6.1). The property tax is the largest component of local governments' own-source income, and about 28 percent of their total revenues. Six percent of local revenues comes from locally adopted sales taxes, 2 percent comes from individual income taxes, and about 24 percent comes from charges and miscellaneous fees. Municipalities have the most diversified revenue structure. Compared to counties, municipalities are less dependent on state aid and property taxes. They rely more on federal aid and sales and income taxes. School districts rely the most on state aid (over half of their revenues come from this source) and property taxes. Nearly 90 percent of their funds come from these two sources. Special district governments depend more than the others on federal aid (particularly funds for housing and community development and for sewage systems) and less than the others on state aid. Over half of their revenues comes from charges for various services.

Over the years, local governments as a whole have steadily moved away from reliance on property taxes. The decline has been fairly consistent since 1922, when property taxes provided 77 percent of local general revenues; by 1997 they provided only 18 percent and, more recently, 27 percent in 1999 (see Appendix A). Over much of this time, local officials have actively encouraged a shift away from property taxes in the belief that they would be better off with a more diversified revenue structure. Movement away from property taxes since the late 1970s has been virtually compelled by taxpayer pressure and court decisions.

Property-tax collections actually declined nationwide in the late 1970s under the wave of activity prompted by the adoption of Proposition 13 in California.[10] From 1980 to 1990, however, local property-tax revenues increased nationally by an astounding 128 percent, mostly as a result of growth in assessed values, rather than from tax-rate increases. Property taxes continued to outpace inflation during the 1990s. Because residential property values increased more than commercial property values during this period, much of the property-tax burden shifted from commercial- to residential-property owners, creating financial difficulties for many homeowners. Revenue increases, local officials argued,

Table 6.1

Local-Government Revenues, Fiscal Year 1997

	Dollars				
Item	All local governments	Counties	Munici- palities	Special districts	School districts
General revenues (in millions)	747,030	191,271	222,190	67,653	257,342
Percent federal aid	3.9	2.6	5.3	14.9	0.6
Percent state aid	34.5	33.5	20.6	8.7	53.3
Percent property tax	27.9	24.7	22.2	11.9	36.0
Percent sales tax	6.1	7.9	12.3	2.6	0.4
Percent income tax	1.9	1.2	6.1	—	0.3
Percent charges	23.5	26.9	29.2	52.1	7.7

Source: U.S. Bureau of Census, Department of Commerce.

were needed to make up for the loss or slow growth of intergovernmental aid and to meet the increased costs of unfunded mandates and increased service demands.

These explanations, however, did little to calm the waters. Faced with public demands for property-tax relief, lawmakers in many states adopted tax freezes and capped assessment rate increases. Still others provided relief by phasing out automobile property taxes and expanding homestead exemptions. More significantly, several states reduced pressure on property taxes by shifting much of the burden of financing education from these taxes to other taxes, such as state sales taxes. Michigan did this in dramatic fashion in 1993. During the mid- to late-1990s, general-revenue increases from a healthy economy allowed the states to provide property-tax relief without cutting programs or increasing other taxes to offset the lost revenues. As the result of state relief efforts, property taxes began to stabilize. As the economy began to sour shortly after the turn of the century, the pressure to turn to property taxes returned.

Taxpayer unhappiness has brought property-tax rate and assessment limits, some property-tax rollbacks, and relief programs for low and fixed income families. Charges of unfair assessments have also prompted state agencies to become more involved in overseeing the application of uniform assessment policies.[11] Some counties have opted to let the state take over the property-tax assessment function. This step has been supported by elected county officials as a means of securing property-tax relief. Many county officials, however, have been reluctant to give up local control and to see the function slip out of the hands of an elected local official (the county assessor) into those of some state employee.[12] Property-tax reform in some states has taken the form of giving local officials added discretion in dealing with the problem. Local officials, however, have sometimes been reluctant to use this discretion. In Pennsylvania, for example, voters and the legislature gave school districts and other local units the authority, with voter approval, to give property-tax relief to senior citizens. Yet school districts have been hesitant to act, not being sure of the revenue loss involved and how they could make up for this lost revenue. Similarly, county officials in South Carolina, though under considerable pressure from state lawmakers to take action, have been reluctant to use the powers granted them under a 1999 state law that allows them to delay property-tax assessments and to cap property value increases on homes.

Overall, the property tax remains, as it has been for the last few decades, one of the nation's most controversial and unpopular taxes.[13] Citizen discontent with the property tax has been reflected not only in public-opinion polls but also in organized activities and, at times, in voting behavior resulting in the defeat of bond issues and the favoring of tax limitation propositions. In 1998, for example, some Arkansas citizens took it upon themselves to initiate a proposed constitutional amendment that would abolish all property taxes in the state. This proposal was thrown off the ballot through a court suit because of violations of the law in collecting signatures. The same group, however, appeared willing to try again. In an effort to take the steam out of the anti-property-tax campaign, the Arkansas state legislature came up with a constitutional amendment that, as approved by the voters in November 2000, puts limits on property-tax increases but also brought a half-cent increase in the sales tax to offset the expected loss in property-tax revenues. In 2000, Alaska voters came to the rescue by overwhelmingly rejecting a property-tax initiative modeled after California's Proposition 13 that would have capped municipal property taxes statewide at 1 percent of assessed value and frozen assessments, allowing them to rise no more than 2 percent annually for inflation unless the property was transferred or built upon. A year later, however, antitax groups in Washington State secured voter support for an initiative that limits property tax increases to 1 percent a year without a public vote. The previous limit was 6 percent a year. New Jersey, with the highest per-capita property taxes in the nation, has struggled with the property-tax question on a regular basis in recent years, finally settling on a rebate program for homeowners to relieve them from property taxes. The program was initiated in 1999 by Governor Christie Whitman after the property-tax issue nearly cost her a bid for reelection.

In California, Proposition 13 remains popular with voters, who have also given their approval to a variety of other property-tax limitation measures. The current controversy, however, is not so much voter driven as it is a struggle between local governments and the state over the revenue stream.[14] The state of California came to the relief of local governments following the adoption of Proposition 13 by giving localities greater financial aid, picking up some of the program costs that local governments had been bearing, and granting localities new authority to raise revenues.[15] In the early 1990s, however, with the state mired in a recession, the legislature shifted over $2 billion in property taxes from local governments to the state education budget. Without the transfer, through what is known as the Education Revenue Augmentation Fund (ERAF), the state would have had to raise taxes or take money out of the general fund to pay for education and thus cut the level of other state services. County governments were particularly hard hit by the loss of property-tax revenues. Some counties reacted in dramatic fashion to this "tax grab" by directing their auditors not to turn the money over to the state and by taking the state to court on the grounds that the action violated the counties' state constitutional rights. These efforts amounted to very little. Since 1992, the amount of money lost to local governments has grown because of inflation and new development. In 2000, it totaled close to $4 billion. Under the existing system, moreover, localities are encouraged to promote the development of commercial enterprises. This type of development generates sales-tax revenues that localities can keep. Increases in property-tax revenues coming from other developments, on the other hand, are swallowed up by the state. Revenue considerations thus have encouraged land-use decisions favoring such developments as shopping centers and auto malls.

Proponents of capping, if not ending, the diversion of funds had some hope of success in the late-1990s because of an improvement in the state's economy, the election of a governor, Democrat Gray Davis, who was thought to be more sympathetic to the local governments' position, and the movement of more former council members and county supervisors into the legislature, some of whom had direct experience with the turmoil caused by the diversion. One legislator, who had been a city council member during that period, remembered it this way: "It forced the cities to be the bad guys. . . . For my city, the choice was either cut back on services or raise fees."[16] In the fall of 2000, however, Governor Davis vetoed a measure that would have placed a cap on the amount of money diverted, thus preserving the revenue stream coming into the state.

In addition to the legal limits imposed by taxpayer revolt and the political limits imposed by its unpopularity, the usefulness of the property tax has been further reduced by state-enacted exemptions reducing the property-tax base. Counties, for example, often find that 60 percent or more of the property-tax base has been exempted.[17] Figures are nearly as bad for city government in the District of Columbia and for many municipalities in the state of New York. A survey of 173 cities in 2000 found that, on the average, property-tax exemptions had caused the cities to lose more than 13 percent of their total budgets.[18] Governments, educational institutions, religious bodies, charitable organizations, and hospitals are prominent among the owners of tax-exempt property. Veterans and elderly residents are the principal recipients of exemptions for residential property.[19] While states sometimes make payments in lieu of taxes (PILOTs) for property-tax exemptions, PILOTs are often far lower than what local governments would have collected in taxes had the property not been exempt. Along with losses from tax exemptions, some local governments lose property-tax revenues because of inadequate funding for collections. A study on property-tax administration by the California Institute of County Governments, for example, concluded that increased spending on property-tax collection could boost revenues by hundreds of millions of dollars in that state.

Historically, the property tax has been a rich and relatively stable source of income that local officials could pretty much call their own. Local officials have been able to raise or decrease the tax rate depending on their budgetary needs. Public-choice theorists like the property tax because it gives individuals a highly visible tax price for the public services that are being offered, thus clarifying their choices. Yet, one might argue, it is this very high visibility of the tax that makes it unpopular and encourages local officials to turn away from it to more hidden sources.[20] While many applaud the decline in the relative importance of the local property tax, this movement has had its costs. As the states have assumed greater control over property-tax rates and assessments, they have cut into local autonomy, deprived local officials of the discretionary use of a viable revenue source, and, in a general sense, reduced both the incentive citizens have to participate in local affairs and their ability to do so on a rational basis.[21] Localities also have turned to other own-source revenues, which have their own liabilities and limitations.

States and localities are competitors for the taxpayer's dollar. Being in the driver's seat, states have historically taken advantage of their position to limit that competition by forcing localities to rely on the property tax and, moreover, have limited the amount that localities can raise from that source. Localities have had a difficult time getting state support to tap other revenue sources. In recent years, largely because of the forces pushing state as well as local governments away from relying on the property tax, however, the revenue structure has become more diverse for general-purpose governments.

Local governments have received increased authority to levy new taxes, particularly on sales, and to impose fees for various services, such as police, fire, and ambulance services. Also available to some jurisdictions are cable-franchise fees (for example, on bars and restaurants that have cable television for their customers) and fees for local government delivery of online services. Legislatures have usually made the adoption of new taxes subject to voter approval. The local-option sales tax is now allowed in thirty-three states; many of these permit counties, municipalities, and special districts to levy the tax, while some restrict the right to either municipalities or counties. The tax has the advantage of shifting or "exporting" some of the tax burden to nonresidents but, overall, it tends to be regressive in its impact. Like the property tax, however, the local-option sales tax is riddled with exemptions, costing some states and local governments billions of dollars each year in lost revenue. Thus far, the tax is also losing out because it does not extend to services or to the ever-increasing volume of Internet sales and mail-order purchases. Another disadvantage is that local dependence on this source tends to put jurisdictions in intense, sometimes ruinous competition for building shopping centers in order to expand their revenue streams. As has been noted in regard to California, this has led to the "fiscalization of land use," or "zoning for dollars," that is, making of planning and land-use decisions that favor sales-tax-generating developments such as shopping centers and auto malls rather than housing and other nonretail activities.

Politically, the local-option sales tax is unpopular in the business community and among local officials in rural areas because people in these areas commonly shop and pay their local-option sales tax in urban areas. Business and rural community forces have combined to scuttle local-option sales taxes in several states, including Montana, Maine, and New Hampshire.[22] Expansion of the sales tax so that it may be drawn upon by hard put local jurisdictions is also likely to be opposed by local jurisdictions already drawing upon the source. In 2002, for example, cities and counties in Missouri opposed, though unsuccessfully in this case, a measure giving fire and ambulance districts the authority to levy a sales tax up to one-half cent. County and city spokespersons pointed out that they stood to suffer; the other units were likely to escalate the sales tax rate and, as a result, create greater pressure for more sales tax exemptions and encourage more purchases from the Internet and catalog sales and thus avoid all sales taxes.

Fifteen states authorize the use of local income taxes, but the tax is relied upon only in a handful of these, particularly Pennsylvania and Ohio. Apparently, many jurisdictions fear that a local income tax would hurt the development of the local economy.[23] During the past two decades, user fees have become a popular means of financing water, sewage, transportation, and other services. The notion that the direct user of a service should pay for it appears popular throughout the country. Because of this, user fees are a relatively acceptable way of raising revenues. They are also attractive to local officials because they can usually levy fees without a grant of permission from state legislatures. However, some courts have declared user fees (such as transportation fees) to be disguised taxes and therefore invalid in the absence of specific state authorization.[24]

Localities also have significant discretion to impose impact fees on developers to help offset the costs engendered by projects such as the building or expanding of roads, sewers, and parks. Builders commonly argue that impact fees are excessive and far beyond the actual cost of providing the new infrastructure rendered necessary by development. Local officials contend that fees only help offset the costs and are a more equitable means of doing so because those who benefit from the improvements pay for them. In recent years, however, several states have acted to ensure that fees are reasonable and related to reliable estimates of the impact of particular developments.

Nationwide, the number of exactions (required improvements, property set-asides, fees, and taxes) imposed by local governments on developers has increased greatly in recent decades. To some extent, the increase in exactions reflects the notion that growth must pay for itself. The increase, however, has also stemmed from the financial difficulties of many localities. Just as the federal and state governments tried to cope with their economic problems by passing costs on to local governments, local governments have attempted to ease their economic difficulties—and the burden on current taxpayers—by passing costs on to developers. That developers have not offered more resistance may stem from the fact that they can, in turn, pass the costs on to residential or commercial buyers.[25]

Historically, localities have collected varying amounts of franchise fees from telecommunications companies for use of the public right of way, charging the companies whatever the market will bring. Companies, in recent years, however, have gone to state legislatures to limit the amounts. As a result, state laws now commonly limit local compensation to the actual costs they incur in managing the right of way and doing the pavement-degradation repair work necessary after companies tear up streets to bury cable and other equipment. In some places, such as Michigan, the process has become more centralized as the state collects a uniform franchise fees—one that local officials claim fails to cover their costs—for cable and telephone companies and distributes the funds to localities.

Additional revenues are available in some jurisdictions from state or locally owned enterprises or legalized gambling. On the local level, one finds municipal power systems that bring large amounts of revenue into city treasuries and/or sell power to consumers at relatively low rates. Overall, however, municipalities receive less than 2 percent of their revenues from this source. The legalization of gambling has improved local finances in several places. Local governments in Louisiana, for example, receive 25 percent of the state taxes and fees on poker devices in bars, restaurants, and truck stops. In addition, municipalities and parishes (which are equivalent to counties) receive an entry fee of $2.50 per person for fifteen casino-type riverboats located in major metropolitan areas. A land-based casino authorized for the city of New Orleans provides an additional revenue source. Thirty-seven states have lotteries, some of which contribute to local revenues. In these cases, however, local gains may be more apparent than real. While some states earmark lottery funds for education and other local programs, such revenues are fungible—that is, they may have simply replaced what would have been spent out of other sources for the same programs—and thus do not necessarily amount to a net gain in revenues.[26]

The State-Aid Battle

State financial aid to local governments consists of grants and shared taxes. Grants are usually designated for specific programs in such areas as education and transportation, though most states also provide unrestricted grants for general purposes. In the case of shared taxes, states act as tax collectors, returning all or a portion of the yield from a shared tax according to an allocation formula or on the basis of the revenues' origin. Sales, income, and gasoline taxes are among the state taxes that are often shared. Altogether, states share more than $23 billion with local governments.[27] As in the case of grants, states earmark much of this shared revenue for specific purposes—requiring, for example, that localities spend their share of the state gasoline tax on highway or street improvements. Some shared revenue, however, is unrestricted and can be spent as local officials see fit. Much of the unrestricted aid comes to local governments as compensation for a state action—for example, a state-required property-tax exemption that reduced local revenues—or to help local governments pay for state-mandated services.[28] As far back as 1905, Wisconsin legislators exempted railroad property from local property taxation and decided to make up for this by dedicating part of a state gross earnings tax to reimburse cities. Many of the revenue-sharing programs with cities took root in the Depression years of the 1930s as a result of political campaigns waged by state municipal leagues. Municipalities at that time were looking for a new and stable source of income and were often willing to agree to limitations on their taxing power in exchange for a share of these revenues.[29]

Formulas for the distribution of state aid are often quite controversial, provoking conflict between various regions and types of local government, each of which wants its "fair share" of the revenues. For example, New Yorkers have commonly complained that although much of the state government's revenue comes from their city's taxpayers, the formulas used to distribute state aid favor upstate areas.[30] Generally, states distribute aid according to a criterion such as population or place of origin, rather than on the basis of local need. Use of such criteria allocates funds more evenly among jurisdictions, but it may also aggravate local fiscal disparities. For political reasons, even the best-intended state-aid programs are likely to be scuttled by a legislature if the allocation formula creates too many losers, be they regions or local governmental units. Such was the outcome, for example, in Wisconsin in 2001, when a special commission headed by University of Wisconsin political scientist Donald Kettl proposed to the legislature that it replace a program that distributed shared revenues on a per capita basis among the state's 1,850 municipalities with one that used a formula rewarding municipalities that worked collaboratively on a regional basis to provide services. There was little legislative support for changing the system after a study by the nonpartisan Legislative Fiscal Bureau disclosed that while 60 percent of the municipalities were likely to gain funds, 40 percent were likely to lose funds under the new formula. The president of the League of Wisconsin Municipalities later commented, "It was a horrible mistake to do those regional runs. There were too many losers. In order to make this work, you need a substantial amount of winners and you need to be able to have a hold-harmless provision for the losers. We could have corrected that, had we gotten a chance."[31] Unfortunately, the group didn't get the chance. Legislators in Wisconsin had gone into the process with an eye for getting a fair share of the aid for local governments in their districts, some reportedly being painfully aware that this could affect their reelection prospects.[32]

Nationwide, state aid to local governments is a major source of local revenue, accounting for better than a third of all local general revenues. During the 1990s, it was around 35 percent, down from a high of 38 percent in 1971 (see Appendix B). State spending on aid as a percentage of its total spending also has been somewhat on a decline from the late 1970s, falling from about 38 percent to 33 percent (see Appendix A). Differences among states in the level of local assistance are associated with a number of factors, ranging from per capita income to the percentage of Democrats in the state legislature. The importance of particular factors varies with the type of assistance.[33] Overall, state aid has a modest equalizing effect, only somewhat reducing the revenue gap between poorer and wealthier localities.[34] Only a handful of states make a conscious effort to target funds on the basis of local need.[35] On the other hand, as detailed in the following chapter, states often assist financially distressed local governments when the need arises.

Over the years, the bulk of state aid (from 60 to 64 percent since 1975) has gone to education. Following education in funding are public welfare (now around 12 percent of the total), general local-government support (around 8 percent, down from 10 percent in the 1980s), and highways (a category that has experienced a steady, long-term decline from over 20 percent in the 1940s to the current 4 percent). State aid has also appeared in relatively new areas such as corrections, housing, and transit in recent years. However, relatively little state aid (only about one out of every eight dollars) goes to support traditional municipal-government programs such as police and fire protection.[36] As Table 6.2 suggests, a majority of the aid goes to school districts; counties come in second, and municipalities wind up third. Around 83 percent of all the funds that go for education go to independent school districts; the remainder goes to municipal or county governments in the few states, including Maryland, North Carolina, and Virginia, where these units rather than independent school districts have responsibility for school systems. Counties receive the bulk of the funds earmarked by the state for welfare and for health and hospitals, while state aid on highways is relatively equally distributed between counties and localities. Municipalities received 58 percent of the general, unrestricted support funds.

State aid, while vital to local governments, is not altogether dependable. The amount ebbs and flows, in part, with changing economic conditions. Being largely based on sales and income taxes, it can be relatively high in times of prosperity but also relatively low when the economy is in trouble. Even in times of widespread prosperity, aid may be limited because it competes poorly with demands for tax relief. Also, even in good economic times, state aid may not fare well because lawmakers, for ideological or political reasons, do not look favorably on the aid system—some feeling, as a Wisconsin legislator declared not long ago, "I don't view my role as being an ATM machine for local governments."[37] At the very least, local requests for state aid are likely to be greeted with skepticism and suggestions that the localities are being fiscally mismanaged by people who lack discipline and the courage to make hard decisions.[38] What happens when states decide to cut aid? One local official's answer: "It's not rocket science. . . . It's pretty much raise taxes or cut services. That's what it boils down to."[39] How cities go about adjusting to aid cutbacks—for example, whether they make across-the-board budget cuts and choice of programs to be reduced—varies widely. Whatever adjustments to aid cutbacks are made, though, tend to be short-term rather than permanent.[40]

One municipal league leader has suggested that whatever else local officials might do about cutbacks, they should pass up the opportunity to replace the state dollars that are cut with local funds: "If local officials refuse to replace the state dollars that are cut, then the effects associated with those cuts will be significantly more visible to the public.

Table 6.2

**Percentage Distribution of State Aid by Type of Local Government,
Fiscal Year 1997** (total aid = $260,367 million)

Item	Counties	Municipalities	School districts	Other
Education	8.0	7.4	83.4	1.2
Welfare	72.5	26.8	—	0.7
Health	77.2	15.7	—	7.1
Highways	50.4	42.3	—	7.3
General support	33.0	58.2	—	8.8
Total	24.8	17.8	53.1	4.3

Source: U.S. Bureau of Census, Department of Commerce.

State legislators—not just local-elected officials—may have to answer to the citizens for the consequences of the budget reductions back in their home districts. If local officials continue to try to do the "right thing" by replacing lost state money so that programs don't suffer, the state is likely to reward them with more of the same treatment. One thing is certain—if the members of the General Assembly don't experience any significant backlash from citizens, they will continue to rely disproportionately on local governments to help solve their budget problems."[41]

States, at times, have risked local official if not citizen backlash by taking a hard look at the revenues they share with cities and counties. In recent years, for example, long-established revenue-sharing programs have been cut drastically in Alaska and Arizona, and Tennessee's long history of shared taxes, giving municipalities and counties over $700 million each year, has been threatened because of state budget shortfalls. In 2002, the Tennessee Municipal League (TML) and the Tennessee County Services Association were working together—one of the very rare times this had ever occurred—to protect state-shared money. Drawing on the state-partnership idea, Mayor Randall Higgens, the president of the TML, announced: "Our goal right now is to let the legislators know that their constituents and our constituents are the same."[42] About the same time, in an effort to fight off a proposed cut in the local government share of state tax revenues, an Illinois Municipal League official declared that municipalities had a firm partnership with the state in the revenue-sharing program and one that prohibited the state from "unilaterally changing the terms."[43]

The same year provided evidence of the effectiveness of highly mobilized local lobbies in Wisconsin and Michigan where, as elsewhere, large revenue shortfalls contributed to the conflict. In the first of these, Governor Scott McCallum, faced with a large budget deficit, proposed scaling down and eventually phasing out the state's ninety-year program of shared revenues with municipal governments and counties. The governor did little to help matters by characterizing local officials as "big spenders." Localities struck back with an intense lobbying and public relations campaign to save the $1.03 billion yearly program. A spokesman for the Wisconsin Alliance of Cities later noted, "You can't understate how engaged we were in shared revenues. . . . Thousands of public employees would have lost their jobs. Those are people patching potholes in the street and fighting crime. Their loss would have been felt immediately and sorely."[44] The legislature, under considerable pressure, decided to retain the current funding level at $1.03 billion and to trim it by only $40 million in 2004.

In Michigan meanwhile, Governor John Engler alarmed local officials by vetoing some $854 million in local revenue-sharing payments for local governments. The governor declared that the freed-up funds would be needed if voters approved various propositions on the 2002 ballot; if the voters rejected the measures, he would reinstate the revenue-sharing along with some $7.4 million in fire department grants he was vetoing on the same grounds. The governor contended that the discretionary revenue funds provided the only pot of money he could draw upon to head off a possible financial emergency. A spokesperson for the Michigan Municipal League countered, "It's an atom bomb approach to addressing three initiatives the executive branch doesn't like. . . . He's holding the entire state hostage by threatening to wipe out cities, villages and townships all over the state."[45] The issue was resolved the way aroused local officials insisted it should be when the state legislature overwhelmingly overrode the governor's veto (by a 36–1 vote in the Senate and a 105–1 vote in the House), something that had not happened in 25 years. Addressing a gathering of some 2,000 local government workers on the Capitol grounds on the day of the vote, a city official who helped lead the charge against the proposed cuts declared: "When you put together a force this powerful, good things are going to happen today in Lansing."[46]

Still, some, perhaps many, state lawmakers around the country remain critical of the idea of state aid—seeing no reason why the state should be raising money that local officials spend—and have suggested that the state, as an alternative, give local communities greater authority to raise their own revenues. Critics of this approach, however, argue that it overlooks the fact that localities differ greatly in their tax bases and in their ability to raise revenues. Increased authority to raise revenues is unlikely to be of much value in a jurisdiction with a limited tax base. State aid, on the other hand, can make it possible for jurisdictions with lower tax bases to afford at least a minimal level of service. Because of structural changes in their economies, some cities have a particularly strong need for continued intergovernmental aid.[47]

On the question of state aid, the debate has often proceeded as one might expect—from a "where-you-sit" perspective. From where they sit, state officials find state-aid programs objectionable because state officials are the ones who must suffer the pain of raising revenues, while local officials get credit for providing the services that the aid supports. Along with this view comes the suspicion that local officials seek the aid only because they are afraid to ask their own taxpayers to support services, and because they want to use state money to keep local tax rates low. From where they sit, local officials see state aid as justified because it makes up for state laws that limit local governments' ability to raise revenues and because it offsets costly state mandates on localities. With state mandates in mind, local officials claim that the states are the guilty parties when it comes to claiming credit for programs that other governments finance and when it comes to imposing expenditures on other governments to keep their tax rates as low as possible.

Shifting Support: The Case of Education

Considering state financial aid in isolation gives an incomplete and somewhat misleading picture of state efforts to ease fiscal pressures on local governments. For example, a state that provides minimal direct financial aid to local governments may actually be providing more indirect aid than many or most states, because it assumes the cost of expensive functions that in other states are borne by local governments.[48] In recent years, several states have helped out by taking on more financial responsibility for courts and corrections, indigent health care, mental health care, and cash welfare assistance as well as education. Looking across the nation, the state share of spending generally is highest in Hawaii (78 percent), where the state assumes the costs of education, but also in the relatively lightly populated states of Alaska, Delaware, Vermont, and Rhode Island. It is lowest in California (33 percent) and under 40 percent in Arizona, Colorado, Florida, Minnesota, Nevada, New York, and Wisconsin.[49]

State assumption of expenditures could reduce spending disparities that result from reliance on the local property tax as well as provide and free up property-tax revenues for other local functions. Yet the price is likely to be a loss of local control and perhaps a decline in service quality. In fact, some programs now under state administration may be better off under direct local control. Some observers have suggested, for example, that a decentralized court system, which can allow for more flexibility in judicial administration, may be preferable to a court system financed and administered by the state. Rather than assume full financial and administrative responsibility for courts, states could provide relief through grants in aid and cost-reimbursement plans but give local governments some control over the administration of the system.[50]

Among the most important disruptions in state-local financial relations in recent years has been the shift in the financing of educational services from the local property tax to revenue resources controlled by the state. This shift has been encouraged by both the taxpayers' protests against the property tax, much of which is used to finance local education, and court decisions finding local property taxes to be an unfair method of supporting education.

One of the most dramatic reactions to mounting citizen discontent with education-related property taxes was the July 1993 decision of the Michigan legislature to simply eliminate property taxes for elementary and secondary education. This action followed several years of the legislature's groping with ways to reform the property-tax system. The tax had been steadily increasing, largely in an effort to keep up with the costs of education. The property-tax burden, putting the state far above the national average, eventually led voters to reject proposed property-tax increases for schools. In 1993, some schools ran out of money and had to close down before the official end of the school year. Nevertheless, in June of 1993, voters rejected a statewide proposal that would have increased the state sales tax by 50 percent in exchange for a cap on local property taxes and a guaranteed minimum of $4,800 spending for every pupil in school.

Republican governor John Engler proposed in the summer of 1993 to cut school property taxes by 20 percent. Democrats in control of the legislature felt that the governor's offer was a gambit, rather than a sincere proposal, and attempted to put him on the spot by offering legislation eliminating all property taxes for operating local schools. The governor, however, did not, as the Democrats hoped, back away from property-tax reform, but instead called the legislature's bluff by announcing that he would sign the Democrats' bill should it be passed. As it turned out, virtually no one in the legislature dared to oppose the proposed tax cut, and the governor, also committed by his words, signed the "scorched earth" measure into law. The decision, produced through a brinkmanship process, seemed risky—if not reckless; the property tax had been eliminated without a plan for replacing the lost revenues of some $7 billion. One newspaper editor, noting that the lawmakers hadn't the slightest idea of how they were now going to pay for schools, greeted the decision by wondering, "Is Michigan celebrating the '90s by going mad?"[51]

Late in 1993, the legislature gave its approval to two alternative school-finance proposals. They submitted one of these for voter approval on March 15, 1994, with the understanding that if it were rejected, the other plan would go into effect. Compared to the 1993 ballot issue, which gave citizens a choice of *yes* or *no* on the proposed reform, they were put in a position of having to choose between a plan that featured a 50 percent increase in the sales tax—the one on the ballot—and the one in reserve, which called for a 30 percent increase in the state income tax. At the time, Michigan had a relatively low sales tax and a relatively high income tax. Not surprisingly, in this context, in a heavy turnout, 70 percent of the voters chose the sales-tax alternative. This plan also added a statewide property tax and either increased or added a mixture of other taxes and a new lottery game to make up for the lost property-tax revenue. The change did not provide overall tax relief but only a shift in taxation, that is, away from the local property tax to other sources, particularly the sales tax. The measure, however, by reducing reliance on the property tax, increasing state support for poorer schools, and limiting what school districts could spend, narrowed the gap in spending between poor and rich school districts throughout the state.

Engler, looking at the returns, noted, "It is a huge vote. . . . The property tax had been a terrible problem in the state because of the relentless increases for schools. We were approaching an educational meltdown, and it was the root of the inequities in the per pupil spending among districts."[52] More profoundly, approval of the plan shifted much of the control over the financing of schools from local school boards to the state government. The action in Michigan stimulated similar reform in several states during the 1990s, though most wound up making incremental rather than dramatic shifts to state funding. Still, there have been some exceptions. In 1996, for example, after having put a freeze on local property taxes, the Wisconsin legislature decided to fund two-thirds of the school costs. Five years later, Minnesota provided tax relief for all classes of property by shifting much of the funding for schools from local property taxes to state revenues. In 2002, the Indiana legislatures did likewise, providing property-tax relief, through increasing sales, gasoline, and cigarette taxes.

While politicians and citizen groups around the country have protested what they have seen to be excessively high local property taxes for education, others have gone to state courts arguing that reliance on the local property tax to finance education discriminates against students in areas where property values are the lowest and thus violates provisions in the various state constitutions. Thus far, state courts in about half of the states have forced state legislatures to change how education is funded and remedy inadequacies in expenditures or educational quality brought about by the reliance on local property taxes. Nationwide, the public seems to favor change. A national survey in the late 1990s, for example, found only 20 percent of the population in favor of relying on property taxes as a way of funding schools, while 50 percent favored shifting funding to state sales taxes or income taxes.[53]

Among the most notable developments in education finance in recent years is the Vermont legislature's adoption in 1997 of a reform measure (Act 60) that created a new statewide property tax to finance elementary and secondary schools. This legislative action followed a decision of the Vermont Supreme Court earlier in the year that the state's school-funding system based on local property taxes was invalid because it caused a wide disparity in the amount of money that various towns spent on education. Though the court did not demand precisely equal funding, it did require the state to move toward equality of educational opportunity through the state and rejected the contention that the state constitution required only a minimal level of expenditure in each district. Act 60 replaced a school-financing system that relied on local property taxes to pay 70 percent of the cost of education while the state picked up the remaining 30 percent. Under the new system, the state property tax pays 70 percent of the cost, while local property taxes pay 30 percent. The legislative plan became controversial because it conflicted with state's tradition of local authority—provoking cries from citizens that Montpelier was taking over their lives—and because it called for a redistribution of tax money from richer communities to poorer ones. For a time, some of the wealthier towns refused to pay the additional taxes.

In 1999, the New Hampshire legislature also made an abrupt change in school funding. Responding to a state court order that made it illegal to support public education with widely varying local property taxes as the primary source of funding, the legislature came up with a statewide property tax and a plan under which the state pays more than 60 percent of the cost of education. Prior to the act, New Hampshire had raised over 90 percent of its funds for schools from local taxes. Constitutional challenges brought by property-rich towns—which, under the new plan, are taxed to aid students in property-poor towns—were dismissed by the state supreme court. In their anger, some of the property-rich towns, known as "donor towns," went so far as to threaten to secede from the state.

In some parts of the country, much of the responsibility for financing the growing costs of education continues to rest with local governments—principally, independent school districts—and the local property tax. In many places and in the nation overall, however, because of citizen pressure and judicial decisions, the share borne by state governments has increased over the past several years. In 1971–1972, state governments contributed about 38 percent of all revenues for public elementary and secondary schools. In fiscal year 2001, this proportion was over 50 percent. Research suggests that responsibility for education funding has been most likely to be shifted to the state in states where (1) resistance to increases in property taxes has been greatest and (2) the degree of "localism" in the state's culture and history—and thus the resistance to state control—is weakest.[54]

Throughout the country, shifting education funding to the states has been an effective means of addressing the problems of overall support and equity. It has, however, also created other difficulties. For one, it makes financial support of education less stable by tying it to the ups and downs of the fiscal health of the state and, often, to revenue sources that are less dependable than the property tax, especially in a recessionary period. Pinning education finance to the sales tax makes support for education particularly volatile. Even in good times, moreover, there is considerable uncertainty as to the level of support because education has to compete with a host of other demands on state funds. For educators, the growth of state financial aid has had the added downside of being accompanied by caps on local educational expenditures and increases in state regulations. States also have stepped up their involvement in the provision of educational services. As one state legislator put it, "When we control the money, it's hard to get out of the details."[55] They have shown an increased concern with curricula, class size, special education, and, in the interest of accountability, statewide academic standards and mandated tests. Legislators commonly evaluate the performance of public schools in their states by national education standards and have instituted a variety of programs to improve the quality of education, ranging from vouchers and charter schools to the direct takeover of school districts. With increased state funding, governors, legislators, and state administrators feel perfectly justified in demanding a greater "bang for the buck," that is, a better educational product. Meanwhile, the push toward greater equity in spending among districts has also provoked its share of conflict between rich and poor communities, with residents from rich communities condemning "Robin Hood" plans benefiting the poor at the expense of affluent communities, and state legislators representing rich districts opposing forced reductions on the amount of money that their constituents can spend on education.

Helping Out: The Broader Picture

State governments can help local officials meet their financial problems in a variety of ways: chiefly by increasing revenue authority, extending aid, and picking up the cost of certain functions. States could also help by cutting local costs, for example, by eliminating mandates or fully funding them, fostering greater efficiency at the local level, or encouraging greater cost-sharing cooperation among local governments. In several states, municipalities, counties, and school boards have taken advantage of the services of state management specialists to identify cost savings. Moving in this direction in 1999, the Florida legislature passed enabling legislation (but no funding) for a Local Government Financial Technical Assistance Program, intended to provide financial technical assistance to smaller municipalities and independent special districts throughout the state.

States can also help in other ways. Legislation adopted by the 1997 Georgia legislature, for example, allows municipalities and counties to ask the state Revenue Department to withhold unpaid local taxes, fees, and fines from an individual's state income tax refund. A similar program in South Carolina has been highly successful. Some reformers also have suggested that states can help out by exempting local governments from state taxes. County, municipal, and school district governments could, for example, save millions of dollars if the gasoline used to fill official vehicles were exempt from state gasoline taxes. When it comes to the gasoline tax, however, transportation officials and road builders are likely to oppose exemptions on the grounds that they would reduce the pool of funds earmarked for road projects.

In many places, there continues to be a mismatch between fiscal needs and resources—the needs being disproportionately in the central cities and the resources being disproportionately in the suburbs. Residents of central cities have to tax themselves at a higher rate than suburban residents simply to generate the same revenues and at a substantially higher rate to generate sufficient revenues to address their special needs. Yet, if they try to raise revenues to the necessary level, they are likely to encourage more people to leave for the suburbs. Solutions to the mismatch problem have sought, through reforms, state aid programs that would more directly target large cities with financial problems. Some states have shown increased interest in plans calling for local governments in metropolitan areas to share burdens. For example, some state legislatures and courts require each municipality to assume its share of responsibility for providing low-income housing. Some state lawmakers around the country have also considered encouraging local governments in a given region to share revenues rather than depend on state aid or extended revenue authority. The Regional Tax Base Sharing Program, in Minneapolis-Saint Paul, is an example of neighboring governments pooling resources: a portion of the increase in the area's industrial tax base is placed in a regional pool, from which all jurisdictions in the area draw revenues. The financial strain on central cities and hard-pressed smaller communities in many places could also be relieved by burden-shifting—if, for example, various functions were moved from the municipal to the county level. Many of the issues surrounding annexation, incorporation, and consolidation further involve moves that could head off fiscal problems or, hopefully, end fiscal imbalances and promote or create equity in services delivered in metropolitan areas (see Chapter 8).

To a large extent, the real issues of state-local relations revolve around financial matters rather than abstract concerns about local home rule.

Not surprisingly, state-local tensions vary with ups and downs in the general economy. More routinely, local officials want more state aid to make up for what they see as unfair state policies and their lack of control over revenue decisions. "It would be nice," a city attorney noted recently, "if we had a system in which local governments could make revenue decisions and be held accountable for them. But at the moment these decisions are made by the Legislature, often by the courts and only rarely by the elected local officials that are accessible to the people."[56]

When it comes to revenue authority, county governments appear most in need of help. Although in many states, increased urbanization and suburbanization have blurred the distinction between municipal and county services, county governments lag behind municipal governments in their ability to raise revenues. In California, where there have been some recent moves to reform the system of county finance, researchers report that "the fundamental dilemma of counties remains: (1) counties have little control over their expenditures or revenues, and (2) county supervisors are elected locally but have few tools to respond to local preferences."[57]

7

The Takeover Problem

Local officials often bristle over having to get state permission to do even the most routine activities and over the lack of state financial support. On occasion, they also have reasons to feel even worse—as if they are the displaced or exiled leaders of a territory occupied by some distant power. This has happened at various times when state governments have, in effect, suspended local self-government to take varying degrees of direct control over local activities.

State takeovers of financially distressed, general-purpose local governments (municipalities and counties) and "academically bankrupt" school districts have been the most noticeable in recent years. In the first case, takeovers have stemmed from a state's determination that a local government is facing a financial crisis. The general objective of state intervention has been to restore financial stability. States have been encouraged to get involved out of fear that a failing municipality will lower the credit rating of other localities and the state itself, thus making the state less attractive to business investments. Takeovers have been further encouraged on the grounds that the state, as the legal parent, has an obligation to assure that local units live up to their contractual obligations and that there be no disruption in the provision of necessary services.[1] For academic bankruptcies, the reasons for intervention and the goals sought have been more varied. Some interventions, for example, have been based on state findings that a school district is guilty of improper hiring practices or of simple mismanagement. Such problems, however, have often been tied to broader charges that local school officials are failing, or have already failed, in their primary mission of educating children.

A general idea behind both types of state takeovers is that existing units of local government having trouble need not be destroyed but can be saved by suspending democracy for a time, making painful adjustments, and implementing long-term, largely managerial, reforms. In a legal sense, states need not be overly concerned about their ability to take over and operate a local government. Yet, the desire to intervene in local affairs is countered by a variety of political considerations—not the least of which is community resistance—that work against the exercise of state authority. State administrators also face the possibility that faulty assumptions about the nature of a problem or about the effectiveness of particular remedies will prevent them from finding long-term solutions. The broader question raised in the following discussion is whether state officials should be actively involved in monitoring the performance of local governments, demanding corrective action when they deem necessary, or largely sit back and wait for local governments to request assistance.

Municipal Interventions

State legislatures have historically taken two types of action regarding municipal financial distress. At times, they have acted on an ad hoc basis with legislation for specific municipalities in dire financial straits, giving them financial and technical assistance and imposing various controls on their activities. Such action has frequently been prompted by a request for state action from the locality involved. Taking a more proactive route, some legislatures have authorized state agencies to monitor the fiscal affairs of municipalities generally or broad classes of municipalities and to intervene more extensively in the affairs of those localities that they find heading toward financial trouble. Municipalities found to be in fiscal trouble receive a mixture of aid and regulation. Inability to resolve problems may lead to a complete state takeover as a state agency or a state-appointed receiver assumes the reins of government from local officials.[2] Most takeovers in recent years have occurred as the result of the implementation of general-distress legislation.[3]

A state takeover of a financially troubled local government usually involves the creation of a financial control board to manage the local jurisdiction's financial affairs. Such state agencies are usually comprised of private citizens with expertise in financial matters. In some places, all the members are appointed by state officials, while in others, at least some of the members are appointed by local officials. The allocation of appointment authority between state and local officials may have an impact on the board's overall policy direction: boards controlled by state appointees appear to bring a more state-directed perspective to their job than do those controlled by local appointees.[4] In either case, however, the boards are not directly accountable to local residents and usually have considerable authority to manage the jurisdiction's debt. Free to ignore local political pressures, financial control boards may take swift and decisive action to restructure the debt, dedicate revenues for its repayment, control additional borrowing, compel the affected local jurisdiction to make hard choices in regard to services and taxes, and ensure that local officials have a balanced budget and a sensible financial plan for future years.

This is not to suggest, however, that control boards always have an easy time of it. For example, the Financial Advisory Authority, appointed in 1991 by Illinois state officials to oversee the finances of East St. Louis, a distressed city of some 40,000 people, has found it difficult to prod the city into timely corrective action. It has been handicapped by an Illinois Supreme Court ruling in 1999 that its power extends only to approving or rejecting city budgets and does not include the right to impose a budget of its own on a local government. Confrontations and resistance have also taken place in Camden, New Jersey, another financially troubled city under state supervision. There, the city council unsuccessfully challenged in court the right of the state to appoint a business administrator.

For municipalities, the modern era of state intervention and takeovers began in 1975 when New York City officials, faced with a massive debt and an inability to sell city bonds, passed up bankruptcy and reluctantly turned over much of their authority to the state. The New York State Emergency Financial Control Board (EFCB), dominated by the governor and his appointees (a small group of businesspeople), assumed responsibility for most major municipal financial decisions. Local control was largely suspended during the "crisis regime" of state supervision from the mid-1970s to the mid-1980s.[5] While the city still had its own elected officials, the EFCB, the Municipal Assistance Corporation (MAC) (which the state had formed earlier to help the city get out from under its short-term debt), and other state officials, including a deputy comptroller for New York City, supervised and monitored city finances. As the locus of authority began to change, journalists became awed with the "men of power" who took control of city affairs, and protest groups moved from city hall to the offices of the EFCB, where the power then resided.[6] In the new arrangement, city officials felt frustrated in their efforts to influence the allocation of funds. As the deputy mayor of New

York City, with an eye on some surplus revenues that MAC had been able to generate, noted, "It's our money, but it's in their cash register."[7]

The new regime ushered in a politics of retrenchment, which, within a few years, produced a loss of some 60,000 municipal jobs, large increases in taxes and fees, and severe cuts in services. State agencies took the lead in changing the financial planning process, revising policies toward municipal unions, and finding ways to improve control over semiautonomous agencies.[8] By the mid-1980s, scholars took the experience of the crisis regime in New York as evidence that state and local officials, working together, were not altogether powerless in resolving financial difficulties.[9] Yet, by the early 1990s, the city was once again experiencing considerable fiscal strain, and observers began to express doubts about the ultimate success of the kind of recovery effort practiced in New York.[10]

By the early 1990s, state interventions were well under way elsewhere in New York, such as Yonkers, and in hard-pressed municipalities in Pennsylvania, Connecticut, and Massachusetts. In Pennsylvania, a dozen small municipalities came under the supervision of the state Department of Community Affairs. Most of these were communities in the western part of the state that were under stress because of the decline in the steel industry, though fiscal mismanagement also helped account for their problems.[11] For the municipalities involved, state intervention into their financial planning process came essentially as a tradeoff for varying forms of state assistance. Supervision brought much-needed financial relief and considerable financial restructuring. Much of the latter came at the expense of municipal employees in the form of wage freezes and cuts in job benefits. Labor unions had unsuccessfully challenged the state's intervention in court.[12]

Although initially reluctant to help out Philadelphia, the Pennsylvania legislature provided aid when it appeared that the city was about to default on its bond payments. In 1991, the state created the Pennsylvania Intergovernmental Cooperation Authority (PICA) and gave it the power to issue bonds and divert the proceeds to the city for its fiscal needs. The legislature also gave PICA the right to exert certain controls over the city's financial affairs, including the approval of a long-term fiscal plan and the power to withhold certain state funds from the city if the city did not follow the plan. Philadelphia's financial plan, which was approved by the state board, contained many cuts in workers' salaries and benefits, a development strongly resisted by municipal unions. In addition, the city made a host of changes, including improving tax collection, finding new ways to save on utility costs, and contracting out more work through a competitive-bidding procedure. The city's economic condition greatly improved, though it continued to have structural problems, as reflected in high levels of poverty.[13]

The first of PICA's chairpersons later remarked that the success of the intervention rested on the board's functioning as an "oversight" group that allowed city officials considerable discretion in operating the city and framing remedies to its financial woes rather than as a "control group" that tried to dictate specific policy steps. PICA's chief value to city officials, in the eyes of its chairperson, may have been in giving the elected officials the political cover that they needed to make unpopular decisions. When something unpopular had to be done, the city's officials could blame the board.[14] From the city's point of view, the oversight board functioned like a "friendly banker," though much of its effectiveness rested on the board's possession of a "nuclear weapon" in the ability to cut off funds to the city.[15]

During the early 1990s, few cities facing financial distress received as much media coverage as Bridgeport, Connecticut, the state's largest city, with a population of about 140,000. In addition to a general recession, Bridgeport suffered from a loss of manufacturing jobs, shrinking federal and state aid, white flight to the suburbs, increased welfare costs, and, some observers charged, slipshod financial management. Its troubles, evidenced by a pyramiding debt of some $60 million, prompted the state, at the city's request, to come up with special legislation in 1988 to create the Bridgeport Financial Review Board, hereafter referred to as the FRB, to oversee the city's finances. Along with this, the state agreed to guarantee $35 million in bonds for the city. The following year, the city sold bonds to cover its operating deficit and began a three-year plan to regain financial stability. By June 1991, it had cut services and workforce expenditures but still had a $16 million deficit. Mayor Mary C. Moran tried without success to cover this debt by securing concessions, such as reduced pensions and fringe benefits, from unions. Moran had difficulties with the FRB, perhaps, at least in part, because she was a Republican, elected to office on a partisan ticket, and the FRB was controlled by Democrats. The board also had what some considered to be a state orientation because six of the nine members were either state officials or appointed by state officials.[16]

On June 5, 1991, the FRB ordered for the city a budget calling for drastic spending cuts and an 18 percent increase in the property tax. Mayor Moran contended that Bridgeport could not afford the tax increase; indeed, city attorneys argued, such increases would make matters worse by encouraging more homeowners and businesses to leave the city. On the following day, the mayor took the unusual step of filing for protection under Chapter 9 of the federal bankruptcy code, making it the largest city in the nation ever to have declared bankruptcy. The mayor reportedly sought bankruptcy to avoid the changes ordered by the board—particularly the property-tax increase, which she felt would hinder her reelection, less than six months away.[17] By filing for bankruptcy, she prevented the board from forcing the increases. The petition for bankruptcy, however, did little to reduce her political problems. Political opponents denounced the mayor's bankruptcy move as a cynical political maneuver to detract attention away from her inability to handle the city's affairs. The move also created some economic panic as investor services downgraded the city's credit rating, banks refused to cash city workers' checks, and some vendors, fearful of not being paid, asked the city to return various goods. Some politicians worried that the action would reflect poorly on the entire state, scaring off needed investments.[18] The FRB contended that the mayor had acted illegally—that the city could not apply for bankruptcy without the board's permission. The bankruptcy judge rejected this position but went on to deny the city's petition on the grounds that city officials had not proven that the city was insolvent and would therefore be unable to meet its future financial obligations.

Democratic challenger Joseph P. Ganim easily defeated Mayor Morgan in her bid for reelection, the bankruptcy petition being a major issue. Coming into office in 1991, Mayor Ganim successfully negotiated with the FRB to avoid major tax increases, brought reductions in the city's budget by imposing a freeze on hiring and spending—gaining some concessions from unions—and ended the city's attempt to declare bankruptcy. Ganim developed particularly close ties with Independent governor Lowell P. Weicker Jr., who helped the mayor relocate various projects into the city. By the mid-1990s, the FRB had closed up shop and the city returned to normal.

The ultimate in recent state takeovers came in Chelsea, Massachusetts, an impoverished city of around 28,000 people, about one-third of whom are Hispanic, on the northern edge of Boston. The city experienced a severe financial decline in the mid-1980s, even though the rest of the state was enjoying rapid growth. The state initially responded with loans, grants, and fiscal oversight. State financial assistance started in 1986. In June 1991, the state gave Chelsea an infusion of $960,000. At the time, the city had a $48 million budget, of which the state was contributing more than half, and a $9 million debt. It faced a myriad of financial problems: a shrinking tax base, increased costs, union reluctance to make concessions, and voter refusal to approve tax increases to help close the budget gap.

In September 1991, a state board appointed to straighten out the financial mess refused to accept an interim budget for the city, leaving it without the means to pay its bills. Mayor John Brennan reacted by announcing that he would immediately ask the state to put Chelsea in receivership—a position he had publicly taken earlier in the year after citizens had turned down a tax increase. The state agreed to the receivership to save Chelsea from financial collapse and, it was hoped, to enable it to survive on its own. Prodded by Governor William Weld, on September 11, 1991, the legislature agreed to an emergency proposal that brought Chelsea under state control. The law gave the governor authority to appoint a receiver to run the city for up to five years, eliminated the post of mayor, and reduced the status of other locally elected officials to an advisory capacity. This was the first time since the Depression of the 1930s that a Massachusetts municipality had been placed in receivership.[19] Since 1991, the state has put other cities under financial review boards that must approve the cities' spending plans, but none of the boards has had the exceptional power given to the receiver in Chelsea.

The legislation gave the receiver broad authority to cut municipal spending, eliminate services, revise agreements with unions representing municipal workers, issue service contracts, and even restructure the local government to eliminate corruption and improve the future ability of local officials to govern efficiently. The idea of receivership got mixed reviews in Chelsea. While some citizens were elated, several Chelsea aldermen, faced with a loss of authority, accused the governor of abolishing democracy in the city.[20] "It stinks" was the conclusion offered by a firefighter concerned that the receiver would lay off people in his position and reduce the salaries of those not laid off.[21]

The receiver brought in a management team and went to work on the first phase of his program: developing a balanced budget. By cutting the payroll, renegotiating union contracts, bringing in a $5 million advance payment from the Massachusetts Port Authority, and taking various other steps, such as increased user fees and the privatization of some services, the receiver helped the city move out of insolvency.[22] Savings on the labor front resulted from the reduction of the city bureaucracy from 309 to 224 people. Negotiating from a position of strength, the receiver secured a new contract with the firefighters that eliminated costly minimum staffing, sick leave, vacation, and overtime requirements. A state official was quick to point out that the new firefighters' contract was not altogether popular and "was only possible because the receiver did not have to run for reelection and face the wrath of an organized, focused opposition."[23] Having balanced the operating budget, the receiver tackled the long-term problem of enabling the community to function on its own. Toward this end, he developed long-term capital and infrastructure plans and, working with a citizens' panel, devised a new form of government for the city. The new form, approved by the voters in June 1994, called for an elected 11–member city council and an appointed city manager with strong powers over budgetary and personnel matters. Backers of the plan offered it as a way of avoiding corruption—Massachusetts courts had recently convicted several former Chelsea mayors and police officers on corruption charges—as well as improving financial management. The new plan was used in December 1994 as the basis for the city's first fully democratic election in over three years. While en route to hiring a city manager—a step that had to be completed before state control could end—the new city council demonstrated its assertiveness by strongly protesting the receiver's decision to fire a long-time city clerk because of the way absentee ballots were counted in the December election and declaring that it needed no help from the receiver in selecting a manager.

School District Interventions

State intervention in the affairs of local school districts, like intervention in the affairs of municipalities, has a long history. Actual takeovers of operationally or academically troubled school districts, however, are a relatively new phenomenon, dating back to the late 1980s. State legislatures have sometimes passed statutes that mandate direct takeovers of particular districts—either through a state-appointed official or a local official, such as a mayor. At other times, takeovers have resulted from court orders. The 1995 takeover of the school system in Cleveland, Ohio, containing about 73,000 mostly minority students, for example, resulted from an order by the federal court judge who presided over the district's desegregation litigation. The judge found the district to be so bogged down in conflict, indecision, mismanagement, and fiscal irresponsibility that it could no longer be depended upon to run its own affairs, and he ordered a state takeover.[24]

Most commonly, however, takeovers have come as a last-resort remedy in a process provided for in what are called academic bankruptcy laws, now found in 23 states.[25] Under this legislation, a state agency periodically evaluates the governance, management, fiscal operations, and educational programs of each of its school districts. Early intervention may simply consist of warnings of the need for corrective action. This is followed by a succession of sanctions if matters do not improve. To encourage change, state education departments may withhold state aid from districts or revoke their accreditation. State officials, as the ultimate remedy, may take direct control over the district, dismissing elected school board members and local administrators. The superintendent and entire school board may be replaced, even if only a few schools are failing to perform up to standards. As with financial-distress laws, academic bankruptcy status usually brings financial and technical assistance.

Although academic takeovers have been rare, in part because of the cumbersome procedures required by the laws, there have been more than 40 takeovers in 18 states since the late 1980s.[26] Some takeovers have involved small rural systems with inadequate funding, poor management, and poor academic performance. Others have involved large, urban school systems with similar but more expansive problems—the most recent being the state of Pennsylvania's takeover in late 2001 of the Philadelphia school district, with 260 schools and 220,000 students. Takeovers have lasted from a year or less to several years, with five years being common. In some cases, a state has taken over a school district more than once—this is true, for example, in regard to the Barbour County School District in Alabama and the Floyd County School District in Kentucky. In some cases, the state has also had to deal more than once with chaos attributed to the same superintendent—an example being J. L. Handy, who was fired from his job as superintendent of the Compton, California, Unified School District in 1992 when it was well on its way toward state control and who surfaced eight years later as superintendent of the Emeryville, California, Unified School District, as it too stood on the brink of a state takeover. "We've seen poor oversight and administration now for the second time by the same guy. . . . It's an exceedingly high batting average," noted a state education department spokesman.[27]

In some places, a superintendent sent in by the state during intervention acts not only as a superintendent but as the school board as well. This situation, as the state-appointed superintendent in Paterson, New Jersey, noted, "is every superintendent's dream."[28] For those on the receiving end, as a school official in a South Carolina district put it, intervention is likely to be a "hell of an embarrassment to the kids as well as the community."[29] Looking back, the official recalled, "We went through hell for a couple of years. . . . They came in with an Impairment Committee, picked by the state . . . and they were instructed not to find anything good going on in your district."[30] In the end, however, the official gave intervention good marks for goading the community into passing a needed bond issue for the schools and providing technical assistance that helped upgrade the quality of education offered.

A similar story unfolded after the state of California took over the Compton Unified School District, with about 30,000 students, mostly Hispanic and black, south of Los Angeles. The state took control of Compton's schools in 1993, at a time when the district was in debt to the tune of nearly $20 million and confronted with problems of poorly qualified teachers (some of whom had been fired by other schools), inadequate facilities, and some of the lowest standardized test scores in the state. "You have to try to get students to achieve that poorly," the fifth state-appointed administrator sent to the district, Randolph E. Ward, thought when he took over in 1996.[31] Ward improved management practices, cut the payroll, reduced the debt problem, and found funds to purchase textbooks and make needed building repairs. In the end, test scores also improved, though the students continued to lag behind most other students in the state. Ward was proud of the improvements, though he noted that these would not have been made without his having been given complete control.[32] As state control began to phase out in July 2000, several members of the community were more than happy to see the state-appointed administrator go and downplayed the extent of the gains made. From the beginning, many had seen the state's presence as an "occupation" and "a total dictatorship very demeaning to the people of the community."[33] In Compton, as in other districts, the state takeover was viewed by some in the community as a matter of putting blacks and Hispanics down.

Some of the most studied school interventions have occurred in New Jersey, where, under a pioneering procedure adopted in 1988, the state department of education systematically reviews each district's governance, management, fiscal operations, and educational programs every five years. Local governments have an opportunity to correct problems that arise. If the problems are not resolved, a state monitoring team steps in for further investigation and makes a report. State officials, acting on this report, can order the district to show cause why it should not be taken over. District officials can present their side in a hearing and may also challenge a proposed takeover in court. In the end, the commissioner of education may appoint a superintendent who is responsible to the state education department to run the district, replacing the local school boards and local administrators. This New Jersey law grew out of a school-improvement plan devised for the state in 1975. Originally, local school systems were offered grants and other forms of state assistance to strengthen their effectiveness. State education administrators, however, found pockets of resistance at the local level and eventually went back to the legislature and received greater regulatory authority to intervene in deficient school systems.[34]

Thus far, the state education department has issued "show cause" orders leading to takeovers in districts in Jersey City, Paterson, and Newark. The takeover in Jersey City, in 1989, initiated the current round of academic bankruptcy actions. It was the first solvent school district in the country to have its authority transferred to the state. Jersey City is an aging industrial city, where nearly 80 percent of the approximately 28,000 students in the school system are black or Hispanic. State officials said that they were reluctantly taking control because school officials had not corrected numerous deficiencies discovered over a three-year monitoring process. By one account, frustrated by the resistance encountered in a long and contentious monitoring relationship, the department of education simply declared war on the district and threw just about every charge it could against the school district's officials.[35]

The state found that the district had not provided an environment conducive to learning. School administration was, according to the state, plagued by political patronage in hiring, corruption, and excessive union demands. Jersey City officials bitterly fought the takeover and resorted to court action as a last-ditch effort to avoid state control. One analysis suggests that the takeover aborted what could have been an effective reform effort led by a new management team that had taken office in

1985.[36] Following intervention, a 1993 independent audit of Jersey City's schools found significant improvements in the system's management, finance, facilities, and educational programs, but student achievement continued to be a problem.[37] In 2000, the schools began a transition back to local governance.

New Jersey's education commissioner took over Paterson's school district in April 1991. In this instance, the central charges were mismanagement of the 22,000-student system and the inability to make corrections noted in successive rounds of state inspections since 1984. The report detailed nearly three dozen problems relating to the district's management. The mayor of Paterson endorsed the state's action, but several of the displaced school board members complained that the state had acted on inaccurate information and in a heavy-handed way, with detrimental effects on the community. An independent audit conducted three years after the takeover was similar to that of Jersey City in finding substantial progress in financial management, the learning environment, and other areas. Student standardized test scores, however, were no better than before the takeover.[38]

The case against Newark schools, as detailed in a five-volume report prepared by the state, centered on what the state department of education found to be corrupt and incompetent school district management, which had "consistently failed or . . . been unable to take corrective action necessary to establish a thorough and efficient system of education" for the 48,000 children in the system.[39] The department's investigation found two worlds in the Newark system: "the world of the schools themselves, with misdirected instruction, badly neglected buildings, inefficient practices, and inequitable distribution of even the most basic resources," and "the world of comfortable offices and important-sounding titles in the district central office, detached from the everyday reality of the schools."[40] School officials in Newark denied the accusations. They also contended that the school takeovers in Jersey City and Paterson have made little improvement.[41] On a more positive note, they devised a plan for improving the schools. State officials characterized the plan as being too little, too late. In a press release, the state concluded that "It is highly unlikely that such 11th-hour remedies, applied by the same leaders, will be able to bring about the major change needed if the students in Newark's public schools are to achieve the education services they deserve."[42]

By the summer of 1994, state education officials apparently had given up on the leadership of the Newark school system and had concluded that it had to be replaced. By this time, however, the district had also organized to prevent the state from taking control. Some acts of aggression had already occurred: the state had conducted a 2 A.M. raid on district offices to seize some files, while, on the other hand, an elderly state official had been handcuffed and dragged from one of Newark's schools.[43] State officials in February 1995 filed a petition with an administrative law judge seeking permission to proceed to the takeover stage without going though the standard hearing process. The judge accepted the petition. However, unlike state officials, who placed emphasis on incompetent administrators in defending the need for intervention, the judge defined the problem differently, placing emphasis on the failure of Newark schoolchildren on statewide school proficiency tests.[44] While there has always been some confusion as to the purpose of the takeover in Newark, it did lead to some academic gains, for example, in school attendance and test scores. Unlike the other interventions, however, the state produced little in terms of improved budgeting. The state-appointed administrators left the district some $70 million in debt as it began its transition back to local control.[45]

School district takeovers in New Jersey have required education officials to make a strong case that local officials are unwilling or unable to comply with state mandates. In practice, nothing much is likely to happen until state education administrators lose all confidence in (or respect for) the officials in charge of a suspect system, decide that it would be futile to wait any longer for change, and feel that they can make their case in court, if necessary, against the district. The department of education has given local school-district officials several warnings before taking drastic action. They have discovered that the mere threat of a takeover can sometimes get the attention of local school officials and galvanize them into taking corrective action without further state involvement.

When takeover proceedings begin, however, they have been resisted fiercely by many local school officials, teachers, and at least some community leaders who, though unhappy about the schools, are even more unhappy about state interference. State intervention has often conflicted with deeply rooted traditions of local control of public schools. Interveners have faced severe uphill battles posed by local culture and tradition. As an observer of the takeover in Jersey City noted, "People in Jersey City have spent generations developing a certain way of thinking about and dealing with their schools. So how easy will it be for a superintendent who is parachuted in by the department of education to change these attitudes?"[46] Community opposition to school takeovers in some places has also reflected the fear of job loss, as schools supply many of the few jobs available.[47] Often, racial overtones have also been apparent. Some states have run afoul of the federal Voting Rights Act of 1965. Mindful of the law, the U.S. Department of Justice has viewed takeovers as potentially violating rights to elect local officials and has required certain states to obtain the department's clearance before taking over a school district.

Evaluation

State takeovers can lead to a considerable amount of controversy. What appears to count most in establishing the number of takeovers, their tone, and the level of disruption they create is whether the basic policy approach is reactive or proactive. Illustrative of the first of these is the general approach taken in regard to financial distress in such cities as New York and Philadelphia. Illustrative of the proactive approach are those taken under general legislation extending to distressed municipalities and academic bankruptcy legislation. Under the proactive approach, one is likely to see virtually the whole range of administrative control techniques—reports, inspections, advice, grants, approval, review—before the last resort, the takeover or, as it is sometimes euphemistically known, "substitute administration." Under the reactive approach, these devices are employed, if at all, after the decision is made to take over a local operation. Under the proactive approach, the basic decision of whether to take over the municipality or school district is in the hands of administrators, while state legislatures make these decisions in the reactive model. All other things being equal, takeovers seem more likely when the decisions are in the hands of state administrators rather than state legislators. The latter have reason to fear that they will upset constituents through such actions. Some legislators also claim that they tend to back away from intervention out of a natural reluctance to usurp the power of fellow elected officials.[48] Administrators are not limited by these considerations.

The reactive approach is more consistent with the norm that local governments should conduct their own affairs and devise solutions to their own problems. The state becomes involved only because matters have reached a point at which it is clear to local officials that they cannot take care of the situation on their own and decide to ask the state for help. From the local point of view, the loss of control is understandable; it is the price that local officials have to pay for financial and technical assistance and for a way out of an emergency situation. The state's role is narrowly targeted and only temporary. The downside of the reactive approach is the danger that by the time the state decides to get involved, considerable damage may have already occurred and the problems may have become far more difficult to resolve.

Under the proactive approach, the state is on a mission to detect problems or to bring about general improvement in the quality of a service. Underlying this perspective is the pessimistic assumption that some or many of the local units monitored are likely to go wrong and will fail to correct their ways without state intervention. Thus, without a constant outside threat and continuous monitoring, some municipalities may be expected to create havoc by running up debt to the point at which they can no longer find someone to lend them money and may even sacrifice the education of children because of incompetent administration, poor teaching, or local political interference. The proactive approach leads to greater local controversy because it is uninvited and more directly conflicts with the norm of local autonomy. Though actual takeovers are infrequent, they are likely to be hostile in nature. With the emphasis on continuous surveillance, moreover, this approach also annoys a larger number of local officials, even (or, perhaps, especially) those doing an outstanding job.

All other things being equal, states that take a more reactive than proactive approach to intervention may minimize friction with local officials. Other factors, of course, may be involved. Intervention, for example, is more supportable when the goals of the state are clear—and this has not always been the case, as, for example, with regard to New Jersey schools—and state officials can demonstrate that treading on local autonomy is justified because of the seriousness of the problem or because a well-documented record based on information gathered over several years indicates the unwillingness or inability of local officials to handle a situation or live up to performance standards. Union opposition can be minimized with restrictions on the ability of state officials to violate collective-bargaining agreements or remove employees—restrictions that, of course, could greatly limit the ability of the new managers to cut expenses.

On the receiving end, resistance is reduced if a takeover is accompanied by the infusion of needed revenues and efforts to minimize the loss of power. Friction may have been greater in New York than in Pennsylvania, for example, because the former tended toward "control," while Pennsylvania chose an "oversight" strategy that gave local officials more discretion. Allowing elected officials—be they council members or school board members—to stay in office, with reduced powers or, at least, in an advisory capacity, takes a bit of the sting out of the takeover and may be a good idea for no other reason than that local officials stand to be better prepared to assume responsibility when the state relinquishes control. Equally, if not more, beneficial in terms of community acceptance are provisions, now often found in laws shifting control over schools to state boards or to mayors, that give citizens the opportunity somewhere down the road to vote on the question of whether to retain the newly created reform boards.

Takeovers stem from the conclusion—be it by governors, state legislators, or state administrators—that there is a need for an immediate change in management. Often, the tone is one of frustration—that things are not going to improve unless the people who are running things are gotten rid of or, at least, until they can safely be pushed aside to minimize the damage they can do. On a more positive note, interventionist programs assume that states can help bring both immediate and long-term improvements that survive long after the state-appointed interveners have departed. For distressed municipalities, state intervention appears most useful in dealing with short-term emergency problems. Financial control boards, while often facing considerable opposition from the elected local officials that they have replaced in power and from segments of the community, have generally been successful in getting municipalities through their immediate financial crisis. They have made it possible to continue city operations, though with reduced services and higher taxes, while meeting the demands of the city's creditors. Indeed, the mere creation of the board helps reassure municipal creditors that matters are on the right track. Beyond this, boards bring new borrowing authority through which they can secure additional funding and reestablish the creditworthiness of the distressed locality.[49] The "crisis regimes" in our examples have been able to cut costs in large part through reductions in employment, employee benefits, and citizen services. Unpopular changes along these lines have been possible because local democracy has been suspended and because local officials have had the cover provided by an oversight agency to make these changes.

Before returning the reins to local officials, financial control boards usually attempt to institute long-term changes in procedures or practices. Although management improvements and greater internal efficiencies are desirable in their own right, there is some doubt about whether they can play a significant role in avoiding financial disasters.[50] Fiscal distress often stems from economic conditions largely beyond local control, such as demographic shifts and structural changes in the economic base. If the underlying problem in a distressed municipality is, indeed, the inadequacy of the locality's economic base, the state should be thinking in broader terms of, for example, targeting economic development projects into the area, bringing about service-sharing agreements with other governments, or, as some of the more recent distress legislation now authorizes, merging the distressed area into a healthier economy through annexation or the consolidation of local governments.

School takeovers have also often placed heavy emphasis on managerial changes, for example, eliminating political patronage and freeing the systems from bloated bureaucracies and inept administrators. As in the case of state interventions in financially distressed municipalities, there is the nagging question of whether state takeovers of school systems adequately address the underlying problems. Intervention may improve district finances, management, and curricula, but when it comes to educational achievement, particularly in large urban systems, there may be little reason to believe that state administrators can do a better job than local administrators.[51] For systems in large urban areas, the underlying problems serving as barriers to student achievement may be economic or social in nature. These problems are not likely to disappear with changes in school personnel and operating practices, as desirable as these may be on other grounds. As the president of the Newark School Board suggested, if the state could provide the school system with answers to the problems of poverty, low self-esteem, and broken families which afflict many Newark students, it should do so. Otherwise, it should stay out of the district's affairs.[52]

As an alternative to getting directly involved in trying to repair poorly performing local governments, either proactively or reactively, states could, in essence, do nothing and simply allow localities to work out their own problems. This is the home-rule solution. For localities faced with mounting debt and an inability to find lenders, bankruptcy may serve as a substitute for state intervention. Bankruptcy brings relief from meeting short-term budgeting problems. It may lead to the rewriting of municipal labor contracts and to the restructuring of some debt. Indeed, the mere threat of filing for bankruptcy may give local officials considerable leverage in dealing with unions and creditors. Local governments, however, have generally resisted bankruptcy out of fear of the long-term damage that it might have on their credit rating and thus on the cost of borrowing. State governments have also been reluctant to allow local governments to pursue this route—they have the power to bar such action—preferring that local governments in trouble pursue the remedies provided in distress legislation. The few local governments that have sought bankruptcy have usually done so not because they were insolvent and could not pay creditors but, as noted in the Bridgeport discussion, because they were trying to avoid politically distasteful actions—for example, raising taxes—or to reduce a legal claim against the government. Bankruptcy, however, does remain an option and an alternative to state monitoring and financial review boards. Another option is to simply dissolve or disincorporate local units that are performing poorly and consolidate them with other units. For various reasons, not the least of which is the opposition of the local units involved, states have generally steered away from this course.

School districts also can go through the bankruptcy and dissolution process. In some states, state education officials have the authority to dissolve deficient school districts, leaving other districts to absorb the schools, teachers, and students. Indeed, courts have been encouraged to take greater advantage of statutes that allow states to disestablish (withdraw authority from) school districts because they relieve judges of the difficult task of devising solutions to educational problems.[53] Taking a somewhat innovative approach, the state of Florida allows students attending a failing school the option of receiving a voucher to attend a public or private school of the family's choice.

For school districts, too, an increasingly popular alternative to a direct state takeover is the transfer of control over schools to mayors. Takeovers of this nature have taken place in Baltimore, Boston, Chicago, Cleveland, Detroit, Philadelphia, and, most recently, in New York City, among other places. This approach, while not so objectionable from the local control point of view, like direct state takeovers, has generated considerable friction and has had varying results in regard to school performance. It has also raised additional questions, such as, "What basis is there for believing that a mayor or any other politician or board has answers that have eluded educational professionals? If the answer to urban school woes is to place more power for hiring and firing teachers, setting budgets, and so on in the hands of one person, why not make the superintendent or the school board president this person?"[54]

Many mayors view the quality of schools as essential to the survival of their cities and have been more than willing to work out governing arrangements with governors and legislators for the operation of school systems. In part, the mindset of mayors reflects the feeling that "cities are increasingly being judged—by both the business community and the citizenry—on the reputation of their public education."[55] In a more negative fashion, as one mayor has put it, "We're going to get blamed for the schools anyway, whether we're responsible for them or not, so we might as well try to fix them."[56] Still, the mayors have met with resistance, especially from school district officials. The 1999 decision to turn Detroit schools over to Mayor Dennis Archer, for example, provoked considerable resistance and turmoil, including a ten-day teacher strike. School district officials protested "Lansing's takeover" of their schools and conducted a fierce—albeit unsuccessful—fight through lobbyists, public relations firms, and court action directed at the "undemocratic scheme" that "stripped the right to vote from citizens of Detroit."[57]

State officials have been generally reluctant to let nature take its course when it comes to a financially failing municipality, especially when its leaders ask for help. Even when such municipalities do not ask for help, states often have strong economic and political incentives to get involved: the financial failure of a medium-sized to large city could do much to damage the state's economy and create political shockwaves throughout the state. State officials apparently also feel obligated—if only in a paternalistic way—to help even the smallest jurisdiction in financial difficulty. Constant financial monitoring and the use of financial review boards appear to have become an established and increasingly important part of state operations. The drive for accountability has underlain much of the drive for school district takeovers, but local control, meaning local control by general-purpose governments, has become the preferred approach in many places. The switch may be attributed in part to the excessive zeal of state agencies that, although talking about trying to help districts help themselves, gave the impression of being nothing much more than a group of outsiders attempting to force their norms on a community.

8

The Restructuring Problem

Rather than trying to repair poorly performing local governments, state legislatures or administrative agencies have from time to time abolished particular local governments or forced their consolidation with other units. Over the years, state legislators and administrators have most notably pushed for the dissolution and consolidation of school districts. By making fewer but larger districts, they have sought to enlarge the property-tax base for schools and to make them more administratively efficient. During the 1940s and 1950s, states often helped produce popular votes in favor of consolidation by requiring or strongly encouraging the creation of local citizen committees to study the problem and make a recommendation. The idea behind this system was that local committees, once informed of the situation, would almost always recommend consolidation. This proved to be the case.[1] In some places, states further encouraged consolidation by offering grants-in-aid that made this course of action financially advantageous. In others, states simply abolished districts and transferred responsibility for schools to the county level. Thanks in large part to state leadership, the number of school districts dramatically declined. From 1942 to 1962, the number fell from 108,579 to 34,678. With the continuation of the movement, by 1997, the figure stood at 13,726.

States have sometimes dissolved municipalities through legislation, making their citizens turn to the county for basic services and giving the county control over what assets were owned by the municipalities. On July 1, 1995, for example, 186 towns in Georgia that had become virtually inactive, failing to provide much if anything in terms of service, ceased to exist. The state law that mandated the abolition of these small rural units also encouraged their eventual consolidation into municipalities that would be able to stand on their own.[2] Yet, while one can find examples of similar state action elsewhere, state legislatures on the whole have not been inclined to reach out and abolish municipalities, particularly in urban areas. Indeed, when it comes to metropolitan areas, state legislators have generally thought less about abolishing existing municipal units than about creating new ones. Much of what restructuring has occurred, moreover, has been through voluntary disincorporation laws, found in some thirty states, under which citizens have voted to dissolve their municipal government.[3]

Scholars have been particularly divided over how many independent local units—even considering only municipalities—there should be in each of the nation's approximately 330 metropolitan areas. In the classic civic reform tradition dating back to the early 1900s, a long line of urban scholars and observers have contended that the fragmentation of governmental authority among a large number of local jurisdictions has several ill effects. Among these are the needless duplication of services, taxing and service inequities, ruinous competition among governments, and difficulties in trying to address areawide problems.[4] In regard to the last of these, reformers have argued that because what once were local problems, such as growth control, are now metropolitan problems, more authority has to be vested in units of local government with metropolitan jurisdictions.

Reformers also argue that people in metropolitan areas already have a common set of interests binding them together; all they need is a general-purpose government to express their will. In this tradition, some have called for the consolidation of governments in a given metropolitan area into a single (one-level) government with general authority over the jurisdiction. Others have favored a two-level federation, with a central government performing areawide functions and local governments handling local functions. The consolidation of local units, civic reformers have argued, is necessary to create local governments that are capable of solving their own problems without the support of the national and state governments and that therefore are truly entitled to exercise home-rule powers. More recently, proponents of the "new regionalism" have argued that greater consolidation of some type is needed to enable regions to be competitive in the global economy.

Public-choice theorists, on the other hand, argue that a large number of local governments in a given area is desirable because it facilitates the ability of citizens to choose the lifestyles and levels of service that they desire and keeps government more accessible and accountable to the people.[5] Those who take this viewpoint also often emphasize the value of competition among local units, for example, in keeping taxes down and encouraging more efficiency. They contend, moreover, that local entities are capable of meeting common problems through a makeshift system of interlocal governance.[6]

If state lawmakers were to follow the advice of the civic reformers, they would (1) make it easier for municipalities to extend their boundaries through annexation; (2) make it more difficult to form (incorporate) new municipal governments in urbanizing areas; (3) make it easier to consolidate local governments; and, (4) make it more difficult for communities to secede from established municipalities. In recent years, civic reformers have generally been losing out on all four counts. Existing municipalities, likewise, have had little to cheer about when it comes to incorporation and annexation, although, from their point of view, the lack of emphasis on consolidation has been a blessing. Movements in all four areas of policy have been compatible with the interests of emerging suburban communities and the prescriptions of public-choice theorists. The states have also helped the public-choice cause by directly and indirectly contributing to the makeshift governance system. They have done this, for example, by encouraging the transfer of functions among jurisdictions (for example, from city to county), an elaborate system of interlocal contracts and agreements, local government participation in metropolitan or regional councils, and the creation of special districts and authorities to deal with specific problems (thus furthering the fragmentation of authority). There is reason to doubt, however, that the makeshift system can be effective in addressing areawide problems such as sprawl. As alternatives, consideration has been given to building a stronger regional approach on the foundation of county governments or existing regional councils. One also finds, however, that pressing metropolitan problems, particularly in regard to land use, have encouraged the states to abandon looking for structural changes to local government in favor of greater state controls and top-down regionalism.

Making Adjustments

Prior to the early twentieth century, states generally encouraged annexation by giving municipalities the right to extend their boundaries by unilateral action. Big cities, eager to become even bigger, took advantage of these laws. Extending their boundaries into unincorporated areas allowed them to keep their boundaries concurrent with population growth, extend their tax base, prevent dwellers on their fringes from benefiting from city services without paying for them, and stymie the development of rival governments. To critics, annexation was a way for the "imperial city" to gobble up neighborhoods and place them in political subjugation: "to destroy the suburban governments and quash their independent commercial growth and political power, as well as to burden their residents with proportionately the greater costs of central administration."[7]

As big-city municipalities expanded their boundaries, they began to frighten people in unincorporated suburbs and rural areas. This produced an alliance of suburban and rural interests in state legislatures that moved to make annexation more difficult. They achieved this goal through laws granting outlying property owners the sole right of initiating annexation proceedings and through laws providing that cities could annex only after voters in the area to be annexed indicated their approval in a referendum election. Along with these changes, state legislatures made it easier for outlying areas to incorporate and thus avoid annexation.

Some states continue to give municipalities considerable power to annex contiguous land. In North Carolina, for example, this can be done without the owner's consent. Over the years, however, there has been a tendency around the country to reduce the ability of municipalities to act unilaterally and to increase the ability of residents to influence annexation proceedings through referenda and other means.[8] North Carolina and about a dozen other states also give municipalities the ability to veto the incorporation of new municipalities forming outside their boundaries. Elsewhere, however, there has been some strong pressure to ease the process of incorporation and thus facilitate the creation of a larger number of independent entities.

In 1997, for example, a setback for municipalities in regard to incorporation occurred in Tennessee with the passage of a bill in the waning hours of the legislative session that allowed virtually any community of 225 or more people to incorporate next to existing municipalities. A number of places near Memphis and Chattanooga, including an apartment complex, sought to incorporate and thereby block the ability of existing municipalities to annex them. A similar situation occurred the same year in Arizona with the adoption of a measure directed at Pima County (Tucson) that eliminated a legal barrier to incorporation—the requirement that areas wanting to incorporate obtain permission from existing cities within six miles of the proposed community's boundaries. The act stimulated the incorporation of several small communities near

Tucson. In both Tennessee and Arizona, the efforts to form new units were later frustrated by court decisions, but the general issue has stayed alive in the state legislative bodies.

Similar developments are found elsewhere. For example, Houston, Texas, which has benefited from generous annexation rules, has been finding more and more political opposition to its use of the law because of the growth of suburban power in the legislature.[9] The Texas Municipal League, meanwhile, has opposed strongly any attempt to erode annexation authority, seeing it as a life-or-death issue. In 1998, for example, the League argued, "Extensive research shows that cities that cannot or do not expand have more segregation, more poverty, lower bond ratings, and many other problems not experienced in expanding cities. It is systematically true—and it's been shown time and time again—that expanding cities prosper, while the others don't. In short, there is a clear correlation between urban decline and the absence of strong annexation authority."[10] These comments echo those of David Rusk, former mayor of Albuquerque, New Mexico, who has argued that annexation policies should be geared toward creating elastic cities that can expand their boundaries into suburban areas and thereby secure a wealthier tax base.[11]

A related development, equally, if not more, disturbing to large cities, has been growing sentiment in various parts of the country that supports the breakup of large cities and the formation of new municipalities out of the pieces of these cities or, in a more limited fashion, the allowing of various districts to secede from the cities and become independent units. Secessionist movements in the name of self-determination have been recently evidenced in Boston, Dallas, New York City, San Francisco, and, most actively, Los Angeles. In the latter, a measure to allow the secession of the San Fernando Valley, with 1.4 million people, failed on the ballot in November 2002. Grumbling over city services and their lack of political clout in city hall, San Fernando Valley residents threatened succession back in the 1970s. The effort, however, was crushed when Los Angeles Mayor Tom Bradley got the state legislature to give cities veto power over secessions. By 1997, however, the San Fernando Valley secessionists had been able to marshal enough strength in the legislature to reverse that decision. In October 1997, Governor Pete Wilson signed a bill into law that removed the power of a city council anywhere in the state to veto secessions. Some prominent supporters of the measure hailed the victory as one for self-determination but talked not so much in terms of communities actually using the law to secede from cities as they did of communities such as in the San Fernando Valley using the threat of secession as a means of leveraging their power in city politics to secure a fairer share of services. Said one of the bill's sponsors, "The people in those communities need no longer to throw up their hands and walk away. They now have a reason to stay and fight."[12]

States, of course, can make the process of secession as easy or difficult as they wish. The California legislation requires only that there be separate favorable majority votes in both the entire city and in the districts seeking independence, and that a comprehensive fiscal analysis of the effects of the separation be done before the question can be submitted to the voters.[13] In other places, state laws have sometimes locked cities out of the process of deciding if a community will break away.[14] Generally, the process of secession is complex and time-consuming, with success dependent on getting the approval of legislatures, administrative bodies such as boundary commissions, and voters.

Though not popular with existing governments, state study commissions have sometimes looked with favor on the consolidation, either complete or partial, of local governments. Taking stock of New Jersey, a property-tax commission appointed by Governor Whitman in 1997, for example, pointed to "an overabundance of local units of local government"—including 21 counties, 566 municipalities, and 611 school districts—as a central factor driving up the cost of local government in the state and recommended consolidation as a possible remedy.[15]

Thus far, however, relatively few total consolidations have occurred within metropolitan areas. The most prominent of these have been locally initiated city-county consolidations such as those in Nashville-Davidson County, Tennessee, and in Jacksonville-Duval County, Florida. Much of the consolidation has involved only the integration of certain departments such as police, health, and welfare to end the duplication of services, increase efficiency, and save the city taxpayers from paying for county services that they do not receive.

Municipal governments in metropolitan areas, as political scientist Victor Jones once observed, have proven to be virtually indestructible "tough organizations with many political and legal protections against annihilation or absorption by another government."[16] Many states require that voters in each affected jurisdiction approve consolidation, and voters, for various reasons, regularly reject consolidation proposals. "Good government" groups in the civic reform tradition and business interests that see change as helping economic development are likely sponsors of consolidation. On the other hand, consolidation is likely to find the determined opposition of incumbent officeholders—both elected and appointed—who are fearful of losing their jobs and of those who wish to retain the identity of their local units or fear an increase in taxation. Consolidation proposals aimed at reuniting central cities and suburbs are likely to have little support in either jurisdiction. Minority groups, having come into power in central cities, do not want to risk losing that power by being swallowed up by a larger government. Suburbanites also fear that consolidation would threaten their control over schools, land use, and tax resources and force them to subsidize lower-income people in the cities. As Anthony Downs of the Brookings Institution has remarked, it is almost impossible to persuade "people that adopting metropolitan government is truly in their interest."[17] Even one of the strongest proponents of metropolitan consolidation has had to admit that "successfully challenging racial and class attitudes underlying the fragmentation of many metro areas is the toughest political task in America. Rarely will a White county commissioner or Black mayor champion actions to unify metro areas (in more than a limited and voluntary way) *and* survive local voter backlash (White or Black)."[18]

States are free to simply order consolidations, bypassing the need for voter approval in the affected jurisdictions. An example is the Marion County-Indianapolis "Unigov" state-ordered consolidation in 1969. This was a limited consolidation, exempting a large number of governments, that took place under exceptional political circumstances. Hatched by Republicans, the plan encountered little political resistance because Republicans controlled the city, county, and state governments.[19] Future actions of this nature seem unlikely because of their general unpopularity with the public. Both state-ordered and locally initiated actions may also be less likely in the future given the disappointing experience in Toronto, Canada, with metropolitan government; although, overall, the record in the United States in regard to consolidation is mixed.[20]

Makeshift Government

In the absence of metropolitan government, local jurisdictions have, with the help of the states, taken various steps in an attempt to address problems that spill over local government boundaries. Local governments, for example, often enter into agreements with each other for the joint planning, financing, or delivery of services. Also popular are interlocal contracts through which one local government purchases services such as police or fire protection from another local government. Examples of efficient service delivery through this type of interlocal cooperation, or "interlocal self-governance," can be found throughout the nation.[21] In the mid-1990s, in Connecticut alone there were 900 instances in which services were being delivered through inter-municipal cooperative ventures.[22] States throughout the nation have encouraged this type of activity through joint-powers acts that give localities broad authority to undertake cooperative ventures.

Research suggests, however, that there are limits to what can be accomplished through contracts and agreements. Local officials, it appears, still much prefer to provide their own services and voluntarily enter into such arrangements only if compelled to do so by cost considerations.[23] Interlocal agreements on services or facility use, while saving money, do little to promote a general areawide perspective or to solve areawide problems. They are entered into by a limited number of jurisdictions on a project-by-project basis with very specific purposes in mind. Contracting in some places may have actually contributed to the fragmentation of governmental authority. It is likely, for example, that many small municipalities in Los Angeles County would have been incorporated into larger neighboring cities had they not been able to secure various services such as police and fire protection from the county.[24] County contracting practices in the Los Angeles area have also led to interlocal friction built around complaints from large cities that their residents are forced to subsidize the provision of county services to other municipalities.[25]

In addition to a system of contracts and agreements, one finds thousands of local special districts in metropolitan areas usually providing a single service on a multijurisdictional basis. Local special districts are a relatively painless way of coping with problems that spill over local boundary lines in that they do not greatly threaten the power of existing municipalities. They are popular with municipal officials for this reason and also because they provide greater fiscal flexibility by allowing them to bypass state taxation and debt limits placed on their units. Special districts, however, further fragment governmental authority and add to the complexity of local government in metropolitan areas. They often operate in isolation from other units of local government and fail to coordinate their programs and plans with them. Because their governing bodies are usually not elected—they are appointed by local or state officials—and seldom attract much attention, special districts also fail to meet the criteria of public accountability. Scholars have generally preferred vesting responsibilities in multipurpose units such as counties and municipalities over special-purpose districts and authorities because the former are more visible and accountable to the citizens. Special districts, however, continue to increase in number, thanks in part to permissive state statutes and to limits, especially financial limits, imposed by the states on general-purpose local governments.[26]

Of greater concern to existing local units has been the emergence of special districts or authorities that operate on an areawide basis to provide programs in areas such as transportation, pollution control, sewage disposal, water supply, and hospitals. These independent agencies come to life through state legislation, and their creation often involves the transfer of authority over particular functions from existing local governments to them. State-enabling legislation has tended to be liberal when it comes to the creation of these agencies.[27] The transfer of authority is likely to have been prompted by some type of crisis in the provision of services. These agencies also suffer because they are usually insulated from local popular control and further the problem of fragmentation along functional lines.

One recent example of this type of government is the fifteen–member superagency created by the Georgia legislature for the Atlanta area. Under the control of the governor, this agency has broad powers to attack problems of traffic, smog, and sprawl. The agency, known as the Georgia Regional Transportation Authority (GRTA), can, among other matters, control highway building in the thirteen–county area and build and operate a mass-transportation system for the region. The state acted, in part, in response to a warning from the federal Environmental Protection Agency that Atlanta's air-quality problems were so serious that it risked losing federal funds for new highway projects. Atlantans were spending more time in their cars than residents anywhere else in the country. Elected local officials from suburban areas who seemed destined to lose influence over how land in their jurisdiction would be used appeared willing to go along with the creation of the new superagency, feeling that they had no choice. As the chairperson of one of the state's county commissions put it, "Ten years ago . . . whoever was sitting in this seat would have taken it as a threat to local authority. Now most of us look at it as a blessing."[28] Still, the agency has not had an altogether easy time of trying to balance local priorities with regional concerns. When it comes to a mass-transit system for the area, one observer noted in 2000, "Regionalism remains a slow train coming."[29]

Counties and COGs

The makeshift system of governance one finds in metropolitan areas seems destined to endure, given the resistance of localities to major restructuring and, partly because of this, the unwillingness of state governments to force such action. Still, there are some signs of change toward stronger multipurpose regional governing bodies built on the foundations of county governments and voluntary councils of government (COGs).

In recent years, the public, the academic community, and governmental reformers have paid considerably more attention to county governments as service providers and as units of possibly even greater importance in the regional future. Those concerned with shifting responsibilities to multipurpose, politically accountable entities with broad metropolitan or regional jurisdictions naturally think first of county governments. Compared to municipalities, the larger jurisdictions of counties make them potentially better able to effectively deal with problems such as environmental protection and transportation. Shifting responsibilities to the county may provide a broader focus, economies of scale, and a larger and more stable tax base. Turning to the counties is more politically feasible than attempting to create a new regional entity or trying to convince municipal officials that they should surrender their identity by consolidating with their neighbors.[30] Compared to special authorities, counties are well-established general-purpose governments directly accountable to the voters.

Many counties, thanks to empowering state legislation, are now providing functions and services on a regional basis that were once provided only by municipal governments. Some have larger budgets and more complicated programs than municipalities within their boundaries. Counties grapple with enormous and vexing problems involving such matters as human services, the criminal justice system, and environmental protection. Counties also have become major players as partners in interlocal networks—undertaking various types of cooperative projects through contracts, agreements, and participation in interjurisdictional associations. Indeed, as one authority has noted, "If counties had not existed at the beginning of the decade, something like them would probably have been invented by the end of it to deliver sub-regional and regional services"[31]

Along with changes in services and functions, many counties have become more centralized and streamlined in structure and have been brought under the direction of professionally trained officials. The increased professionalism of administrations has made it easier for counties to cooperate with neighboring jurisdictions because they are often run by people with essentially the same training and outlooks. Political scientists Vincent L. Marando and Mavis Mann Reeves have concluded, "Differentials between the professional competence of counties and cities need no longer stand in the way of effective partnerships. Professional parity between county and city administrators fosters communication, increased interaction, and the search for joint approaches to problem solving."[32] Some research indicates that county officials generally feel that their units are willing and able, both politically and administratively, to undertake new responsibilities, but that the lack of state financial support severely limits their ability to perform their functions.[33] An improved role for counties in many places would require increasing their discretionary authority in regard to areawide problems as well as their revenue-raising abilities.

One approach to making greater use of county governments is simply to transfer functions to them on a piecemeal basis, as has been done in various parts of the country over the last several decades. Counties have assumed responsibilities from municipal governments in such areas as jails, libraries, and street repairs to end duplication of services and effect economies of scale. Also increasingly shifted to counties are regionally important services such as transit, solid-waste management, and health. Alternatively, reformers could increase substantially county responsibility through charter reorganization. Using the Dade County, Florida, model, reformers could create a two-tier or federated system in which counties perform various activities considered best provided on an areawide basis, while municipal governments assume more specialized local functions—a blend of regionalism and localism. A federated system would be easier to bring about than a complete one-tier consolidation of city and county governments in that it would reduce the amount of change involved.

The potential for counties, it should be noted, is stronger is some parts of the country than others. Counties, for example, have been historically strong in the South but never have played much of a role in the Northeast. Indeed, Massachusetts is in the process of abolishing all of its counties. In this state, counties have generally fallen on fiscal hard times and have, over the years, seen a gradual transfer of their functions for such matters as road building to the state. In sprawling areas extending into two or more counties, county units are already obsolete as natural regional entities. In these situations, one thinks of existing regional agencies such as COGs as the logical building blocks. COGs have been a principal means of bringing greater coordination in metropolitan areas. They help to encourage the exchange of information, encourage cooperative endeavors, and often perform coordinating activities that are required by federal transportation and other programs. They are fundamentally limited by the parochial-individualistic inclinations of their members. Some, however, have pursued an aggressive regional agenda. As they gain the confidence of their members and develop staff facilities, moreover, they may go through an evolutionary process toward becoming regional policymaking and action councils. Going beyond the conventional COG, for example, is Portland, Oregon's, Metropolitan Service District (Metro), created in 1978. This is a metropolitanwide, multipurpose government run by officials directly elected by voters. The government has the authority to perform a wide variety of services, including regional transportation and land-use planning, and, with voter approval, may draw on its own revenue sources. The full development of councils as viable units of regional government elsewhere awaits large-scale efforts to increase citizen participation in the governing system.[34] Several COGs have taken steps away from primary reliance on elected officials to more direct citizen involvement through, for example, the creation of short-term task forces and the use of advisory committees.

Regionalism and Controls from Above

Local officials have shown a strong inclination to seek out partnerships and agreements with other local governments. Indeed, in recent years, the tensions and uncertainties of dealing with state governments have encouraged local officials to look even more to each other for support and to come together to address common problems. Evidence gathered in the mid-1990s suggests that while local officials had soured on their relations with state governments, they saw considerable improvement in their relations with other local officials in the same geographic area.[35] Much of the interlocal cooperation one finds around the country is consistent with public-choice theory in that it is voluntary and, in a sense, a natural development awaiting only favorable state laws such as joint-powers acts to be put in place. To some extent, however, what passes for "voluntary" cooperation among local officials also reflects the carrot-or-stick approach behind federal or state laws encouraging certain types of metropolitan or regional planning. It may also reflect the fear among local officials that if local units do not cooperate or at least go through the motions of cooperating, the state or federal government will mandate solutions to areawide problems. Organizations representing local officials have been among those warning their members of this danger. In the early 1990s, for example, the International City/County Management Association's Future Visions Consortium warned, "Increasingly, local governments face problems that cannot be addressed by single jurisdictions. Our future depends on comprehensive solutions to issues that range from transportation, solid-waste management, and air-quality control to drugs, homelessness, and poverty. . . . If local governments do not willingly collaborate to address regional issues, solutions are likely to be mandated by the state."[36]

One already finds several examples of the federal government and the states using their fiscal and regulatory powers to require greater metropolitan or regional governance. The federal government, for example, requires comprehensive local planning for transportation, air quality, and growth management on an areawide basis through metropolitan planning organizations (MPOs). In addition to their other functions, voluntary councils of government sometimes serve as MPOs. States, though reluctantly and incrementally, have become more involved in imposing regulations in the area of growth management that not only require greater metropolitan or regional planning but mandate that such plans be consistent with state objectives. Under such legislation, local governments must work together in preparing metropolitan or regional plans addressed to the interrelated goals of controlling growth, combating environmental problems such as air and water pollution, and providing an adequate infrastructure. States review local plans to make sure they are consistent with statewide planning goals. States, however, give local governments varying degrees of control over the specific details of the content of plans. In some places, one finds a bottoms-up system in which local governments make their own plans, and in others a top-down system in which state planning agencies have considerable impact on what goes into a local plan, forcing, for example, local governments to adopt plans that call for higher densities.

While there are variations in application, all the state-growth management acts are premised on the belief that there is a need to guide urban development more effectively than local governments can achieve on their own.[37] Enactment of such statutes has generally come only after many decades during which states have generally authorized local governments to control the location and nature of development. One reason why state legislators have been sluggish in pushing for strong regional growth-management agencies, some observers suggest, is that they are about as parochial as the local officials themselves. Their lack of an areawide perspective may be traced to their personal and political ties to local governments and the fact they are usually elected from districts that encompass only a small part of the metropolitan area, if any at all.[38] Their lack of support also may be tied up in cost-benefit calculations. The potential benefits to legislators in terms of reelection seem slight and less important that the costs of alienating local officials or, indeed, state agencies such as highway departments that also fear the loss of power to new growth-management agencies.[39] Legislators, on these as well as other issues, may be especially fearful of being perceived as being hostile to local governments within their districts, threatening their autonomy and thereby the welfare of the community.

State planning mandates have generally improved the amount and quality of local planning and have brought local planning more in line with state and regional concerns in areas such as environmental protection.[40] State-imposed planning, however, has also generated considerable costs for local governments, and in some places, local and state governments have struggled over their respective roles in growth management, especially with regard to infrastructure financing.[41] On the downside, critics contend that state growth-management programs have really not had all that much of an impact on developmental patterns, for example, in curbing urban sprawl. Some see the lack of local support as the central problem. Land-use expert Douglas Porter has written, "All the states involved in growth management have encountered some local officials whose outright hostility, foot-dragging, and even incompetence have required endless negotiations to obtain even partially satisfactory responses."[42] Faced with the vigorous opposition of local officials to state intervention, state officials and growth-management supporters have generally given local governments a significant role in growth management and permitted time-consuming delays in securing local compliance with planning requirements.[43] State agencies, however, seemingly can prod localities only so far toward changing their ways or getting them to do what growth managers feel is the right thing. The underlying problem is that local officials and state administrators disagree not only on who should be in control of land-use decisions, but also on the need to manage growth in the first place. Many local governments qualify as parts of "growth machines" heavily influenced by business interests committed to low-density development.[44] Some observers see the lack of commitment on the part of local officials to state goals as the central problem in putting together effective plans.[45]

Some states, partly as a result of difficulties encountered with local officials in growth-management planning, have turned to less directly confrontational approaches to guide metropolitan growth. The state of Maryland, under the leadership of Governor Parris Glendening, for example, enacted landmark "Smart Growth" legislation in 1997 that targets state funds for local road, water, sewer, and other infrastructures toward priority funding areas. It does not affect local government zoning powers but generally limits state aid to projects within existing municipalities in order to discourage development in areas that will require new public facilities. In still other places, the states have looked to areawide special authorities to address transportation and related problems—an approach which, as in Atlanta, may be met with minimum resistance because of the obvious severity of the problem to be dealt with.

The states have moved into the land-use area in large part because the historical performance of municipalities and counties regarding control of growth has been spotty at best. Some jurisdictions appear to have no interest in planning and have not adopted plans, even though they have the power to do so. In some jurisdictions, plans are given only lip service, and zoning and subdivision controls are often imposed without reference to a plan. Historically, developers often have been able to lobby city councils or county boards to change plans put together by commissions or to override the more restrictive decisions of boards of adjustment. Because of the variation in land-use control among cities and counties in a given metropolitan area, developers have been able to shop around and gravitate to areas with the fewest controls or lowest impact fees, if any at all, on proposed projects. Local land-use choices also seem heavily driven by how much tax revenue a municipality can attract in the short term, rather than by what is in the community's long-term best interest. In California, as noted, decisions seem driven by state policies restricting local revenue choices to the sales tax, making it more profitable for localities to pursue sales-tax-rich retail projects over housing, industry, and public uses.

The most basic problem of remaining reliant on local units for growth management is that each is likely to consider its own needs first and only incidentally the needs of the broader metropolitan area or region. Failing to think beyond the confines of the city limits, one city may give its blessings to a development that has major adverse effects on the well-being of a neighboring jurisdiction. When it comes to control, imposing a moratorium may help a rapidly developing city, at least in the short run. This action, however, is not likely to do anything to help neighboring jurisdictions and, indeed, may prove harmful to them and to the region as a whole.

When it comes to urban sprawl, because authority over the problem is fragmented among several jurisdictions, no particular government has much of an incentive to take the lead in addressing the issue, let alone to try to impose any regional antisprawl policy.[46]

The Limits of Reform

To some extent, it is useful to look at the interaction among local governments in metropolitan areas as resembling the interaction among rival nation states.[47] From this perspective, each local government is primarily concerned about itself—its survival as a legal entity, its ability to maintain or extend its territory, and its economic resources—rather than the welfare of the metropolitan area or region of which it is a part. In dealing with other units of government, officials represent their people as ambassadors represent other countries. Within metropolitan areas, there are counterparts to "major" and "minor" powers. A central city, for example, may be a major power because it has control over the area's water supply. As with nations, cooperation is frustrated by long-standing feuds and rivalries between local units. Like national leaders, officials in the various local units see their own problems as being unique and are suspicious of the agendas of leaders representing other local units. This narrowly focused, me-first, semiparanoiac approach may produce harmful conflict bordering on war if not war itself, the neglect and compounding of common problems, and long-simmering disputes that seem unresolvable. As on the international level, one can only hope that enlightened self-interest will set in and produce diplomatic contacts, treaties, agreements, and other cooperative endeavors among local governments to avoid conflict and solve common problems.

The international relations analogy is helpful in pointing out the difficulties in either restructuring local governments or effecting cooperation among local governments in metropolitan areas. Councils of government are as inherently weak or potentially strong as the United Nations. One finds thousands of regional arrangements whereby local officials get together, but as in the case of conferences among nations, these are not likely to change the basic behavior of participants: they still function to represent the parochial viewpoints of their governing units.

In the real world, local governments, of course, are not like autonomous nation-states. They are part of the vertical intergovernmental system, subject to control from above, especially at the state level. Yet, within this system, local governments have demonstrated considerable clout in generally being able to fight off efforts to establish strong metropolitan or regional governments—although there are enough exceptions to give reformers some hope. They have also demonstrated the ability to withstand the prodding of state agencies when it comes to the imposition of state growth-management goals on their areas. States, for their part, seem excessively fond of local governments. With the exception of school districts, state policies have been tilted toward retaining as many existing local units as possible. State officials, as noted in Chapter 7, seem more comfortable with the idea of fixing specific local governments that are not working well through managerial changes than with the idea of abolishing them or consolidating them. States have generally rejected the course of action most objectionable to local officials and their citizens: The abolition of local units and their absorption into multipurpose regional governments. At the same time, states have been generally friendly to the proliferation of new local units ranging from special districts and authorities to suburban toy towns and new municipalities formed out of old ones.

Maintaining a highly fragmented local governing system and one in which one finds a wide variety of units—some wealthy, some poor— has meant considerable work for state officials. They have been virtually compelled to umpire disputes among local entities and, in a more positive fashion, to try to find ways to bring cooperation among them. Some of the more prominent conflicts have been between cities and counties. The two have fought, for example, over the issue of double taxation, that is, of municipal residents paying for municipal services and similar county services that the county does not provide in the municipality. Another issue has been annexation. While municipalities commonly see annexation as vital to their continued growth and economies, counties often complain that annexation siphons off their tax revenues, that is, allows municipalities to bring in and tax lucrative, developed areas but removes such property from the taxing authority of the counties. Counties and municipalities also have fought over their relative responsibilities in regard to service delivery.

States have demonstrated a variety of responses to these conflicts, often inviting the units to take part in their resolution. In 1998, for example, the California State Association of Counties and the League of California Cities got behind a bill that established a process, including the use of a neutral third party, for working out disputes between cities and counties in reaching property-tax-sharing agreements on proposed annexations.[48] In Tennessee, the legislature in the late 1990s finally reached a point at which it tired of refereeing annexation-taxation fights between cities and counties and came up with far-reaching annexation, planning, and incorporation legislation that requires cities and counties to work out land-development policies. On the tax issue, the law allows counties to retain the tax revenue that they have been receiving from an annexed area for fifteen years and lets municipalities collect any growth in that revenue. After fifteen years, municipalities receive all the taxes. When it comes to service delivery, Georgia made a mark in 1997 when it required municipal and county officials to meet and figure out a way to eliminate duplication of local services, decide which government should do what, and engage in service-delivery planning.[49]

While accepting the notion that existing local units are here to stay, state officials have stopped short of concluding that therefore the state should do all it can to help these governments serve the people or to make sure the system of local government is working well. Still, many are actively engaged in encouraging interlocal cooperation, local efficiency, and innovation. They do this through grants but also, in some cases, by giving temporary waivers or exceptions from state rules or regulations that appear to get in the way of these objectives. One also can find numerous examples of study commissions taking seriously their assigned tasks of exploring problems in state-local relations and finding solutions. Some have come up with creative recommendations regarding the shifting of functions and responsibilities between state and local governments and among types of local governments, the altering of state aid programs and local tax structures, and governmental reorganization at the local level. Proposals involving innovative ideas, however, often wind up simply collecting dust on the shelf because of the lack of political support. For example, in the mid-1990s, the California Constitutional Revision Commission proposed a creative new form of local home rule that would have allowed municipalities, counties, school districts, and special districts, to restructure themselves, consolidating some or all of their operations. The plan, however, threatened existing entities and was ignored by the legislature. The executive director of the commission concluded, "If you want to be dragon slayers, pick your dragons carefully.[50] For similar reasons, the Wisconsin legislature gave a cool reception to the 139 recommendations made by the Kettl Commission in 2001.

9

Concluding Note

During arguments before the Georgia Supreme Court on the validity of a state law preempting the ability of localities to sue gun manufacturers, an attorney representing the state told the court, "This case is about the ability to govern. . . . [The lawsuit] is nothing less than the city of Atlanta trying to usurp, to seize, governmental power that is placed solely by the Georgia Constitution in the General Assembly."[1] One judge, who seemed less than favorably disposed toward the city's position, asked city attorneys, "If the General Assembly has the power to abolish the city of Atlanta, why wouldn't it have the power to abolish its right to pursue this litigation?"[2]

Local officials have found it difficult to come up with convincing answers to such questions. Given the basic legal status of local governments, even the freest local unit is still subject to considerable state control, if the state chooses to exercise its control. States, however, have often chosen not to exercise the full extent of their powers. In an arrangement comparable to the system of permissive federalism said to characterize federal-state relations, states have given localities considerable leeway to act on their own.[3] Among the forces that may help account for this have been a general cultural attachment to the idea of local home rule (and through it the values of self-government, self-determination, and self-sufficiency), the local orientation of state legislators, the political influence of local governments in the state political system, and, simply, the practical limit on the number of localities and activities that can be supervised by the states.

This study has looked at elected local officials and their organizations as major, albeit imperfect, forces of localism. They have been fighting for the survival of existing units, demanding resources from the state, and fending off unwanted interference in local operations. Many local governments and local government organizations enjoy a reputation of being among the most effective interest groups in their states. In their long history of encounters with the states, local officials have often demonstrated political strength and, over the long run, have been able to carve out a place for themselves in the governing system. Working individually or through associations, local officials have had considerable influence on the development of state policies affecting localities, the distribution of state funds, and the extent to which state policies are implemented.[4] The bottom line may be that when it comes to state-local relations, local units "are not passive objects allowing themselves to be willy-nilly shoved anywhere. The shoved can and do sometimes become the shovers."[5] On a day-to-day basis, it is probably sort of a stalemate: "neither state nor local officials are free to deal with each other as they like."[6]

Local officials have room to initiate policy, though, sometimes, as has been noted, they have had to get permission to undertake even the most trivial activities. As agents, the role of local officials has not been simply to do what state or federal officials want them to do, but to modify federal and state programs in light of local needs and interests. They have had an input based on their knowledge of local problems and sentiments. Municipalities, in particular, have a meaningful role that is something less than that of a state within a state and something more than an administrative arm of the state or federal government. What one finds, in short, is a state-local relationship in which the states are constitutionally dominant, but localities, in practice, often have considerable operational autonomy and an opportunity to influence both the making of state and federal policies. While not autonomous, local officials are neither passive nor powerless.

All this is not to say, however, that things couldn't be better. While not discounting the political impact of the forces of localism, the world of local officials is an increasingly unhealthy one when it comes to local home rule. It is filled with state mandates, preemptions, prohibitions, monitoring, and the possibility of state takeovers. Throughout the country, state officials are relatively free to act without regard to how their decisions might impact local authority. Local officials have seen the states move into areas where local decision makers once had the last say. Local governments have also lost out in their competition with state governments over the control of financial resources. Being at the tail end of a shift-and-shaft vertical system, they face the constant prospect that state governments, especially when confronted with revenue difficulties of their own, will cut back on aid and shift as many costs as possible to local government. The political going is especially rough in times of economic stress. One law of intergovernmental relations is that in times of economic stress, local officials can expect to receive less intergovernmental aid and to have more of the costs of government shifted their way. Recent experience also suggests that during these periods, relief from the states is likely to take the form of authorizing increased local revenue authority, rather than aid, so that it is local government officials who must take the heat for raising taxes.

Some obstacles to local government influence exist in good or bad economic times. Local officials, for example, are hard put to compete with business groups and other interests for the attention of lawmakers and face legal handicaps when it comes to electioneering. Also among the persistent obstacles at the state level has been the tendency of state lawmakers to view local officials as special pleaders or irresponsible children rather than as legitimate partners in the intergovernmental system. Against these images, local officials have proudly, though somewhat ineffectively, presented themselves as spokespersons "of semi-sovereign subnational governments rendering the bulk of the nation's domestic services and functions."[7] Because of population shifts, the political climate has been a particularly difficult one for older central cities in recent years.

Where to from here? Historically, local officials have acknowledged their basic political weakness in state legislatures and have turned to strong and clear legal guarantees of local home rule, preferably in state constitutions, as a way of putting what they see as basic local governing rights beyond the reach of legislative politics. As an official with the Association of Washington Cities wrote some time ago, "Legislative bodies are subject to extreme political pressures from special interest groups with private axes to grind. The will of these groups is often given much greater consideration because of campaign contributions, etc., than the recommendations of the duly constituted local authorities. Unless cities are given specific powers which the legislature cannot constantly override, the whole concept of home rule is in shambles. The legislature, in other words, will constantly go over the heads of local officials to appease an interest group, hamstringing an administration, or place undue burdens on cities without providing the funds to pay the bill."[8] Local officials continue to look for legal remedies or changes in the rules of the game to protect themselves from legislatures, but, as evidenced in Michigan and New Hampshire in recent years, these are not easy to secure.

Nor can it be said that such protections already on the books have given localities anything close to autonomy. On balance, legal provisions for local home rule have but modestly enhanced the ability of local officials to make policies without having to first go to the legislature for specific authority and have given local governments only limited ability to protect themselves against state interference in matters of local concern. Perhaps more than anything else, home rule has given citizens a better opportunity to develop governmental structures appropriate to their local needs. As a political force, the existence of a local home-rule constitutional provision or statute gives local lobbyists some ammunition—an arguing point in dealing with state lawmakers—and serves to remind state legislators and administrators of the importance of local rights.[9]

The case for complete autonomy is weak insofar as it rests on the argument that people in specific geographical areas—be they counties, municipalities, or, for those in favor of further decentralization, neighborhoods—have certain problems that concern only themselves, and that they should have full discretion as to how those problems are resolved. They should, in other words, have the last say on matters that do not affect nonresidents. Yet it is difficult to identify problems that can be said to be exclusively local in nature. The number of purely local problems, if any, is likely to be very small. Assuming that there are such problems, one wonders if they can be resolved locally without running the risk of infringing upon the rights of minorities within the area— even neighborhoods are not likely to be completely homogeneous. Although we sometimes look at local governments as reflecting community norms, in practice, the norms they reflect are likely to be those of just one segment of the population.[10] Public-choice theorists argue that those unhappy with the decisions of local government officials can leave and shop around for a set of policies more agreeable to them. Yet, in practice, mobility for many people, particularly the poor, is limited. Historically, there has been little recourse but to rely upon federal and state power and the power of the courts to protect the constitutional rights of minorities from local action and to prevent localities from doing things that adversely affect nonresidents. States, too, have been considered justified in intervening in local affairs on any number of other grounds, for example, to assure an equitable distribution of services and to protect citizens against corrupt or incompetent local officials.

Local home rule, in the pure and absolute sense, is poor working theory.

Even where the legal guarantee of home rule is at its strongest, one cannot describe local officials as leaders of autonomous, self-sufficient governmental entities. Even if this status were possible to reach through legal provisions, local officials have shown little inclination to go it alone, and many would be hard pressed to try to do so.

Local governments, however, do not have to be entirely autonomous entities with a set of exclusive functions to be important. They can matter because of the roles they play in a broader intergovernmental system in which they share powers and responsibilities with other units, functioning as both initiators of local policy and as agents for federal and state programs. One could argue that it is desirable to give local governments as much policy-making discretion as possible within this broader system because there is a lot to be done and the federal government and states cannot do everything, because there is something to be said for recognizing diversity and the need for a local input in devising solutions to problems, and because local units are valuable as a means through which citizens can participate in civic affairs—and, indeed, if localities don't have the authority to make important decisions, there is no rational reason why citizens should participate. Enhancing local discretion, in other words, is worth doing because it contributes to policy experimentation, better-tailored governmental programs, the training of governmental leaders, meaningful citizenship, and a sense of civic responsibility. Local home rule, especially in regard to the power of initiation, may be most effectively granted by allowing municipalities and counties the leeway to act unless prohibited by state law rather than by attempting to carve out separate spheres of state and local authority. Still, in any given state, it may be worthwhile to examine the existing distribution of functions between the state and local units and to both clarify and strengthen home-rule authority.

When it comes to state intervention in local affairs, the hard question is not whether the states should become involved, because clearly they have legitimate interests in doing so, but when and under what conditions. When it comes to controls, a limited-interference approach would have states intervening in a reactive way, that is, only when invited by local officials or to meet emergency conditions. A more intrusive rule would have the states setting minimum statewide performance standards and acting in a proactive way to assure compliance with the standards. The limited-interference rule is most consistent with local home rule. It furthers the goals of local self-government, self-determination, and self-sufficiency. The era that spawned the home-rule movement was one in which intervening state legislatures demonstrated that local officials had no monopoly on incompetence or corruption. Autonomy-threatening intervention continues to live, though in a less-corrupt form, in constant monitoring by administrative agencies and occasional episodes of "substitute administration." Several of the takeovers in cities and towns and in school districts around the nation have taken on the aura of a crusade by state officials who feel that they are coming to the rescue of local citizens faced with incompetent or corrupt local officials. Interventions of this nature clearly conflict with the norm of local self-governance and self-determination and run the risk of considerable local resistance from the community as well as the affected local officials.

Many of the unresolved issues between localities and the states involve financial matters. The agenda of local officials has not generally been one that would have been taken by someone insistent on building economically self-sufficient units of local government. A more central institutional goal pursued by local officials in the intergovernmental area has been easing the financial problems of local governments. This pursuit has led to various types of autonomy-threatening partnerships with other governments. States, for their part, long ago discovered that the local desire for revenue can be employed to help facilitate state objectives. Generous amounts of state aid can, for example, help take the sting out of state takeovers, and threats of denying aid may convince local officials to pay more attention to problems of urban sprawl.

One could make state aid less autonomy-threatening by separating who pays for a service from who has control over the provision of a service.[11] This, however, has been a hard sell at the state level. It conflicts with the notion that local governments should finance, control, and deliver their own set of services. It further conflicts with the views that the state legislators cannot be accountable to their taxpayers unless they can control how the funds they raise are being spent. Another route would be for localities to move in the direction of financial self-sufficiency. Former Mayor Rudy Giuliani of New York City has been among those urging a movement in this direction. Speaking in 1996, he called for his city to become a model for the "new urban agenda" of self-reliance. Giuliani declared, "We are asking of New York City precisely what we are asking of people on welfare and everyone else in the city: self-reliance. . . . The old agenda was based on looking to others to solve our problems—look to Albany, look to Washington, someone will come along and bail us out. The new urban agenda should declare that we can solve our own problems, without direction from state or federal authorities."[12] The mayor suggested that cities could go a long way toward solving their own problems without state and federal aid if they were freed from costly state and federal mandates.

Mandate relief and increased revenue authority could go a long way in helping out many localities, enabling them to become more self-sufficient. Still, the potential revenue bases of local jurisdictions vary widely, and even with the relaxation of mandates, state aid is likely to come in handy as a means of upgrading and, by targeting it to places where there is the most need, of equalizing service levels. In building a revenue structure, localities need state cooperation in securing a balanced set of taxes, such as a sales and income tax, which are plentiful when the economy is good but lose value when it is bad, and property taxes, which come in handy during a recession but are not as responsive as other taxes to economic growth. To make meaningful decisions that matter in the community, localities need both a reliable own-source revenue stream and the power to raise or lower tax rates—to make the hard decisions that citizens care about. The property tax, as unpopular as it has been, has historically been the means by which local governments have managed their affairs. In today's climate, it might make more sense to shift funding for education to state resources and reserve the property tax for cities, counties, and special districts.[13] Still, as long as we rely on local property taxes or, for that matter, any locally raised tax, there will always be inequities in the level of local services, be it for education or for any other purpose. Such inequities may well be the price of any move toward local financial self-sufficiency.

While many may agree that there are good reasons to both remove restrictions on local authority and delegate as much authority as possible to local units, there is less agreement as to what should be done, if anything, about the structure of local government itself. On this issue, many see local government leaders as part of the problem. They have fought mightily against secession, consolidation, and the creation of regional entities—efforts to both reduce and increase the size of existing entities. When it comes to consolidation and regional governments, local officials defend their opposition in the name of self-government and self-determination. The same arguments, however, are used against them by secessionists. The values of home rule insofar as they involve citizen involvement and control could, in fact, be furthered by breaking down large municipalities into smaller ones, although the financial im-plications for both new and old units of separation have to be carefully considered. Local autonomy, otherwise, seems best served in the ever-changing makeshift governance system. The politics of reform has been and seems likely to continue to be one of making pragmatic adjustments to accommodate problems that spill over boundary lines or are areawide in nature without threatening the survival of existing units or, at least, by doing the least possible damage to them. States have facilitated the system of makeshift governance. They have, however, been pressured by problems, especially in regard to urban sprawl, into examining the adequacy of these arrangements. Discharging their responsibilities in the modern era may well increasingly require localities to do so within a larger regional framework in which the states provide a number of in-centives and sanctions to encourage not only cooperation among local governments, but also the attainment of statewide standards that local governments do not favor.

Delegation of authority to local units is consistent with the long-standing American "dogma," noted by James Bryce many years ago, that "where any function can be equally well discharged by a central or by a local body, it ought by preference to be entrusted to the local body."[14] The catch phrase here, is "equally well discharged." Localities, under the dogma, are expected to perform; local home rule is not an end in itself, nor is it the natural right of every local jurisdiction.

Appendices

Appendix A

State and Local Revenues, Selected Years, 1902–1999 (revenue totals in millions of dollars)

Fiscal year	State and local general revenues	Federal aid, percent of general revenues	Percent of federal aid to states	State, percent of general revenues	Local general revenues	State aid, percent of local general revenues	Property tax, percent of local general revenues
1902	986	1.0	42.8	15.9	854	6.1	73.1
1913	1,912	1.0	50.0	18.9	1,637	5.6	72.8
1922	4,781	2.0	91.7	24.1	3,866	8.1	76.9
1927	7,271	1.5	92.3	25.9	5,903	10.1	73.8
1932	7,267	3.2	95.7	30.6	5,690	14.1	73.1
1934	7,678	13.2	91.8	33.7	5,820	22.6	65.3
1936	8,395	11.3	75.8	39.1	6,179	22.9	62.6
1938	9,228	9.7	79.9	41.1	6,651	22.8	63.1
1940	9,609	9.8	70.6	42.3	6,939	23.8	60.1
1942	10,418	8.2	93.5	44.7	7,122	24.9	59.9
1944	10,908	8.7	97.1	45.0	7,340	25.1	59.4
1946	12,356	6.9	93.8	47.1	8,227	23.7	57.6
1948	17,250	8.9	88.3	48.8	11,373	28.9	51.4
1950	20,911	11.9	91.5	47.9	14,014	30.1	57.0
1952	25,181	10.2	90.8	48.4	16,952	29.8	48.9
1953	27,307	10.5	89.5	48.1	18,371	29.3	49.0
1954	29,012	10.2	91.4	47.7	19,562	29.0	49.0
1955	31,073	10.0	88.2	47.3	21,092	28.4	48.9
1956	34,667	9.6	89.2	48.2	23,137	28.5	48.8
1957	38,164	10.1	94.2	47.9	25,530	29.1	48.5
1958	41,219	11.8	94.1	46.8	27,723	30.2	48.7

Year							
1959	45,306	14.0	96.9	46.7	29,621	29.3	48.7
1960	50,505	13.8	90.4	47.4	33,026	28.6	47.8
1961	54,037	13.2	89.9	46.8	35,859	28.4	48.4
1962	58,252	13.5	90.6	46.9	38,347	28.4	48.0
1963	62,269	13.9	91.2	47.8	40,558	29.3	47.2
1964	68,443	14.6	91.4	48.2	44,085	29.4	46.5
1965	74,000	14.9	91.1	48.6	47,527	29.8	45.9
1966	83,036	15.9	93.6	49.4	53,173	31.8	44.8
1967	91,197	16.8	92.7	49.8	58,232	32.7	43.2
1968	101,264	16.9	98.0	51.4	63,182	34.7	42.5
1969	114,550	16.7	93.2	51.9	71,943	34.4	41.3
1970	130,756	16.7	96.6	52.8	80,917	35.7	40.7
1971	144,927	18.0	91.0	51.6	91,963	37.5	39.9
1972	167,541	18.7	90.6	51.9	105,243	34.9	39.5
1973	190,222	20.6	82.1	53.3	118,392	34.4	37.1
1974	207,670	20.1	78.1	53.8	131,434	34.7	35.3
1975	228,171	20.6	76.7	53.4	146,307	34.8	34.2
1976	256,176	21.7	76.5	53.5	162,940	34.7	33.7
1977	285,157	21.8	76.3	54.1	179,045	34.6	33.7
1978	315,960	22.0	73.8	55.1	194,748	33.7	32.9
1979	343,236	22.0	73.0	56.3	211,987	35.1	29.5
1980	382,322	21.7	76.3	56.6	232,452	35.6	28.2
1981	423,404	21.3	77.7	56.2	257,180	35.5	28.0
1982	457,654	19.0	77.4	55.6	281,045	34.4	28.1
1983	468,753	19.2	77.9	54.5	298,393	33.4	28.8
1984	542,730	17.9	79.3	55.9	323,236	32.9	28.6
1985	598,121	17.7	82.6	56.0	354,146	33.8	28.2
1986	641,486	17.6	84.6	55.8	380,663	34.1	28.2
1987	686,860	16.7	84.9	55.5	410,947	33.8	28.4
1988	726,762	16.2	88.3	55.5	433,976	34.3	29.3
1989	786,129	16.0	92.2	55.6	468,549	35.3	29.3
1990	849,502	16.1	88.5	54.8	512,322	34.2	29.2

(continued)

Appendix A *(continueed)*

Fiscal year	State and local general revenues	Federal aid, percent of general revenues	Percent of federal aid to states	State, percent of general revenues	Local general revenues	State aid, percent of local general revenues	Property tax, percent of local general revenues
1991	902,207	17.0	90.0	54.6	541,791	34.4	29.8
1992	979,137	18.2	91.6	54.9	573,724	35.1	29.9
1993	1,041,567	19.0	94.6	55.4	601,805	34.9	30.0
1994	1,110,441	19.5	91.0	55.1	639,242	34.8	29.5
1995	1,169,505	19.6	88.5	55.6	676,361	34.4	28.7
1996	1,222,774	19.2	90.5	55.6	709,216	34.9	28.1
1997	1,289,239	18.9	88.3	55.9	718,837	35.9	29.0
1998	1,365,762	18.7	88.1	56.1	794,250	34.7	27.6
1999	1,434,028	18.9	88.3	56.1	839,029	35.3	27.1

Source: U.S. Bureau of Census, Department of Commerce.

Appendix B

State Aid to Local Governments, Selected Years, 1902–1998 (state aid total in millions of dollars)

Fiscal year	Total	Percent of state spending	Percent General support	Education	Highways	Welfare	All other
1902	52	27.9	9.6	86.5	3.8	—	—
1913	91	26.9	5.5	90.1	4.3	—	—
1922	312	23.2	11.2	64.7	22.4	1.4	0.3
1927	596	30.2	16.4	48.9	33.1	1.0	0.6
1932	801	28.9	17.5	49.6	28.6	3.4	0.9
1934	1,318	39.6	11.0	39.6	18.7	16.0	21.3
1936	1,417	38.9	11.5	40.4	18.7	17.3	10.7
1938	1,516	37.0	11.9	39.7	20.9	22.8	1.1
1940	1,654	37.7	10.9	42.3	20.1	25.4	1.3
1942	1,780	39.1	12.6	44.4	19.3	21.9	1.7
1944	1,842	40.8	14.9	46.7	16.2	20.0	2.2
1946	2,092	39.9	17.1	45.6	16.2	17.9	3.2
1948	3,283	34.7	13.0	47.3	15.4	19.7	4.4
1950	4,217	28.6	11.4	48.7	14.5	18.8	6.6
1952	5,044	28.7	10.9	50.0	14.4	19.3	5.3
1953	5,384	28.6	10.9	50.8	14.9	18.2	5.0
1954	5,679	27.3	10.6	51.6	15.3	17.7	4.8
1955	5,986	26.3	9.9	52.6	15.2	17.5	5.2
1956	6,536	26.5	9.7	54.2	15.1	16.4	4.8
1957	7,440	27.5	8.9	56.6	14.5	15.2	4.6
1958	8,089	27.2	8.5	56.8	14.4	15.4	4.8
1959	8,689	27.3	8.3	57.0	13.9	16.2	4.5
1960	9,443	27.5	8.6	57.8	13.2	15.7	4.7

(continued)

Appendix B *(continued)*

Fiscal year	Total	Percent of state spending	Percent General support	Education	Highways	Welfare	All other
1961	10,114	27.0	8.1	58.9	12.5	15.8	4.6
1962	10,906	27.2	7.7	59.4	12.2	16.3	4.5
1963	11,885	34.6	8.5	58.9	11.9	16.1	4.6
1964	12,968	28.7	8.1	59.1	11.8	16.3	4.8
1965	14,174	29.1	7.8	58.9	11.5	17.2	4.6
1966	16,928	31.4	8.0	60.1	10.2	17.0	4.6
1967	19,056	32.0	8.3	62.2	9.8	15.2	4.6
1968	21,950	34.1	9.1	60.7	9.2	16.2	4.9
1969	24,779	33.5	8.6	59.9	8.6	17.8	5.1
1970	28,892	34.7	10.2	59.1	8.4	17.3	4.9
1971	32,640	34.4	9.9	59.1	7.7	17.6	5.6
1972	36,759	34.3	10.2	57.7	7.2	18.9	6.1
1973	40,822	35.5	10.5	57.1	7.2	18.4	6.7
1974	45,600	36.6	10.5	59.4	7.0	16.2	6.8
1975	51,004	35.9	10.1	61.0	6.3	14.0	8.7
1976	56,678	35.8	10.0	60.1	5.7	14.6	9.5
1977	61,984	36.1	10.4	60.5	5.9	14.3	8.8
1978	65,815	36.3	10.4	61.0	5.8	13.0	9.8
1979	74,461	37.4	11.0	62.0	5.6	11.6	9.7
1980	82,758	36.5	10.4	63.7	5.3	11.2	9.4
1981	91,307	37.7	10.5	62.7	5.2	12.1	9.5
1982	96,950	37.1	10.4	62.6	5.2	12.3	9.5
1983	99,544	35.5	10.4	63.4	5.3	11.4	9.5
1984	106,651	35.0	10.1	63.3	5.3	11.2	10.1

1985	119,608	35.2	10.3	62.7	5.0	10.6	11.4
1986	129,860	35.0	10.3	63.1	5.0	10.9	10.7
1987	138,970	35.0	10.3	63.5	4.9	12.5	8.9
1988	149,009	35.1	10.0	64.0	4.7	11.9	9.5
1989	165,415	35.2	9.5	63.2	4.5	11.9	10.9
1990	175,028	34.4	9.5	62.5	4.4	12.4	11.2
1991	186,469	33.6	9.1	62.2	4.4	12.0	12.3
1992	201,313	33.3	8.1	62.1	4.2	14.6	11.0
1993	210,469	32.5	8.4	62.3	4.4	14.9	10.0
1994	222,031	32.4	8.1	61.2	4.3	13.8	12.6
1995	237,361	32.4	8.0	62.4	4.4	12.9	12.3
1996	248,205	32.9	8.1	64.4	4.3	12.6	10.6
1997	260,367	33.9	8.4	63.0	4.4	13.7	10.5
1998	275,337	33.3	8.2	64.0	4.2	11.7	11.9

Source: U.S. Bureau of Census, Department of Commerce.

Notes

Chapter 1—Introduction

1. For a discussion, see Gordon L. Clark, *Judges and the Cities: Interpreting Local Autonomy* (Chicago: University of Chicago Press, 1985).

2. *City of Clinton v. Cedar Rapids and Missouri River Railroad*, 24 Iowa (1868): 455, at 475. Similarly, the U.S. Supreme Court, in *Hunter v. City of Pittsburgh*, held that "Municipal corporations are political subdivisions of the State, created as convenient agencies for exercising such of the governmental powers of the State as may be entrusted to them. . . . The number, nature and duration of the powers conferred upon these corporations and the territory over which they shall be exercised rests in the absolute discretion of the State." (207 U.S. 161, at 178 [1907]

3. Gerald E. Frug, "The City as a Legal Concept," *Harvard Law Review* 93 (April 1980): 1059–1174.

4. Ibid.

5. Richard Briffault, "Our Localism: Part I—The Structure of Local Government Law," *Columbia Law Review* 90 (January 1990): 1–115 at 111–112.

6. Ibid., 112.

7. Richard Briffault, "Our Localism: Part II—Localism and Legal Theory," *Columbia Law Review* 90 (March 1990): 346–454.

8. Briffault, "Our Localism: Part I."

9. See, for example, Paul Kantor, *The Dependent City Revisited: The Political Economy of Urban Development and Social Policy* (Boulder, CO: Westview Press, 1995); Paul E. Peterson, *City Limits* (Chicago: University of Chicago Press, 1981); Douglas Yates, *The Ungovernable City: The Politics of Urban Problems and Policymaking* (Cambridge, MA: M.I.T. Press, 1977); and Anthony Orum, *City Building in America* (Boulder, CO, Westview Press, 1995).

10. For an overview of urban politics literature, see Michael N. Danielson and Paul G. Lewis, "City Bound: Political Science and the American Metropolis," *Political Research Quarterly* 49 (March 1996): 203–220.

11. Harold Wolman and Michael Goldsmith, "Local Authority As a Meaningful Analytic Concept," *Urban Affairs Quarterly* 26 (September 1990): 3–27.

12. Charles M. Tiebout, "A Pure Theory of Local Expenditures," *Journal of Political Economy* 64 (October 1956): 416–424.

13. Harvey C. Mansfield, "Functions of State and Local Governments," in James W. Fesler, ed., *The 50 States and Their Local Governments* (New York: Knopf, 1967): 108.

14. W. Brooke Graves, *American Intergovernmental Relations* (New York: Charles Scribner's Sons, 1964): 710–711.

15. Remarks by Mayor John V. Lindsay, reprinted in Robert L. Morlan, ed., *Capital, Courthouse, and City Hall*, 5th ed. (Boston: Houghton Mifflin, 1977): 38–39.

16. Quoted by David R. Berman, "Relating to Other Governments" in Charldean Newell, ed., *The Effective Local Government Manager*, 2d ed. (Washington, DC: International City/County Management Association, 1993): 180.

17. See Rufus E. Miles, "The Origin and Meaning of Miles' Law," *Public Administration Review* 38 (September/October 1978): 399–403; and David R. Berman, Lawrence L. Martin, and Laura Kajfez, "County Home Rule: Does Where You Stand Depend on Where You Sit?" *State and Local Review* 17 (Spring 1985): 232–234.

18. Thomas J. Anton, *American Federalism and Public Policy: How the System Works*. (New York: Random House, 1989): 2.

19. Douglas E. Ashford, *Democracy, Centralization, and Decisions in Subnational Politics* (Beverly Hills, CA: Sage Publications, A Sage Professional Paper, 1976).

20. Harold A. Hovey, "Analytic Approaches to State-Local Relations," in E. Blaine Liner, ed., *A Decade of Devolution: Perspectives on State-Local Relations* (Washington, DC: Urban Institute Press, 1989): 163–182 at 164.

21. David R. Berman and Barbara P. Greene, "Counties and the National Agenda," in David R. Berman, ed., *County Government in an Era of Change* (Westport, CT: Greenwood Press, 1993): 123–134.

22. Joseph F. Zimmerman, *State-Local Relations: A Partnership Approach*, 2d ed. (New York: Praeger, 1995).

23. Frank J. Macchiarola, "The State and the City," in Robert H. Connery and Gerald Benjamin, eds., *Governing New York State: The Rockefeller Years*. (New York: The Academy of Political Science, 1974): 104–118.

24. Charles Press, "State Governments in Urban Areas: Petty Tyrants, Meddlers, or Something Else?" *Urban Interest* 2 (1980): 12–21 at 12.

25. Susan H. Fuhrman and Richard F. Elmore, "Understanding Local Control in the Wake of State Educational Reforms," *Educational Evaluation and Policy Analysis* 12 (Spring 1990): 82–96, at 82.

26. See, for example, Wayne A. Logan, "The Shadow Criminal Law of Municipal Governance," *Ohio State Law Journal* 62 (2001): 1409–1472.

27. See, for example, Thomas C. Desmond, "States Eclipse the Cities," *National Municipal Review* 44 (June 1955): 296–300, and Steven Gold, "Time for Change in State-Local Relations," *Journal of Policy Analysis and Management* 6 (Fall 1986): 101–106.

28. In performing this role, one formed by the virtue of holding particular elected positions, local officials may also feel that they are fulfilling their obligations as agents of the citizens who elected them. As I see it, performance of this role also folds into efforts to promote the interests of the particular region in which a locality is located, the type of local government for which the official works, and the interests of local government in general.

29. For a different perspective, see Alberta M. Sbragia, *Death Wish: Entrepreneurial Cities, U.S. Federalism, and Economic Development* (Pittsburgh: University of Pittsburgh Press, 1996).

30. Alvin D. Sokolow, "The Changing Property Tax and State-Local Relations," *Publius: The Journal of Federalism* 28 (Winter 1998): 165–87 at 180.

31. Ibid.

32. Desmond, "States Eclipse the Cities," 297.

33. See, for example, Edward A. Zelinsky, "Unfunded Mandates, Hidden Taxation, and the Tenth Amendment: On Public Choice, Public Interest, and Public Services," *Vanderbilt Law Review* 46 (November 1993): 1355–1415.

34. See Andrew Kirby, "A Smoking Gun: Relations Between the State and Local State in the Case of Fire Arms Control," *Policy Studies Journal* 18 (Spring 1990): 739–754; and Michael. D. Ward and Lewis L. House, "A Theory of Behavioral Power," *Journal of Conflict Resolution* 32 (1988): 3–36.

35. Illinois Municipal League Committee on Home Rule, "The Home Rule Experience," in Lois M. Pelekoudas, ed., *Illinois Local Government* (Urbana, IL: Institute of Government and Public Affairs, University of Illinois, May 1961): 54–59 at 54–55.

Chapter 2—Federal, State, and Local Relations

1. Christopher Swope, "Fighting the Wage War on Local Turf," *Governing* (June 1996): 35–37.

2. See Vivian E. Watts, "Federal Anti-Crime Efforts: The Fallout on State and Local Governments," *Intergovernmental Perspective* (Winter 1992): 35–38.

3. Anne Marie Cammisa, *Governments As Interest Groups: Intergovernmental Lobbying and the Federal System* (Westport, CT: Praeger, 1995).

4. See, generally, Roderick M. Hills, Jr., "Dissecting the State: The Use of Federal Law to Free State and Local Officials from State Legislative Control," *Michigan Law Review* 97 (March 1999): 1201–1286.

5. *Missouri v. Jenkins*, 495 U.S. 33 (1990).

6. On this point, see Daniel J. Elazar, "Local Government in Intergovernmental Perspective," in Daniel J. Elazar et al., eds., *Cooperation and Conflict: Readings in American Federalism* (Itasca, IL: F. E. Peacock, 1969): 416–423 at 417.

7. Hills, "Dissecting the State."

8. Daniel J. Elazar, *The American Partnership: Intergovernmental Cooperation in the Nineteenth-Century United States* (Chicago: University of Chicago Press, 1972); and Morton Grodzins, *The American System: A New View of Government in the United States* (Chicago: Rand McNally, 1966).

9. George S. Blair, *Government at the Grass-Roots* (Pacific Palisades, CA: Palisades, 1977): 43.

10. Paul Betters, J. Kerwin Williams, and Sherwood L. Reeder, *Recent Federal-City Relations* (Washington, DC: The United States Conference of Mayors, 1936): 136.

11. Raymond S. Short, "Municipalities and the Federal Government," *The Annals of the American Academy of Political and Social Science* 207 (January 1940): 44–53.

12. George C. S. Benson, *The New Centralization: A Study of Intergovernmental Relationships in the United States* (New York: Farrar and Rinehart, 1941): 86–97.

13. Betters et al., *Recent Federal-City Relations*, 136.

14. Ibid. See also John J. Gunther, *Federal-City Relations in the United States: The Role of the Mayors in Federal Aid to Cities* (Newark: University of Delaware Press, 1990): 259.

15. Benson, *The New Centralization*, 97.

16. Ibid., 126.

17. Letter from Kenneth L. Seegmiller, Executive Secretary, National Association of County Officials, June 30, 1954, cited in Advisory Committee on Local Government, Commission on Intergovernmental Relations, *Local Government* (Washington, DC: G.P.O., June 1955): 27.

18. Lyndon B. Johnson, "Partnership in Public Service," in *Economies and New Ideas for Cities: Proceedings, American Municipal Congress, 1963* (Washington, DC: American Municipal Association, 1963): 19.

19. Ibid. at 20.

20. Mavis Mann Reeves, "Galloping Intergovernmentalization As a Factor in State Management," *State Government* 54 (3) (1981): 102–108.

21. *Reflections on Being Governor* (Washington, DC: National Governors' Association, 1981): 111.

22. Cammisa, *Governments as Interest Groups*, 2. See, generally, Donald Haider, *When Governments Come to Washington: Governors, Mayors and Intergovernmental Lobbying* (New York: Free Press, 1974).

23. Harland Cleveland, Dean, Maxwell Graduate School, Syracuse University, "The Municipal Balance Sheet: Balancing Urban Needs and Financial Resources," in *Proceedings of the American Municipal Congress, 1960* (Washington, DC: American Municipal Association, 1961): 9–15 at 9.

24. *Reflections on Being Governor*, at 195–196.

25. Ibid.

26. Ibid.

27. Quoted by Marshall Kaplan and Sue O'Brien, *The Governors and the New Federalism* (Boulder, CO: Westview Press, 1991): 99. Other observers have a less positive view of Nixon's "New Federalism." Two scholars, for example, have noted, "The Nixonian New Federalism was simply romantic rhetoric, a facade behind which the national government is to abrogate its domestic role, to reduce its presence merely to that of an onlooker. . . ." Michael D. Reagan and John G. Sanzone, *The New Federalism* (New York: Oxford University Press, 1981): 175.

28. Cammisa, *Governments as Interest Groups*, at 3.

29. Neal Peirce, "Angry States Left with Tab for Social Services," *Washington Post* syndication, August 1989.

30. Helen F. Ladd, "The State Aid Decision: Changes in State Aid to Local Governments, 1982–1987," *National Tax Journal* (December 1991): 477–496. For earlier assessments of the performance of the states, see Helen F. Ladd and John Yinger, *America's Ailing Cities* (Baltimore: John Hopkins University Press, 1989); and Steven D. Gold, "A Better Scoreboard: States Are Helping Local Governments," *State Legislatures* (April 1990): 27–28.

31. Steven D. Gold, "Local Taxes Outpace State Taxes," *PA Times* (July 1993): 15, 17.

32. See, for example, William L. Waugh, Jr., "States, Counties, and the Questions of Trust and Capacity," *Publius: The Journal of Federalism* 18 (1988): 189–198.

33. On "shift-and-shaft federalism," see Stephen D. Gold and Sarah Ritchie, "State Policies Affecting Cities and Counties in 1991: Shifting Federalism," *Public Budgeting & Finance* (Spring 1992): 23–46.

34. Barbara P. Greene, "Counties and the Fiscal Challenges of the 1980s," *Intergovernmental Perspective* 13 (Winter 1987): 14–16.

35. See, for example, Alan Ehrenhalt, "As Interest in Its Agenda Wanes, a Shrink-

ing Urban Bloc in Congress Plays Defense," *Governing* (June 1991): 33–37; Charles H. Levine and James A. Thurber, "Reagan and the Intergovernmental Lobby: Iron Triangles, Cozy Subsystems and Political Conflict," in Allan J. Cigler and Burdett A. Loomis, eds., *Interest Group Politics* (Washington, DC: Congressional Quarterly Press, 1986): 202–220; and B.J. Reed, "The Changing Role of Local Advocacy in National Politics, *Journal of Urban Affairs* 5 (Fall 1983): 287–298.

36. "Mayor Cisneros Comments on State of U.S. Cities," contained in an extension of remarks of Hon. James J. Florio, *Congressional Record* (March 25, 1986): E961.

37. Quoted in Randy Arndt, "NLC Fiscal Survey: Budget Gap on Rise," *Nation's Cities Weekly* (July 8, 1991): 1, 8.

38. D. Michael Stewart, "Counties in the Federal System: The Washington Connection," *Intergovernmental Perspective* 17(Winter 1991): 18–20 at 19.

39. Charles Young. "How States' Mandates Make Local Taxes Go Up," *Sunday Record* (June 19, 1994): NJ-1, NJ-2, at 2.

40. Relevant survey information from municipal officials is found in William Barnes and David Dickinson, "Federal, State Levels Get Poor Rating from Local Officials," *Nation's Cities Weekly* (January 20, 1992): 7; "Unfunded Mandates Rank as Highest Priority Concern of Local Officials," *Nation's Cities Weekly* (January 10, 1994): 8; Jamie Woodwell, *The State of America's Cities* (Washington, DC: National League of Cities, January 1998); and "State of the Cities: 1999, Special Report," *Nation's Cities Weekly* (January 25, 1999): 5–9. See also Victor S. DeSantis, "State, Local, and Council Relations: Managers' Perceptions," *Baseline Data Report* 23 (March–April 1991) and county survey information by William L. Waugh, Gregory Streib, and Tanis J. Salant, in *County Government in an Era of Change*, David R. Berman, ed. (Westport, CT: Greenwood Press, 1993).

41. For commentary on the legislation, see Timothy J. Conlan, James D. Riggle, and Donna E. Schwartz, "Deregulating Federalism? The Politics of Mandate Reform in the 104th Congress," *Publius: The Journal of Federalism* 25 (Summer 1995): 23–39; and John Novinson, "Unfunded Mandates: A Closed Chapter?" *Public Management* (July 1995): 17–19.

42. Theresa A. Gullo and Janet M. Kelly, "Federal Unfunded Mandate Reform: A First-Year Retrospective," *Public Administration Review* 58 (September/October 1998): 379–387.

43. See Congressional Budget Office, "An Assessment of the Unfunded Mandates Reform Act in 1997," Washington, DC: G.P.O., February, 1998.

44. Paul L. Posner, *The Politics of Unfunded Mandates: Whither Federalism?* (Washington, DC: Georgetown University Press, 1998).

45. Janet M. Kelly, "Lessons from the States on Unfunded Mandates," *National Civic Review* 84 (Spring 1995): 133–139.

46. U.S. Census Bureau, *Federal Aid to States for Fiscal Year 2001* (Washington, DC: G.P.O., April 2002).

47. In the welfare area, some questions have arisen over the control of federal funds. In the early 2000s, for example, several states began using excess welfare funds to free up funds for other purposes, for example, schools, road building, and even tax cuts. In Ohio, officials in Cuyahoga County challenged the diversion of welfare funds as a violation of state law and the state's agreement with the county in regard to the administration of assistance and welfare transition programs. Cuyahoga

and other Ohio counties had been counting on the diverted federal welfare funds to support programs to train and educate the poor.

48. Richard L. Cole, Rodney V. Hissong, and Enid Arvidson, "Devolution: Where's the Revolution?" *Publius: The Journal of Federalism* 29 (Fall 1999): 99–112 at 105.

49. Ibid.

50. Bruce D. McDowell, "Advisory Commission on Intergovernmental Relations in 1996: The End of an Era," *Publius: The Journal of Federalism* 27 (Spring 1997): 111–127.

51. On the earliest relations, see Charles R. Adrain and Ernest S. Griffith, *A History of American City Government: The Formation of Traditions, 1775–1870* (New York: Praeger, 1976).

52. Benson, *The New Centralization,* 116–131.

Chapter 3—Localities in State Politics

1. Jonathan Walters, "Lobbying for the Good Old Days," *Governing* (June 1991): 33–37 at 35.

2. Quoted by Christy Hoppe, "More Cities Turning to Lobbyists: High Stakes, Short Session Force Move, Officials Say," *Dallas Morning News* (December 26, 1998): A-1.

3. See Timm Herdt, "County, Cities Pay Big Bucks to Lobby," *Ventura County Star*, Ventura County, California (December 29, 1997): A-1.

4. Quoted by Paul Schatt, "The Bottom Line," *Phoenix Gazette* (January 10, 1993): G-2.

5. Hoppe, "More Cites Turning to Lobbyists."

6. In regard to the Chicago delegation, for example, see James W. Fossett and J. Fred Giertz, "Money, Politics, and Regionalism: Allocating State Funds in Illinois," in Peter Nardulli, ed., *Diversity, Conflict, and State Politics: Regionalism in Illinois* (Urbana and Chicago: University of Illinois Press, 1989): 222–246.

7. "Federalist Paper Number 46," *The Federalist Papers* (New York: Mentor Books, New American Library, 1961): 296.

8. James Bryce, *The American Commonwealth* (New York: Macmillan, 1906): 5.

9. Quoted by Jamie Cooper and Linda Tarr-Whelan, "Turning Urban Nightmares to Dreams," *State Government News* (October 1991): 14–15.

10. William De Soto, "Cities in State Politics: Views of Mayors and Managers," *State and Local Government Review* 27 (Fall 1995): 188–194.

11. Quoted in Judy Walton, "Cities Join Push for Tax Reform," *Chattanooga Times/Chattanooga Free Press* (October 10, 1999): C-1.

12. Harold B. Smith, "Associations of Cities and Municipal Officials," *Urban Government*, Volume 1, Part IV of the Report of the Urbanism Committee to the National Resources Committee (Washington, DC: G.P.O., 1939): 181–211 at 189.

13. Councilman Charles P. Taft, Cincinnati, Ohio, "The Challenge of City-State Relations," in *Proceedings, American Municipal Congress, 1962* (Washington, DC: American Municipal Association, n.d.): 24.

14. Paper, "Effective Lobbying Begins at Home" prepared by the Alabama League of Cities, n.d.

15. Ibid.

16. See Alan Rosenthal, *The Third House: Lobbyists and Lobbying in the States* (Washington, DC: CQ Press, 1993); Anne Marie Cammisa, *Governments as Interest Groups* (Westport, CT: Praeger, 1995); and Donald Haider, *When Governments Come to Washington: Governors, Mayors and Intergovernmental Lobbying* (New York: Free Press, 1974).

17. See the account by Lee S. Green and Jack E. Holmes, "Tennessee: A Politics of Change," in William C. Havard, *"The Changing Politics of the South* (Baton Rouge: Louisiana State University Press, 1972): 190–191.

18. *Proceedings of the American Municipal Congress, 1962* (Washington, DC: American Municipal Association, n.d.): 94.

19. Nancy Hill-Holtzman, "Cities' PAC Gets More Flak Than Influence in State Capitol," *Los Angeles Times* (June 1, 1999): Metro, B-1.

20. Michael Fisher, "Cities' Voice at the State Level Reaches Out LOBBY: The Effort Seeks to Rally Local Groups and Push for Action in Sacramento," *Sacramento Press-Enterprise* (Riverside, CA, August 13, 2001): B-1.

21. Parris N. Glendening and Mavis Mann Reeves, *Pragmatic Federalism* (Pacific Palisades, CA: Palisades Publishers, 1977): 50; and David C. Nice, *Federalism: The Politics of Intergovernmental Relations* (New York: St. Martin's Press, 1987): 32.

22. Meredith Newman and Nicholas Lovrich, "The Hearing of Local Government Interests in State Legislatures: The Effects of Prior Service in City or County Government; A Research Note on Preliminary Findings" (paper prepared for delivery at the 1995 annual meeting of the Pacific Northwest Political Science Association, Bellingham, WA, October 1995).

23. Quoted in Margaret Hammersley, "Masiello, in Swipe at State Mandates, Envisions Unions, Firms Bidding on Services," *Buffalo News* (February 17, 2000): B-5.

24. De Soto, "Cities in State Politics."

25. Tanis J. Salant, "Shifting Roles in County-State Relations" in David R. Berman, ed., *County Governments in an Era of Change* (Westport, CT: Greenwood Press, 1993): 107–122 at 110.

26. Ibid., 111.

27. John T. Bragg, "A View from the Commission," *Intergovernmental Perspective* (Summer 1988): 2.

28. Nancy Hill-Holtzman, "Cities' PAC Gets More Flak."

29. Fisher, "Cities' Voice at State Level Reaches Out LOBBY."

30. Deil S. Wright, *Understanding Intergovernmental Relations* (Pacific Grove, CA: Brooks/Cole, 1982): 398.

31. Jim Miller, "The Legislative Process: What We Must Do," *Minnesota Cities* (February 1994): 5.

32. John F. Jennings, "Advice from a Friendly Insider," *The School Administrator* (August 1996): 10.

33. See Rosenthal, *The Third House*, 50. See also, Tom Loftus, *The Art of Legislative Politics* (Washington, DC: CQ Press, 1994): 129.

34. Clive S. Thomas and Ronald J. Hrebenar, "Interest Group Power in the Fifty States: Trends Since the Late 1970s," *Comparative State Politics* 20 (August 1999): 3–16.

35. David Morgan, "The Use of Public Funds for Legislative Lobbying and Electoral Campaigning," *Vanderbilt Law Review* 37 (March 1984): 433–472.

36. Ibid., at 440.

37. Alabama League of Cities, "Effective Lobbying Begins at Home," n.d.

38. Morgan, "The Use of Public Funds."

39. Walter Johnson, ed., Carol Evans, assistant ed., *The Papers of Adlai E. Stevenson* (Volume III, Boston: Little, Brown, 1973): 15.

40. Ibid.

41. Frank J. Macchiarola, "The State and the City," in Robert H. Connery and Gerald Benjamin, eds., *Governing New York State: The Rockefeller Years* (New York: The Academy of Political Science, 1974): 104–118.

42. Peter Burns, "The Intergovernmental Regime and Public Policy in Hartford, Connecticut," *Journal of Urban Affairs* 24 (2002): 55–73.

43. Also helpful in this respect are legislative staffers specializing in intergovermental matters. See "Coalition to Improve Management in State and Local Government," *Improving Local Services Through Intergovernmental and Intersectional Cooperation* (School of Urban and Public Affairs, Carnegie Mellon University, Pittsburgh, 1992): 11.

44. Ernest S. Griffith, *A History of American City Government: The Conspicuous Failure 1870–1900* (New York: Praeger, 1974): 218.

45. Ibid.

46. Ernest S. Griffith, *A History of American City Government: The Progressive Years and Their Aftermath, 1900–1920* (New York: Praeger, 1974): 235.

47. S. C. Wallace, *State Administrative Supervision over Cities in the United States* (New York: Columbia University Press, 1928): 37

48. John N. Kolesar, "The States and Urban Planning and Development," in Alan K. Campbell, ed., *The States and the Urban Crisis* (Englewood Cliffs, NJ: Prentice-Hall, 1970): 114–138, at 116.

49. Council of State Governments, *State Planning: New Roles in Hard Times* (Lexington, KY: Council of State Governments, 1976): 9–10.

50. Steven D. Gold, "Time for Change in State-Local Relations," *Journal of Policy Analysis and Management* 6 (Fall 1986): 101–106 at 103.

51. See a discussion by Robert E. Deyle and Richard A. Smith, "Local Government Compliance with State Planning Mandates: Effect of State Implementation in Florida," *Journal of the American Planning Association* 64 (Autumn 1998): 457–469.

52. R. Allen Hays, "State-Local Relations in Policy Implementation: The Case of Highway Transportation in Iowa," *Publius: The Journal of Federalism* 18 (Winter 1988): 79–95.

53. See Glenn Abney and Thomas A. Henderson, "An Exchange Model of Intergovernmental Relations: State Legislators and Local Officials," *Social Science Quarterly* 59 (March 1979): 720–731.

54. See "City Government in the State Courts," *Harvard Law Review* 78 (1965): 1596. Reprinted in Edward C. Banfield, ed., *Urban Government: A Reader in Administration and Politics*, rev. ed. (New York: The Free Press, 1969): 88–122.

55. Richard Briffault, "Our Localism: Part I—The Structure of Local Government Law," *Columbia University Law Review* 90 (January 1990): 1–115 at 55.

56. Mark Alan Hughes and Peter M. Vandoren, "Social Policy Through Land Reform: New Jersey's Mount Laurel Controversy," *Political Science Quarterly* 105 (1990): 97–111.

57. Justice William Brennan, Jr., "The Bill of Rights and the States: The Revival of State Constitutions As Guardians of Individual Rights," *New York University Law Review* 61 (October 1986): 535–553.

58. See, for example, Michael A. Lawrence, "Do 'Creatures of the State' Have Constitutional Rights? Standing for Municipalities to Assert Procedural Due Process Claims Against the State," *Villanova Law Review* 47 (2002): 93–116.

59. U.S. Advisory Commission on Intergovernmental Relations, *Local Government Autonomy: Needs for State Constitutional Statutory and Judicial Clarification* (Washington, DC: G.P.O, October 1993).

60. Donald L. Jones, *State Municipal Leagues: The First Hundred Years* (Washington, DC: National League of Cities, 1999): 78.

61. Donald J. Stabrowski, "Oregon and Measure Five: One Year Later," *Comparative State Politics* (October 8, 1993): 32. See also Michael L. Starn, "Tax Limitation in Various States," *Current Municipal Problems* 23 (1997): 523–528. Reprinted from the *Maine Townsman*, published by the Maine Municipal Association.

62. Donald J. Stabrowski, "Oregon's Increasing Use of the Initiative and Its Effect on Budgeting," *Comparative State Politics* 20 (February 1999): 31–45.

63. John A. Straayer, "Direct Democracy and Fiscal Mayhem," *Comparative State Politics* (February 1993): 6–12 at 11, 12.

64. Paul M. Grattet, City Manager of Greeley, Colorado, "TABOR Too Broad a Brush," *Denver Post* (March 29, 1998): J-2.

65. James Jacobs, "Taxpayers Bill of Rights or Wrongs?" *Denver Post* (March 29, 1998): J-01.

66. For a recent account, see David B. Magleby, "Ballot Initiatives and Intergovernmental Relations in the United States,"*Publius: The Journal of Federalism* 28 (Winter 1998): 147–163.

67. *Telford v. Thurston* 95 Wn. App. 149; 974 P.2d 886; 1999 Wash. App.

Chapter 4—Cities and the States: The Historical Perspective

1. In New England, on the other hand, the situation was almost reversed: towns did not have charters protecting them against colonial legislative action, but their citizens enjoyed considerable political and economic freedom. Thus, while the status of Boston as a town put it at the mercy of the legislature (the Massachusetts General Court), unlike cities with corporate charters, town status brought direct citizen participation in town meetings and, as it turned out, relatively unfettered commercial activity. See Jon C. Teaford, *The Municipal Revolution in America: Origins of Modern Urban Government 1650–1825* (Chicago: University of Chicago Press, 1973): 35–44.

2. Teaford, *The Municipal Revolution*, 80.

3. Charles N. Glaab, ed., *The American City: A Documentary History* (Homewood, IL: Dorsey Press, 1963): 1–6, 65–69.

4. Benjamin Baker, *Urban Government* (Princeton, NJ: D. Van Nostrand, 1957): 310.

5. See, generally, Kenneth Fox, *Better City Government: Innovation in American Politics, 1850–1937* (Philadelphia: Temple University Press, 1977); and Leonard

P. Curry, *The Corporate City: The American City as a Political Entity, 1800–1850* (Westport, CT: Greenwood Press, 1997).

6. Letter to Benjamin Rush, September 23, 1800, reprinted in Glaab, *The American City*, 52.

7. Alexis de Tocqueville, *Democracy in America*, trans. by Henry Reeve. 3d American ed. (New York: Appleton, 1899).

8. See Glaab, *The American City*, 51–63.

9. James C. Mohr, *The Radical Republicans and Reform in New York During Reconstruction* (Ithaca, NY: Cornell University Press, 1973).

10. Steven P. Erie, *Rainbow's End: Irish-Americans and the Dilemmas of Urban Machine Politics, 1840–1985* (Berkeley: University of California Press, 1988).

11. Barbara G. Salmore and Stephen A. Salmore, *New Jersey Politics and Government*, 2d ed. (Lincoln: University of Nebraska Press, 1998): 21

12. Ernest S. Griffith, *A History of American City Government, the Conspicuous Failure, 1870–1900* (New York: Praeger, 1974).

13. R. L. Mott, *Home Rule for America's Cities* (Chicago: American Municipal Association, 1949): 11. Quoted by Baker, *Urban Government*, 317.

14. Hon. Seth Low, President of Columbia College, New York, and formerly Mayor of the City of Brooklyn, "An American View of Municipal Government in the United States," in James Bryce, ed., *The American Commonwealth* (New York: Macmillan, 1906): 660–661.

15. George Washington Plunkitt, "New York Is Pie for the Hayseeds," in William L. Riordon, ed., *Plunkitt of Tammany Hall* (New York: E. P. Dutton, 1963): 21–24.

16. Paul M. Green, "Legislative Redistricting in Illinois: A Historical Analysis," *Comparative State Politics* 9 (October 1988): 39–75.

17. Austin F. Macdonald, *American State Government and Administration* (New York: Crowell, 1934): 713.

18. Charles R. Adrian and Ernest S. Griffith, *A History of American City Government: The Formation of Traditions: 1775–1870* (New York: Praeger, 1976): 36.

19. Fox, *Better City Government*.

20. Frank J. Goodnow, *Municipal Home Rule: A Study in Administration* (New York: Columbia University Press, 1916): 9. Originally published in 1895.

21. Benjamin Parke DeWitt, *The Progressive Movement: A Nonpartisan, Comprehensive Discussion of Current Tendencies in American Politics* (Seattle: University of Washington Press, 1915): 279.

22. John C. Stutz, *Proceedings, First and Second Conferences: The American Municipal Association and the Municipal League Compendium* (Lawrence, KS: The American Municipal Association, 1926): n.p.

23. John MacVicar, "League of American Municipalities," *Annals of the American Academy* 25 (1905): 165–167, at 165.

24. Patrick Healy, "Looking Back: How the NLC Was Born," *Nation's Cities* (November 1974): 14–18.

25. Joseph D. McGoldrick, *Law and Practice of Municipal Home Rule* (New York: AMS Press, 1967). Originally published in 1933.

26. *People ex rel. LeRoy v. Hurlbut* (24 Mich 44, 1871).

27. Joan C. Williams, "The Constitutional Vulnerability of American Local Government: The Politics of City Status in American Law," *Wisconsin Law Review* (1986):

83–153. See also Gerald E. Frug, "The City As a Legal Concept," *Harvard Law Review* 93 (1980): 1059–1154.

28. Ernest S. Griffith, *A History of American City Government: The Progressive Years and Their Aftermath, 1900–1920* (New York: Praeger, 1972): 256.

29. Charles Press, "State Government in Urban Areas: Petty Tyrants, Meddlers, or Something Else?" *Urban Interest* 2 (1980): 12–21.

30. See, for example, Lyle E. Schaller, "Home Rule—A Critical Appraisal," *Political Science Quarterly* 76 (September 1961): 402–415.

31. Harold B. Smith, "Associations of Cities and Municipal Officials," *Urban Government*, Vol. 1, Part IV of the Report of the Urbanism Committee to the National Resources Committee (Washington, G.P.O., 1939): 188–189.

32. Ibid., 188.

33. Richard S. Childs, *Civic Victories: The Story of an Unfinished Revolution* (New York: Harper and Brothers, 1952).

34. Thomas C. Desmond, "States Eclipse the Cities," *National Municipal Review* 44 (June 1955): 296–300 at 298.

35. Councilman Charles P. Taft, Cincinnati, Ohio, "The Challenge of City-State Relations," in *Proceedings, American Municipal Congress, 1962* (Washington, DC: American Municipal Association, n.d.): 23.

36. Ibid., 24.

37. A. James Reichley, "The Political Containment of the Cities," in Alan K. Campbell, ed., *The States and the Urban Crisis* (Englewood Cliffs, NJ: Prentice-Hall, 1970): 173.

38. See ibid., 185; Childs, *Civic Victories*, 263; John M. Swarthout and Ernest R. Bartley, *Principles and Problems of State and Local Government* (New York: Oxford University Press, 1958): 104–105; and Gordon E. Baker, *The Reapportionment Revolution* (New York: Random House, 1966): 49.

39. Mayor Ben West of Nashville, Tennessee, "The Effect of Reapportionment on State Actions," in *Proceedings, American Municipal Congress, 1962* (Washington, DC: American Municipal Association, n.d.): 49.

40. *Reynolds v. Sims*, 377 US.S. 533 (1964).

41. Reichley, "The Political Containment of the Cities."

42. Charles Mahtesian, "Semi-Vendetta, Cities and the New Republican Order," *Governing* (June 1996): 30–33.

43. Quote from Doug Finke, "Edgar Nixes Bill Banning Pay Raises," *The State Journal-Register* (Springfield, IL) (April 29, 1995): 1.

44. Quoted by George Strawley in "Politicians in Philadelphia, Pittsburgh Hit a Rough Spot in Harrisburg," The Associated Press State and Local Wire (June 27, 2001), n.p.

45. Quoted by Lee Leonard, "Big-City Democrats; Mayors Demand a Little Respect from Legislature," *The Columbus Dispatch* (October 5, 2002): (6-B). Complaints centered on the failure of the legislature to give cities their fair share of state and federal funds and to give adequate support to urban schools, and its interference with home-rule authority by, for example, preempting the right of cities to regulate predatory lending practices.

46. Lyle E. Schaller, "Home Rule—A Critical Appraisal," *Political Science Quarterly* 76 (September 1961): 402–415.

47. Dr. Thomas H. Reed, in *Government in Metropolitan Areas: Commentaries on a Report by the Advisory Commission on Intergovernmental Relations* (Washington: U.S. Government Printing Office, 1962): 3.

Chapter 5—The Authority Problem

1. John F. Dillon, *Commentaries on the Law of Municipal Corporations* (Boston: Little, Brown, 1911): 145.

2. See, generally, James D. Thomas and William H. Stewart, eds., *Alabama Government and Politics* (Lincoln: University of Nebraska Press, 1988); and Charles J. Spindler, "Alabama," in Dale Krane, Platon N. Rigos, and Melvin B. Hill, Jr., eds., *Home Rule in America: A Fifty-State Handbook* (Washington, DC: CQ Press, 2001): 24–25.

3. David W. Owens, "Local Government Authority to Implement Smart Growth Programs: Dillon's Rule, Legislative Reform, and the Current State of Affairs in North Carolina," *Wake Forest Law Review* 35 (Fall 2000): 671–705.

4. Gordon L. Clark, *Judges and the Cities* (Chicago: University of Chicago Press, 1985): 78–79.

5. Kathy Hunt, *Wyoming Home Rule: A Current Status Report* (Cheyenne: Wyoming Association of Municipalities, 1994).

6. David R. Berman, Lawrence L. Martin, and Laura Kajfez, "County Home Rule: Does Where You Stand Depend on Where You Sit?" *State and Local Review* 17 (Spring 1985): 232–234.

7. Quoted by James W. Zumwalt, "The Local Government Role: Home Rule and Short Ballots," in *Proceedings: A Symposium on the Alabama Constitution* (Center for Governmental Services, Auburn University, February 15, 1996), Internet, www.auburn.edu.

8. Joseph F. Zimmerman, *State-Local Relations: A Partnership Approach*, 2d ed. (New York: Praeger, 1995).

9. Unlike municipalities, which are called into being at the direct request of the persons composing them or, at least, with their consent, the quasi-municipal corporations are created by a state government acting on its own for its own purposes. They are primarily administrative units of the state, though some counties have charters that give them a degree of independence.

10. David R. Berman and Lawrence L. Martin, "State-Local Relations: An Examination of Local Discretion," *Public Administration Review* 48 (March/April 1988): 637–641.

11. See U.S. Advisory Commission on Intergovernmental Relations, *Local Government Autonomy: Needs for State Constitutional, Statutory, and Judicial Clarification* (Washington, DC: G.P.O: October 1993).

12. Lawrence L. Martin and Ronald C. Nyhan, "Determinants of County Charter Home Rule," *International Journal of Public Administration* 17 (1994): 955–970.

13. Kenneth E. Vanlandingham, "Municipal Home Rule in the United States," *William and Mary Law Review* 10 (Winter 1968): 269–314.

14. Susan B. Hannah, "Writing Home-Rule Charters in Michigan: Current Practices in Constitution Making," *National Civic Review* 84 (Spring 1995): 140–148.

15. Stephanie Cole, "Home Rule in Illinois," *Illinois Issues* (August 1975): 243–246.

16. U.S. Advisory Commission on Intergovernmental Relations, *State Laws Governing Local Government Structure and Administration* (Washington, DC: G.P.O., March 1993).

17. Charles Mahtesian, "The Endless Struggle Over Open Meetings," *Governing* (December 1997): 48–51.

18. State directives that prohibit local units from becoming involved in certain policy areas, from performing certain functions, or from taking certain actions (such as raising particular taxes) are also sometimes categorized as mandates, although in this work, they are treated separately. On the definition of *mandates* and the different forms they can take, see Janet M. Kelly, *State Mandates: Fiscal Notes, Reimbursement, and Anti-Mandate Strategies* (Washington, DC: National League of Cities, 1992); Kelly, "Unfunded Mandates: The View from the States," *Public Administration Review* 54 (July/August 1994): 405–408; Max Neiman and Catherine Lovell, "Federal and State Mandating: A First Look at the Mandate Terrain," *Administration and Society* 14 (November 1982): 343–372; Neiman and Lovell, "Mandating As a Policy Issue—The Definitional Problem," *Policy Studies Journal* (Spring 1981): 667–680; U.S. Advisory Commission on Intergovernmental Relations, *State Mandating of Local Expenditures* (Washington, DC: G.P.O., 1978); Georgia Municipal Association, *Calculating the Cost of State and Federal Mandates: Getting Started* (Atlanta: Georgia Municipal Association, March 1993); and Joseph F. Zimmerman, "Some Remedies Suggested for State Mandated Expenditure Distortions," *Current Municipal Problems* 21 (1994): 93–110.

19. Quoted by Alan Ehrenhalt, "Powerless Pipsqueaks and the Myth of Local Control," *Governing* (June 1999): 7–9 at 7.

20. Ibid.

21. Quoted by Jonathan Walters, "Reinventing the Federal System," *Governing* (January 1994): 49–53.

22. Edward Flentje, "State Mandates As Family Values?" *Current Municipal Problems* 22 (1996): 510–512.

23. Joel A. Thompson and G. Larry Mays, "The Impact of State Standards and Enforcement Procedures on Local Jail Performance," *Policy Studies Review* (Autumn 1988): 55–71.

24. Michael Fix and Daphne Kenyon, eds., *Coping with Mandates: What Are the Alternatives?* (Washington, DC: Urban Institute Press, 1990): 21.

25. U.S. Advisory Commission on Intergovernmental Relations, *Mandates: Cases in State-Local Relations* (Washington, DC: G.P.O., September 1990): 21.

26. State and Local Government Commission of Ohio, *Unfunded Mandates: Regaining Control at the Local Level* (Columbus: State and Local Government Commission of Ohio, December 8, 1994).

27. Harry A. Green, Executive Director and Research Director, Tennessee Advisory Commission on Intergovernmental Relations (TACIR), "State Mandates to Local Governments," memorandum to TACIR Commissioners (August 28, 1995).

28. Connecticut Conference of Municipalities, *The State of Municipalities in Connecticut: A Public Policy Report* (New Haven: Connecticut Conference of Municipalities, February 1995): 17.

29. Edward A. Zelinsky, "Unfunded Mandates, Hidden Taxation, and the Tenth Amendment: On Public Choice, Public Interest, and Public Services, *Vanderbilt Law Review* 46 (November 1993): 1355–1415.

30. Robert M. Shaffer, "Comment: Unfunded State Mandates and Local Governments," *University of Cincinnati Law Review* 64 (Spring 1996): 1057–1088.

31. Susan A. MacManus, "Mad About Mandates: The Issue of Who Should Pay for What Resurfaces in the 1990s," *Publius: The Journal of Federalism* 21 (Summer 1991): 59–75. See also Shaffer, "Comment: Unfunded State Mandates."

32. See Janet M. Kelly, "A New Approach to an Old Problem: State Mandates," *Government Finance Review* (December 1993): 27–29. See also Janet M. Kelly, "Institutional Solutions to Political Problems: The Federal and State Mandate Cost Estimation Process," *State and Local Government Review* 29 (Spring 1997): 90–97.

33. See Ann Calvares Barr, "Cost Estimations as an Anti-Mandate Strategy," in Fix and Kenyon, eds., *Coping with Mandates*, 57–61. See also U.S. General Accounting Office, *Legislative Mandates: State Experiences Offer Insights for Federal Action* (Washington, DC: U.S. General Accounting Office, 1988); and Kelly, *A New Approach to an Old Problem*, 42.

34. Janet M. Kelly, "Mandate Reimbursement Measures in the States," *American Review of Public Administration* 24 (December 1994): 351–371.

35. Virginia Legislature, Joint Legislative Audit and Review Commission, *Intergovernmental Mandates and Financial Aid to Local Governments*, House Document no. 56 (Richmond, 1992).

36. Joseph Zimmerman, quoted in "States Take Lead in Mandate Relief," *State Trends Bulletin* (February/March 1996): 8.

37. *Durant v. State of Michigan*, 566 N.W.2nd 272 (Mich. 1997). See also David G. Pettinari, "Michigan's Latest Tax Limitation Battle: A Tale of Environmental Regulation, Capital Infrastructure, and the 'Will of the People,'" *University of Detroit Mercy Law Review* 77 (Fall 1999): 83–154.

38. See Richard H. Horte, "State Expenditures with Mandate Reimbursement," in Fix and Kenyon, eds., *Coping with Mandates*; and Kelly, *A New Approach to an Old Problem*.

39. Sam Mamet, *Mandates: Controlling Your Municipality's Destiny* (Denver CO: Colorado Municipal League, n.d.).

40. National League of Cities, *Annual Survey of City Fiscal Conditions* (news release, July 1, 1999).

41. "State of the Cities: 1999, Special Report," *Nation's Cities Weekly* (January 25, 1999): 5–9.

42. Edward A. Zelinsky, "The Unsolved Problem of the Unfunded Mandate," *Ohio Northern University Law Review* 23 (1997): 741–781.

43. Janet M. Kelly, "Lessons from the States on Unfunded Mandates," *National Civic Review* 84, (Spring 1995): 133–139 at 136.

44. Janet M. Kelly, *State Mandates: Fiscal Notes, Reimbursements, and Anti-Mandate Strategies* (Washington, DC: National League of Cities, 1992).

45. On this point see, for example, Paul Flowers and John T. Torbert, *Mandate Costs: A Kansas Case Study* (Topeka: Kansas Association of Counties, 1993).

46. Christopher Swope, "Rent Control: Invisible No More," *Governing* (January 1998): 28–29.

47. Howie Fain, "Rent Control in Massachusetts: Notes on the Cambridge Electorate," *National Civic Review* 84 (Spring 1995): 161–163.

48. Peter D. Jackson, Jeffrey Wasserman, and Kristiana Raube. "The Politics of Antismoking Legislation," *Journal of Health Politics, Policy, and Law* 18 (Winter 1993): 787–819.

49. Ibid., 794.

50. See the overview by Patricia S. Biswanger, "Preserving Democracy in the Face of Special Interest Might: Local Initiatives to Ban Cigarette Vending Machines," *Current Municipal Problems* 21 (1994): 67–92. An abbreviated version of this article appeared in the November/December 1993 issue of the *Municipal Attorney*, National Institute of Municipal Law Officers, Washington, DC.

51. The leading case is *Morial v. Smith & Wesson Corp.*, 785 So.2d 1 (La. 2001). See reviews by Brent W. Landau, "Recent Legislation: State Bans on City Gun Lawsuits," *Harvard Journal on Legislation* 37 (Summer 2000): 623–638; and Andrew S. Cabana, "Missing the Target Municipal Litigation Against Handgun Manufacturers: Abuse of the Tort System, *George Mason Law Review* 9 (Summer 2001): 1127–1175.

52. See Christopher A. Novak, "Agriculture's New Environmental Battleground: The Preemption of County Livestock Regulations," *Drake Journal of Agricultural Law* 5 (Winter 2000): 429–469.

53. Quoted by Jeremy R. Cooke, "Bill Lets City Teachers Live Outside City," *Pittsburgh Post-Gazette* (July 22, 2001): C-3.

54. Gerald E. Frug, "The City As a Legal Concept," *Harvard Law Review* 93 (April 1980): 1059–1174 at 1150.

55. Richard Briffault, "Local Government and the New York State Constitution," in Burton C. Agata, Eric Lane, and Norma Rotunno, eds., *State Constitutions: Competing Perspectives* (Hempstead, NY: Hofstra University, School of Law, 1996): 79–109 at 82.

Chapter 6—The Revenue Problem

1. News item, *Nation's Cities* (February 1970), 67.

2. S. C. Wallace, *State Administrative Supervision over Cities in the United States* (New York: Columbia University Press, 1928): 254–255.

3. W. Brooke Graves, *American Intergovernmental Relations* (New York: Charles Scribner's Sons, 1964): 729.

4. U. S. Advisory Commission on Intergovernmental Relations, *City Financial Emergencies: The Intergovernmental Dimension* (Washington, DC: G.P.O., July 1973): 71.

5. Chris Hoene, "History, Voters Not Kind to Property Tax," *Nation's Cities Weekly* (May 14, 2001): 3, 5.

6. U.S. Advisory Commission on Intergovernmental Relations, *Tax and Expenditure Limits on Local Governments* (Washington, DC: G.P.O., March 1995). See also Phillip G. Joyce and Daniel R. Mullins, "The Changing Fiscal Structure of the State and Local Public Sector: The Impact of Tax and Expenditure Limitations," *Public Administration Review* 51 (May/June 1991): 240–253; Daniel E. O'Toole and Brian Stipak, "Coping with State Tax and Expenditure Limitations: The Oregon Experience," *State and Local Government Review* 30 (Winter 1998): 9–16; and Alvin D. Sokolow, "The Changing Property Tax and State-Local Relations," *Publius: The Journal of Federalism* 28 (Winter 1998): 165–187.

7. William J. Shultz, "Limitations on State and Local Borrowing Powers," *The Annals* 181 (September 1935): 118–124 at 119.

8. Ibid., 121–123.

9. See Alberta M. Sbragia, *Debt Wish: Entrepreneurial Cities, U.S. Federalism, and Economic Development* (Pittsburgh: University of Pittsburgh Press, 1996).

10. On property tax trends, see Michael Fitzpatrick Lorelli, *Special Report: State and Local Property Taxes* (Washington, DC: Tax Foundation, August 2001; Phillip M. Dearborn, "Local Property Taxes: Emerging Trends," *Intergovernmental Perspective* (Summer 1993): 10–12; and Scott Mackey, "Keeping a Lid on Property Taxes," *State Legislatures* (March 1997): 10–11. See also a series of articles by Steven D. Gold: "The State of State-Local Relations," *State Legislatures* (August 1988): 17–20; "Local Taxes Outpace State Taxes," *PA Times* (July 1993): 15, 17; and "Passing the Buck," *State Legislatures* (January 1993): 36–38.

11. Lorelli, *Special Report: State and Local Property Taxes.*

12. Todd Von Kampen, "State Controls Few Assessors," *Omaha World-Herald* (October 25, 1999): 9.

13. Richard L. Cole and John Kincaid, "Public Opinion and American Federalism: Perspectives on Taxes, Spending, and Trust—An ACIR Update," *Publius: The Journal of Federalism* 30 (Winter/Spring 2000): 189–201. See also U.S. Advisory Commission on Intergovernmental Relations, *Changing Public Attitudes on Government and Taxes* (Washington, DC: Advisory Commission on Intergovernmental Relations, 1990, 1991, 1992).

14. For background, see Noel Brinkerhoff, "The Worst of Times" *California Journal* (September 1997): 17–20; Mary Beth Barber, "Local Government Hits the Wall: Proposition 13 Finally Comes Home to Roost," *California Journal* (August 1993): 13–15; A. G. Block, Danielle Starkey, and Steve Scott, "The 1993–94 Budget: Pete Wilson and Willie Brown Delivered, but Was It a Knockout Punch for California?" *California Journal* (August 1993): 7–11; Danielle Starkey, "Stung By a Grab of Property Taxes by the State, County Governments Are Fighting Back," *California Journal* (August 1993): 21–23; and Hugh Mields, Jr., "The Property Tax: Local Revenue Mainstay," *Intergovernmental Perspective* (Summer 1993): 16–18.

15. Alvin D. Sokolow, "The Changing Property Tax and State-Local Relations," *Publius: The Journal of Federalism* 28 (Winter 1998): 165–187.

16. Michael Gardner, "Payback Time for Cities and Counties? Copley News Service, May 28, 1999, n.p.

17. John P. Thomas, "Financing County Government: An Overview," *Intergovernmental Perspective* (Winter 1991): 12.

18. Randy Arndt, "Fiscal Conditions Remain Strong in Most Cities," *Nation's Cities Weekly* (July 31, 2000): 1, 9.

19. See *Government Finance Review* (June 1991): 4. See also Glenn W. Fisher, *The Worst Tax? A History of the Property Tax in America* (Lawrence: University of Kansas Press, 1996).

20. This argument is made, for example, by Wallace E. Oates, "Local Property Taxation: An Assessment," *Land Lines* (Lincoln Institute of Land Policy, May 1999). Internet, www.lincolnist.edu.

21. Sokolow, "The Changing Property Tax." See also David Brunori, Contributing Editor of *State Tax Notes*, "To Preserve Local Government, It's Time to Save the Property Tax" (2001). Internet, www.tax.org.

22. Brunori, "To Preserve Local Government."

23. Ibid.

24. Reid Ewing, "Transportation Utility Fees," *Government Finance Review* (June 1994): 13–17.

25. Alan A. Altshuler and Jose A. Gomez-Ibanez, with Arnold M. Howitt, *Regulation for Revenue: The Political Economy of Land Use Exactions* (Washington, DC, and Cambridge, MA: Brookings Institution and Lincoln Institute of Land Policy, 1993).

26. See John L. Mikesell, "Lotteries in State Revenue Systems: Gauging a Popular Revenue Source after 35 Years," *State and Local Review* 33 (Spring 2001): 86–100; and Donald E. Miller and Patrick A. Pierce, "Lotteries for Education: Windfall or Hoax? *State and Local Government Review* 29 (1997): 34–42.

27. Fiscal Planning Services, Inc. *Dedicated State Tax Revenues: A Fifty-State Report* (June 2000).

28. See U.S. Advisory Commission on Intergovernmental Relations, *The State of State-Local Revenue Sharing* (Washington, DC: G.P.O., 1980); and Paul D. Moore, "General Purpose Aid in New York State: Targeting Issues and Measures," *Publius: The Journal of Federalism* 19 (Spring 1989): 17–31.

29. Harold B. Smith, "Associations of Cities and Municipal Officials," in *Urban Government* Vol.1, Part IV, of the Report of the Urbanism Committee to the National Resources Committee (Washington, DC: G.P.O., 1939): 189–190.

30. Frank J. Macchiarola, "The State and the City," in Robert H. Connery and Gerald Benjamin, eds., *Governing New York State: The Rockefeller Years* (New York: The Academy of Political Science, 1974): 104–118, at 112–113.

31. Amy Rinard, "Kettl Panel Work All for Naught," *Milwaukee Journal Sentinel* (May 20, 2001): 02Z.

32. Steven Walters, "Kettl Plan a Victim of Budget Wars; Lauded Program for Reform Has No Political Constituency." *Milwaukee Journal Sentinel* (May 16, 2001): B-1.

33. Keith J. Mueller, "Explaining Variation in State Assistance Programs to Local Communities: What to Expect and Why," *State and Local Review* 19 (Fall 1987): 101–107. Compare this with David R. Morgan and Robert E. England, "State Aid to Cities: A Causal Inquiry," *Publius: The Journal of Federalism* 15 (Spring 1984): 67–82.

34. See Thomas R. Dye and Thomas L. Hurley, "The Responsiveness of Federal and State Governments to Urban Problems," *Journal of Politics* 40 (February 1978): 196–207; and John P. Pelissero, "State Aid and City Needs: An Examination of Residual State Aid to Large Cities," *Journal of Politics* 46 (August 1984): 916–935. For more pessimistic views, see Robert M. Stein and Keith E. Hamm, "A Comparative Analysis of the Targeting Capacity of State and Federal Intergovernmental Aid Allocations: 1977, 1982," *Social Science Quarterly* 68 (September 1987): 447–477; and David R. Morgan and Mei-Chiang Shih, "Targeting State and Federal Aid to City Needs," *State and Local Government Review* 23 (Spring 1991): 60–67.

35. See, for example, Robert M. Stein, "The Targeting of State Aid: A Comparison of Grant Delivery Mechanisms," *Urban Interest* 2 (1981): 47–60; Robert M. Stein, "The Allocation of State Aid to Local Governments: An Examination of Interstate Variation," in U.S. Advisory Commission on Intergovernmental Relations, *State and Local Roles in the Federal System* (Washington, DC: G.P.O., 1982): 203–226; and Robert M. Stein and Keith E. Hamm, "Explaining State Aid Allocations: Targeting Within Universalism," *Social Science Quarterly* 75 (September 1994): 524–540.

36. Randy Arndt, "NLC Study Shows Lag on City Aid," *Nation's Cities Weekly* (September 12, 1988): 1, 9.

37. Representative John Gard, quoted in Amy Rinard, "State Lawmakers Cool to More Local Funding," *Milwaukee Journal Sentinel* (April 9, 1999): 1.

38. Macchiarola, "The State and the City," 111–118. See also Wallace S. Sayre and Herbert Kaufman, *Governing New York City* (New York: The Russell Sage Foundation, 1960): 57.

39. Quoted by Kevin McDermott and Patrick J. Powers, "Illinois Cities Protest Plan to Cut Revenue Sharing," *St. Louis Post-Dispatch* (May 11, 2002): News, 12.

40. John R. Bartle, "Coping with Cutbacks: City Response to Aid Cuts in New York State," *State and Local Government Review* 28 (Winter 1996): 38–48.

41. Betty Long, Deputy Director, Virginia Municipal League, "2002 General Assembly Proved Costly for Local Government," *Virginia Town & City* 37 (May 2002), n.p.

42. Randall Higgins, "Rowland Discusses Municipal League," *Chattanooga Times/Chattanooga Free Press* (June 12, 2002): B-3.

43. "Illinois Cities Opposed to Plan to Cut Revenue Sharing," Associated Press State and Local Wire (May 11, 2002).

44. Todd Richmond, "Shared Revenue Hot Button for Budget Repair Lobbyists," Associated Press State and Local Wire (August 21, 2002), n.p.

45. From Chris Andrews and Stacey Range, "Engler Slashes Local Funding," *Lansing State Journal* (MI) (July 26, 2002): A-1.

46. "Comments About Tuesday's Vote to Override Engler's Veto," Associated Press (August 13, 2002), n.p.

47. See, for example, Helen F. Ladd, "Big-City Finances," in *Big-City Politics, Governance, and Fiscal Constraints*, George E. Peterson, ed. (Washington, DC: Urban Institute Press, 1994): 201–269.

48. Gold, "State Aid to Localities," 1–5.

49. *State and Local Source Book 2000*, Supplement to *Governing Magazine.*

50. Barbara Todd, "Counties in the Federal System: The State Connection," *Intergovernmental Perspective* 17 (Winter 1991): 21–25.

51. "Has Michigan Gone Crazy: Killing School Tax, It Stages a Great Experiment," editorial, *Buffalo News* (July 31, 1993): 2.

52. Quoted by William Celis III, "Michigan Votes for Revolution in Financing Its Public Schools," *New York Times* (March 17, 1994): A-1.

53. See the December 1998 poll by Zogby International in *Public Opinion Online* (Roper Center at University of Connecticut, Accession Number 0320743, Question Number 009).

54. Kenneth K. Wong, "Fiscal Support for Education in the American States: The Parity-to-Dominance View Examined," *American Journal of Education* 97 (August 1989): 329–357.

55. Robert C. Johnson and Jessica L. Sandham, "States Increasingly Flexing Their Policy Muscle," *Education Week on the Web* (April 14, 1999).

56. Michael Colantuono, quoted by Claire Cooper, "State High Court OKs Tax Challenges," *Sacramento Bee* (June 5, 2001): A-3.

57. "Why County Revenues Vary: State Laws and Local Conditions Affecting County Finance." Report prepared by Legislative Analyst's Office, State of California, May 7, 1999.

Chapter 7—The Takeover Problem

1. "Avoiding Local Government Financial Crisis: The Role of State Oversight," *CRC Memorandum* (a publication of the Citizens Research Council of Michigan): July 2000.

2. States using a "multijurisdictional policy approach to fiscal stress" include Colorado, Florida, Illinois, Kentucky, Maine, Nevada, New Jersey, Ohio, Pennsylvania, North Carolina, Rhode Island, Tennessee, and Wisconsin. See, generally, Anthony G. Cahill, Joseph A. James, Jean E. Lavigne, and Ann Stacey, "State Government Responses to Municipal Fiscal Distress: A Brave New World for State-Local Intergovernmental Relations," *Public Productivity and Management Review* 17 (Spring 1994): 253–264; Anthony G. Cahill and Joseph A. James, "Responding to Municipal Fiscal Distress: An Emerging Issue for State Governments in the 1990s," *Public Administration Review* 52 (January/February 1992): 88–94; Scott R. Mackey, *State Programs to Assist Distressed Local Governments* (Denver: National Conference of State Legislators, March 1993); and David R. Berman, "Takeovers of Local Governments: An Overview and Evaluation of State Policies," *Publius: The Journal of Federalism* 25 (Summer 1995): 55–70.

3. One example of general-distress legislation is the Pennsylvania Municipalities Financial Recovery Act of 1987, popularly known as Act 47, which applies to all cities except Pittsburgh and Philadelphia. Under Act 47, the State Department of Community Affairs (DCA) collects financial information from municipalities and evaluates it according to eleven indicators of distress. The DCA may declare a municipality officially distressed and appoint a state coordinator to develop and implement a plan to correct the problems. A municipality may reject this plan and develop its own, but the DCA has to approve the municipality's plan. Until it approves a plan, the DCA can withhold assistance provided by Act 47 and also withhold some other revenues given to the locality as regular state funding. For a review, see Drew Patrick Gannon, "An Analysis of Pennsylvania's Legislative Program for Financially Distressed Municipalities and the Reaction of Municipal Labor Unions," *Dickinson Law Review* 28 (Winter 1994): 281–305.

4. See Note: "Missed Opportunity: Urban Fiscal Crises and Financial Control Boards," *Harvard Law Review* 110 (January 1997): 733–750.

5. Robert Bailey, *The Crisis Regime* (Albany: State University of New York Press, 1984).

6. William K. Tabb, *The Long Default: New York City and the Urban Fiscal Crisis* (New York: Monthly Review Press, 1982): 29.

7. Quoted by Gerald Benjamin, "The Political Relationship," in Gerald Benjamin and Charles Brecher, eds., *The Two New Yorks: State-City Relations in the Changing Federal System* (New York: Russell Sage Foundation, 1988): 122.

8. Bailey, "The Crisis Regime."

9. Charles Brecher and Raymond D. Horton, "Retrenchment and Recovery: American Cities and the New York Experience," *Public Administration Review* 45 (March/April 1985): 267–274.

10. Ester R. Fuchs, *Mayors and Money* (Chicago: University of Chicago Press, 1992): 182.

11. Gannon, "An Analysis of Pennsylvania's Legislative Program."

12. Ibid.

13. Testimony of David Cohen, Philadelphia Mayor's Office, before U.S. House Government Reform and Oversight Committee, District of Columbia Subcommittee (March 8, 1995; televised on C-Span2).

14. Testimony of Bernard Anderson, former chairman of the Pennsylvania Intergovernmental Cooperation Authority, ibid.

15. Testimony of David Cohen, Philadelphia Mayor's Office.

16. Dorothy A. Brown, "Fiscal Distress and Politics: The Bankruptcy Filing of Bridgeport As a Case Study in Reclaiming Local Sovereignty," *Bankruptcy Developments Journal*, vol. 11 (1995): 625–656.

17. Ibid.

18. Adam Pertman, "Bridgeport Mayor Files for City's Bankruptcy," *Boston Globe* (June 8, 1991 Metro section): 25.

19. Even before receivership, a private institution, Boston University, had taken charge of the city's schools. This arrangement began in 1989 in an effort to find innovative solutions to school problems.

20. Fox Butterfield, "Mired in Debt, a Boston Suburb Is Taken Over by Massachusetts," *New York Times* (September 13, 1991): A-21.

21. Fox Butterfield, "Insolvent Boston Suburb Faces Threat of Takeover," *New York Times* (September 8, 1991): A-18.

22. See William Cox, "Lessons of Receivership: The Legacy of Chelsea," *Government Finance Review* 9 (August 1993): 21–22, 24; and Ed Cyr, "Thoughts on the Chelsea Receivership," *Government Finance Review* 9 (August 1993): 23–24. Cyr, at the time, was an assistant receiver for administration and finance for the city of Chelsea.

23. Cyr, "Thoughts on the Chelsea Receivership."

24. "Text of Judge Robert B. Krupansky's Order for State Takeover," *The Cleveland Plain Dealer* (March 9 1995): 4B–5B.

25. Updates are found on the web site of the Education Commission of the States, http//www.ecs.org.

26. Education Commission of the States, *State Takeovers and Reconstructions* (Denver, CO: January 2001).

27. Catherine Gewertz, "California Superintendent Leaves Second District in Disarray," *Education Week* 20 (January 10, 2001): 5.

28. Quoted by Laval S. Wilson, "Takeover: The Paterson Story," *The American School Board Journal* 181 (December 1994): 22–26 at 22.

29. Quoted by Dan Weissmann, "State Takeovers, Painful but Productive," *Catalyst* (March 1993): 7–8 at 7.

30. Ibid.

31. Karla Scoon Reid, "'Comeback' from State Control Means Solvency for Compton," *Education Week* 20 (January 31, 2001): 1, 14, 15.

32. Ibid.

33. Jessica Portner, "State Takeover of Troubled Schools Debated," *Mercury News* (November 24, 2001): A-1.

34. See Saul Cooperman, New Jersey State Commissioner of Education, "View from the State," *The American School Board Journal* 175 (November 1988): 24–25, 50.

35. Kenneth J. Tewel, "The New Jersey Takeover Legislation: Help or Hindrance

to Improvement in Troubled School Districts?" *Urban Review* 23 (December 1991): 217–229.

36. Ibid.

37. Jo Anna Natale, "In 20 States a Takeover is 'The Ultimate Audit,'" *The American School Board Journal* 181 (December 1994): 24–25.

38. Jean Rimbach, "Paterson Schools Now in State Hands,"*Record* (Hackensack, NJ, August 8, 1991): D9. See also Jo Anna Natale, "Documenting the State's Case Against Paterson," *The American School Board Journal* 181 (December 1994): 26; and Kimberly J. McLarin, "Schools in Paterson Lagging on Standards, Report Says," *New York Times* (November 4, 1994): B-6.

39. Karen Diegmueller and Drew Lindsay, "NJ Moves Toward Takeover of Newark Schools," *Education Week* (August 3, 1994): 20, 25.

40. Ibid.

41. Ibid.

42. Quoted in Kimberly J. McLarin, "Newark School Officials Pitch a Plan for System,"*New York Times* (July 26, 1994): B-5.

43. Diegmueller and Lindsay, "NJ Moves Toward Takeover of Newark Schools."

44. Neil MacFarquhar, "Judge Orders a State Takeover of the Newark School District," *New York Times* (April 14, 1995): A-1, B-6.

45. Robert C. Johnson, "NJ Takeover of Newark Found to Yield Gains, but Lacks Clear Goals," *Education Week* 19 (May 31, 2000): 17.

46. Marcia Reecer, "Battling State Takeover," *The American School Board Journal* 175 (November 1988): 21–25.

47. Charles Mahtesian, "Whose Schools?" *Governing* (September 1997): 34–38.

48. See, for example, Joseph Berger, "A Long Reluctance to Meddle," *New York Times* (June 7, 1995): B-5

49. See "Missed Opportunity."

50. See Cahill, "State Government Response"; Cahill and James, "Responding to Municipal Fiscal Distress"; Fuchs, "Coping with Fiscal Distress"; and Gannon, "An Analysis of Pennsylvania's Legislative Program."

51. See, generally, Berman, "Takeovers."

52. McLarin, "Newark School Officials Pitch a Plan."

53. Aaron Saiger, "Note: Disestablishing Local School Districts As a Remedy for Educational Inadequacy," *Columbia Law Review* 99 (November, 1999): 1830–1870.

54. Robert L. Green and Bradley R. Carl, "A Reform for Troubled Times: Takeovers of Urban Schools," *The Annals of the American Academy of Political and Social Science* (2000): 56.

55. *Creating Excellence in Education: The Role of Phoenix City Government*, Morrison Institute for Public Policy, School of Public Affairs, Arizona State University; Robert Melnick, Project Director, and Linda Sandler, Principal Author (December 1988): ii.

56. "Strengthening Public Schools," *Nation's Cities Weekly* (July 1, 1996): 4.

57. David Shepardson and Brian Harmon, "Rehire Board, Suit Demands: Coalition Attempts to Reinstate Elected School Trustees," *Detroit News* (September 14, 1999): D-1; and Brian Harmon and Mark Hornbeck, "Fight Builds Over Schools: Detroit Board Battles Back with Reform Plan, Engler Takeover Moves Forward in Lansing," *Detroit News* (February 10, 1999): A-1.

Chapter 8—The Restructuring Problem

1. See Robert L. Morlan, "Local Governments: An Embarrassment of Riches," in James W. Fesler, ed., *The Fifty States and Their Local Governments* (New York: Knopf, 1967): 505–549, at 525.

2. Don Melvin, "Who Needs a Charter?" *The Atlanta Journal and Constitution* (July 1, 1995): C-2.

3. See the views of Allegheny County Controller Frank Lucchino as described in "News from the Nation's Counties," *County News* (March 27, 1995): 22.

4. See a literature review by W. E. Lyons and David Lowery, "Governmental Fragmentation Versus Consolidation: Five Public-Choice Myths About How to Create Informed, Involved, and Happy Citizens," *Public Administration Review* 49 (November/December 1989): 533–543. A contemporary proponent of the civic reform agenda is David Rusk, former mayor of Albuquerque, New Mexico, and author of *Cities Without Suburbs*, 2d ed. (Washington, DC: Woodrow Wilson Center Press, 1995).

5. See Charles Tiebout, "A Pure Theory of Local Expenditure," *Journal of Political Economy* 64 (October 1956): 416–435; and Vincent Ostrom, Charles Tiebout, and Robert Warren, "The Organization of Government in Metropolitan Areas: A Theoretical Inquiry," *American Political Science Review* 55 (December 1961): 831–842.

6. See, for example, Mark Schneider, "Intermunicipal Competition, Budget-Maximizing Bureaucrats, and Levels of Suburban Competition," *American Journal of Political Science* 33 (August 1989): 612–628; and U. S. Advisory Commission on Intergovernmental Relations, *The Organization of Local Public Economies* (Washington, DC: G.P.O., December 1987).

7. Milton Kotler, *Neighborhood Government: The Local Foundations of Political Life* (Indianapolis: Bobbs-Merrill, 1969): 19.

8. Jamie L. Palmer and Greg Lindsey, "Classifying State Approaches to Annexation," *State and Local Government Review* 33 (Winter 2001): 60–73.

9. Juliet F. Gainsborough, "Bridging the City-Suburb Divide: States and the Politics of Regional Cooperation, *Journal of Urban Affairs* 23 (2001): 497–512.

10. "Municipal Annexation Authority Faces Renewed Attacks," *TML Online* (1998): 10.

11. Rusk, *Cities Without Suburbs.*

12. Quote from Paul Hefner, "Valley Cityhood: Voters to Decide," *The Daily News of Los Angeles* (October 13, 1997).

13. The task of making the analysis and deciding whether the question should be submitted to the voters falls to local agency formation commissions. These are state agencies that handle a number of issues involving boundary changes. Under the law, the commissions have to conclude that the new entity will be financially able to provide an acceptable set of services, that is, at the same level residents are presently receiving, and that the split does not leave either side with an unfair financial burden.

14. Richard Briffault, "Voting Rights, Home Rule, and Metropolitan Governance: The Secession of Staten Island As a Case Study in the Dilemmas of Local Self-Determination, *Columbia Law Review* 92 (May 1992): 775.

15. Property Tax Commission, "Report of Recommendations to Governor Christine Todd Whitman," September 1998.

16. Victor Jones, "The Organization of a Metropolitan Region," *University of Pennsylvania Law Review* 195 (1957): 538–552, at 539.

17. Anthony Downs, *New Visions for Metropolitan America* (Washington, DC: The Brookings Institution and Cambridge, MA: Lincoln Institute of Land Policy, 1994): 170.

18. Rusk, *Cities Without Suburbs*, 90.

19. William Blomquist, "Fiscal, Service, and Political Impacts of Indianapolis-Marion County Unigov," *Publius: The Journal of Federalism* 25 (Fall 1995): 37–54.

20. See Frances Frisken, "The Toronto Story: Sober Reflections on Fifty Years of Experiments with Regional Governance," *Journal of Urban Affairs* 23 (2001): 513–541; and G. Ross Stephens and Nelson Wikstrom, *Metropolitan Government and Governance: Theoretical Perspectives, Empirical Analysis, and the Future* (New York: Oxford University Press, 1999).

21. See, for example, U.S. Advisory Commission on Intergovernmental Relations, *Metropolitan Organization: The Allegheny County Case* (Washington, DC: G.P.O, February 1992); Ronald J. Oakerson and Roger B. Parks, "Metropolitan Organization: St. Louis and Allegheny County," *Intergovernmental Perspective* 17 (Summer 1991): 27–30, 34; and Roger B. Parks, "Counties in the Federal System: The Interlocal Connection," *Intergovernmental Perspective* 17 (Winter 1991): 29–32.

22. Connecticut Advisory Commission on Intergovernmental Relations, *Local Government Cooperative Ventures in Connecticut: Executive Summary* (Hartford: Connecticut Advisory Commission on Intergovernmental Relations, June 1996).

23. David R. Morgan and Michael W. Hirlinger, "Intergovernmental Service Contracts: A Multivariate Explanation," *Urban Affairs Quarterly* 27 (September 1991): 128–144.

24. Christopher Hoene, Mark Baldassare, and Michael Shires, "The Development of Counties As Municipal Governments: A Case Study of Los Angeles County in the Twenty-First Century," *Urban Affairs Review* 37 (March 2002): 575–591.

25. Ibid.

26. Scott Bollens, "Examining the Link Between State Policy and the Creation of Local Special Districts," *State and Local Government Review* 18 (1986): 117–124.

27. Ibid.

28. Quoted by Alan Ehrenhalt, "The Czar of Gridlock," *Governing* (May 1999): 20–27 at 24.

29. Craig Schneider, "Regional Solutions Gaining," *The Atlanta Constitution* (January 30, 2000): A-1.

30. Jared Eigerman, "California Counties: Second-Rate Localities or Ready-Made Regional Governments?" *Hastings Constitutional Law Quarterly* 26 (Spring 1999): 621.

31. William R. Dodge, "Regional Problem Solving in the 1990s: Experimentation with Local Governance for the 21st Century," *National Civic Review* 79 (July-August 1990): 354–366 at 358.

32. Vincent L. Marando and Mavis Mann Reeves, "Counties: Evolving Local Governments, Reform and Responsiveness," *National Civic Review* 80 (Spring 1991): 222–226 at 224.

33. William L. Waugh, Jr. and Gregory Streib, "County Officials' Perceptions of Local Capacity and State Responsiveness After the First Reagan Term," *Southeastern Political Review* 18 (Spring 1990): 27–50.

34. Lenneal J. Henderson, "Metropolitan Governance: Citizen Participation in the Urban Federation," *National Civic Review* 79 (March/April 1990): 105–117.

35. See David R. Berman, "State-Local Relations: Patterns, Politics, and Problems," *Municipal Year Book* (Washington, DC: International City-County Management Association, 1994): 59–67.

36. Amy Cohen Paul, *Future Challenges, Future Opportunities: The Final Report of the ICMA Future Visions Consortium* (Washington, DC: International City/County Management Association, 1991). Similarly, a study reported in a National League of Cities outlet concluded, "Cities will either use their powers to protect the environment and conserve natural resources, or higher levels of government will dictate how to exercise them—perhaps in more regulative, bureaucratic, and inefficient ways." Excerpts from a policy statement for Building Sustainable Communities, *Nation's Cities Weekly* (April 16, 1990): 8.

37. Douglas R. Porter, "State Growth Management: The Intergovernmental Experiment," *Pace Law Review* 13 (1993): 481–503 at 496.

38. Downs, *New Visions for Metropolitan America*, 189.

39. Ibid., 190.

40. See, generally, Raymond J. Burby and Peter J. May, *Making Governments Plan: State Experiments in Managing Land Use* (Baltimore, MD: The Johns Hopkins University Press, 1997); and Linda C. Dalton and Raymond J. Burby, "Mandates, Plans, and Planners," *Journal of the American Planning Association* 60 (Autumn 1994): 444–461.

41. Robyne S. Turner, "Intergovernmental Growth Management: A Partnership Framework for State-Local Relations," *Publius: The Journal of Federalism* 20 (Summer 1990): 79–95.

42. Douglas R. Porter, "Reinventing Growth Management for the 21st Century," *William and Mary Environmental Law and Policy Review* 23 (Fall 1999): 705.

43. Porter, "State Growth Management," 483.

44. Henry Molotch, "The City As a Growth Machine: Toward a Political Economy of Place," *American Journal of Sociology* 82 (1976): 309–330.

45. Burby and May, *Making Governments Plan.*

46. William W. Buzbee, "Urban Sprawl, Federalism, and the Problem of Institutional Complexity," *Fordham Law Review* 68 (October 1999): 57–136 at 91.

47. See, for example, Matthew Holden, "The Governance of the Metropolis As a Problem in Diplomacy," *Journal of Politics* 26 (1964): 627–647; Victor Jones, "The Organization of a Metropolitan Region," *University of Pennsylvania Law Review* 105 (1957): 539; and John Kincaid, "Metropolitan Governance: Reviving International and Market Analogies," *Intergovernmental Perspective* (Spring 1989): 23–27.

48. For background on these disputes, see Alvin D. Sokolow, "State-Rules and the County-City Arena: Competition for Land and Taxes in California's Central Valley," *Publius: The Journal of Federalism* 23 (Winter 1993): 53–69.

49. The Georgia legislation is intentionally vague, leaving much discretion to cities and counties in how they go about developing a service delivery strategy. Each strategy, however, must include (1) an identification of all services presently provided in the county by cities, counties, and authorities; (2) an assignment of which local government will be responsible for providing which service in what area of the county; (3) a description of how all services will be funded; and (4) an

identification of intergovernmental contracts, ordinances, resolutions, and so on to be used in implementing the strategy, including existing contracts. See Association of County Commissioners of Georgia, Georgia Municipal Association, Georgia Department of Community Affairs, Carl Vinson Institute of Government, The University of Georgia, *Charting a Course for Cooperation and Collaboration* (June 1997): 1.

50. Editorial, "Untangling Government," *Los Angeles Times* (February 1, 1999): Metro, Part B, 4.

Chapter 9—Concluding Note

1. Bill Rankin, "Fate of Atlanta Gun Suit Up to High Court," *The Atlanta Constitution* (September 20, 2000): B-1.

2. Ibid.

3. Michael D. Reagan and John G. Sanzone, *The New Federalism* (New York: Oxford University Press, 1981).

4. Michael J. Rich, "Distributive Politics and the Allocation of Federal Grants," *American Political Science Review* 83 (March 1989): 198–213; Richard P. Nathan, "State and Local Governments Under Federal Grants: Toward a Predictive Theory," *Political Science Quarterly* 98 (Spring 1983): 47–57; and Christopher Hamilton and Donald T. Wells, *Federalism, Power, and Political Economy: A New Theory of Federalism's Impact on American Life* (Englewood Cliffs, NJ: Prentice-Hall, 1990).

5. Hamilton and Wells, *Federalism, Power, and Political Economy*, 153.

6. Victor Jones, David Magleby, and Stanley Scott, "State-Local Relations in California," Working Paper Number 16, Institute of Governmental Studies, University of California, Berkeley (1975): 3.

7. David B. Walker, "Intergovernmental Relations and the Well-Governed City: Cooperation, Confrontation, Clarification," *National Civic Review* 75 (March/April 1986): 65–87 at 83.

8. Kenneth E. Vanlandingham, "Municipal Home Rule in the United States," *William and Mary Law Review* 10 (Winter 1968): 269–314 at 296.

9. Lyle E. Schaller, "Home Rule—A Critical Appraisal," *Political Science Quarterly* 76 (September 1961): 402–415.

10. Richard C. Schragger, "The Limits of Localism," *Michigan Law Review* 100 (November 2001): 371–472.

11. Harold A. Hovey, "Analytic Approaches to State-Local Relations" in *A Decade of Devolution: Perspectives on State-Local Relations*. E. Blaine Liner, ed. (Washington, DC: Urban Institute Press, 1989): 163–182.

12. Allison Mitchell, "Giuliani Urges New Agenda for Cities: Self-Reliance," *New York Times* (January 12, 1995): B-1.

13. Alvin D. Sokolow, "The Changing Property Tax and State-Local Relations," *Publius: The Journal of Federalism* 28 (Winter 1998):165–187; and Glenn W. Fisher, *The Worst Tax? A History of the Property Tax in America* (Lawrence: University Press of Kansas, 1996).

14. James Bryce, *The American Commonwealth* (New York: Macmillan, 1891) I, 418.

Bibliography

Abney, Glenn, and Thomas A. Henderson. "An Exchange Model of Intergovernmental Relations: State Legislators and Local Officials." *Social Science Quarterly* 59 (March 1979): 720–731.

Adrian, Charles R., and Ernest S. Griffith. *A History of American City Government: The Formation of Traditions, 1775–1870.* New York: Praeger, 1976.

Advisory Committee on Local Government, Commission on Intergovernmental Relations. *Local Government.* Washington, DC: G.P.O., June 1955.

Alabama League of Cities. "Effective Lobbying Begins at Home." Unpublished paper, n.d.

Altshuler, Alan A., and Jose A. Gomez-Ibanez, with Arnold M. Howitt. *Regulation for Revenue: The Political Economy of Land Use Exactions.* Washington, DC, and Cambridge, MA: Brookings Institution and Lincoln Institute of Land Policy, 1993.

Anderson, Bernard. Former chairman of the Pennsylvania Intergovernmental Cooperation, testimony before U.S. House Government Reform and Oversight Committee, District of Columbia Subcommittee, March 8, 1995, televised on C-Span 2.

Anderson, William. *The Nation and the States, Rivals or Partners?* Minneapolis, MN: University of Minnesota Press, 1955.

Andrews, Chris, and Stacey Range. "Engler Slashes Local Funding." *Lansing State Journal* (MI) (July 26, 2002): 1–A.

Anton, Thomas J. *American Federalism and Public Policy: How the System Works.* New York: Random House, 1989.

Arndt, Randy. "Fiscal Conditions Remain Strong in Most Cities." *Nation's Cities Weekly* (July 31, 2000): 1, 9.

———. "NLC Fiscal Survey: Budget Gap on Rise." *Nation's Cities Weekly* (July 8, 1991): 1, 8.

———. "NLC Study Shows Lag on City Aid." *Nation's Cities Weekly* (September 12, 1988) 1, 9.

Ashford, Douglas E. *Democracy, Centralization, and Decisions in Subnational Politics.* Beverly Hills, CA: Sage Publications, A Sage Professional Paper, 1976.

Association of County Commissioners of Georgia, Georgia Municipal Association, Georgia Department of Community Affairs, Carl Vinson Institute of Government, The University of Georgia. *Charting a Course for Cooperation and Collaboration* (June 1997): 1.

"Avoiding Local Government Financial Crisis: The Role of State Oversight." *CRC Memorandum.* A publication of the Citizens Research Council of Michigan, July 2000.

Avoletta, Brenda, and Phillip M. Dearborn. "Federal Grants-in-Aid Soar in the 1990s, but Not for Locals or General Purposes." *Intergovernmental Perspective* (Fall 1990): 3–4.

Bailey, Robert. *The Crisis Regime.* Albany: State University of New York Press, 1984.

Baker, Benjamin. *Urban Government.* Princeton, NJ: D. Van Nostrand, 1957.

Baker, Gordon E. *The Reapportionment Revolution.* New York: Random House, 1966.

Banfield, Edward C., ed. *Urban Government: A Reader in Administration and Politics,* rev. ed. New York: Free Press, 1969.

Barber, Mary Beth. "Local Government Hits the Wall: Proposition 13 Finally Comes Home to Roost." *California Journal* (August 1993): 13–15.

Barnes, William, and David Dickinson. "Federal, State Levels Get Poor Rating from Local Officials." *Nation's Cities Weekly* (January 20, 1992): 7.

Barr, Ann Calvares. "Cost Estimations As an Anti-Mandate Strategy," in *Coping with Mandates: What Are the Alternatives?* Michael Fix and Daphne Kenyon, eds. Washington, DC: Urban Institute Press, 1990, 57–61.

Bartle, John R. "Coping with Cutbacks: City Response to Aid Cuts in New York State." *State and Local Government Review* 28 (Winter 1996): 38–48.

Beard, Charles A. *American City Government: A Survey of Newer Tendencies.* New York: The Century Co., 1912.

Benjamin, Gerald, and Charles Brecher, eds. *The Two New Yorks: State-City Relations in the Changing Federal System.* New York: Russell Sage Foundation, 1988.

Benson, George C. S. *The New Centralization: A Study of Intergovernmental Relationships in the United States.* New York: Farrar and Rinehart, 1941.

Berger, Joseph. "A Long Reluctance to Meddle." *New York Times* (June 7, 1995): B-5.

Berman, David R., ed. *County Government in an Era of Change.* Westport, CT: Greenwood Press, 1993.

———. "Counties, Other Governments, and the Future," in *County Governments in an Era of Change,* David R. Berman, ed. Westport CT: Greenwood Press, 1993, 135–142.

———. "Relating to Other Governments: Patterns, Problems, and Responsibilities," in *The Effective Local Government Manager,* Charldean Newell, ed. Washington, DC: International City/County Management Association, 1993, 167–198.

———. "State Actions Affecting Local Governments," in *Municipal Year Book.* Washington, DC: International City Management Association, 1990, 55–70.

———. "State Actions Affecting Local Governments: Involvement, Problems, and Relationships," in *Municipal Year Book.* Washington, DC: International City Management Association, 1989, 129–142.

———. "State-Local Relations: Authority, Finances, Cooperation," in *Municipal Year Book.* Washington, DC: International City/County Management Association, 2002, 45–61.

———. "State-Local Relations: Authority, Finance, Partnerships," in *Municipal Year Book.* Washington, DC: International City/County Management Association, 2001, 61–75.

———. "State-Local Relations: Authority, Finance, Policies," in *Municipal Year*

Book. Washington, DC: International City/County Management Association, 2000, 31–41.

———. "State-Local Relations: Authority, Finance, and Regional Cooperation," in *Municipal Year Book*. Washington, DC: International City/County Management Association, 1998, 62–75.

———. "State-Local Relations: Authority, Policies, Cooperation," in *Municipal Year Book*. Washington, DC: International City/County Management Association, 1999, 47–68.

———. "State-Local Relations: Devolution, Mandates, and Money," in *Municipal Year Book*. Washington, DC: International City/County Management Association, 1997, 40–52.

———. "States and Their Local Governments: Mandates, Finances, and Problems," in *Municipal Year Book*. Washington, DC: International City Management Association, 1991, 76–81.

———. "State-Local Relations: Mandates, Money, Partnerships," in *Municipal Year Book*. Washington, DC: International City Management Association, 1992, 51–57.

———. "State-Local Relations: Mandates, Money, Partnerships," in *Municipal Year Book*. Washington. DC: International City/County Management Association, 1996, 33–43.

———. "State-Local Relations: Patterns and Problems," in *Municipal Year Book*. Washington, DC: International City Management Association, 1993, 87–93.

———. "State-Local Relations: Patterns, Problems, and Partnerships," in *Municipal Year Book*. Washington, DC: International City/County Management Association, 1995, 55–65.

———. "State-Local Relations: Patterns, Politics, and Problems," in *Municipal Year Book*. Washington, DC: International City/County Management Association, 1994, 59–67.

———. "Takeovers of Local Governments: An Overview and Evaluation of State Policies." *Publius: The Journal of Federalism*, 25 (Summer 1995): 55–70.

Berman, David R., and Barbara Greene. "Counties and the National Agenda." *County Governments in an Era of Change,* David R. Berman, ed. Westport, CT: Greenwood, 1993, 123–134.

Berman, David R., and Kate Lehman. "Counties and the Changing Environment." *County Governments in an Era of Change,* David R. Berman, ed. Westport, CT: Greenwood Press, 1993, 11–19.

Berman, David R., and Lawrence L. Martin. "State-Local Relations: An Examination of Local Discretion." *Public Administration Review* 48 (March/April 1988): 637–641.

Berman, David R., Lawrence L. Martin, and Laura A. Kajfez. "County Home Rule: Does Where You Stand Depend on Where You Sit?" *State and Local Review* 17 (Spring 1985): 232–234.

Berman, David R., and Tanis J. Salant. "The Changing Role of Counties in the Intergovernmental System," in *The American County: Frontiers of Knowledge,* Donald C. Menzel, ed. Tuscaloosa: University of Alabama Press, 1996, 19–33.

Berry, David. "Local Impact of Electric Industry Restructuring." *Public Management* (July/August 1999): 18–21.

Betters, Paul, J. Kerwin Williams, and Sherwood L. Reeder. *Recent Federal-City Relations*. Washington, DC: The United States Conference of Mayors, 1936.

Biswanger, Patricia S. "Preserving Democracy in the Face of Special Interest Might: Local Initiatives to Ban Cigarette Vending Machines." *Current Municipal Problems* 21 (1994): 67–92.

Blair, George S. *Government at the Grass-Roots.* Pacific Palisades, CA: Palisades, 1977.

Block, A. G., Danielle Starkey, and Steve Scott. "The 1993–94 Budget: Pete Wilson and Willie Brown Delivered, but Was It a Knockout Punch for California?" *California Journal* (August 1993): 7–11.

Blomquist, William. "Fiscal, Service, and Political Impacts of Indianapolis-Marion County Unigov." *Publius: The Journal of Federalism* 25 (Fall 1995): 37–54.

Bollens, Scott. "Examining the Link Between State Policy and the Creation of Local Special Districts." *State and Local Government Review* 18 (Fall 1986): 117–124.

Bragg, John T. "A View from the Commission." *Intergovernmental Perspective* (Summer 1988): 2.

Brecher, Charles, and Raymond D. Horton. "Retrenchment and Recovery: American Cities and the New York Experience." *Public Administration Review* 45 (March/April 1985): 267–274.

Brennan, William J. Jr. "The Bill of Rights and the States: The Revival of State Constitutions As Guardians of Individual Rights." *New York University Law Review* 61 (October 1986): 535–553.

Briffault, Richard. "Local Government and the New York State Constitution," in *State Constitutions: Competing Perspectives,* Burton C. Agata et al., eds. Hempstead, NY: Hofstra University School of Law, 1996, 79–109.

———. "Our Localism: Part I—The Structure of Local Government Law." *Columbia Law Review* 90 (January 1990): 1–115.

———. "Our Localism: Part II—Localism and Legal Theory." *Columbia Law Review* 90 (March 1990): 346–454.

———. "State-Local Relations and Constitutional Law." *Intergovernmental Perspective* 13 (Summer-Fall: 1987), 10–14.

———. "Voting Rights, Home Rule, and Metropolitan Governance: The Secession of Staten Island As a Case Study in the Dilemmas of Local Self-Determination." *Columbia Law Review* 92 (May 1992): 775–850.

Brinkerhoff, Noel. "The Worst of Times." *California Journal* (September 1997): 17–20.

Brown, Dorothy A. "Fiscal Distress and Politics: The Bankruptcy Filing of Bridgeport as a Case Study in Reclaiming Local Sovereignty." *Bankruptcy Developments Journal* 11 (1994–1995): 625–663.

Brunoi, David. "To Preserve Local Government, It's Time to Save the Property Tax" (2001). www.lincolnist.edu.

Bryce, James. *The American Commonwealth.* New York: Macmillan, 1891, 1906.

Burby, Raymond J., and Peter J. May. *Making Governments Plan: State Experiments in Managing Land Use.* Baltimore, MD: Johns Hopkins University Press, 1997.

Burns, Nancy, and Gerald Gamm. "Creatures of the State: State Politics and Local Government, 1871–1921." *Urban Affairs Review* 33 (1997): 59–96.

Burns, Peter. "The Intergovernmental Regime and Public Policy in Hartford, Connecticut." *Journal of Urban Affairs* 24 (2002): 55–73.

Butterfield, Fox. "Insolvent Boston Suburb Faces Threat of Takeover." *New York Times* (September 8, 1991): A-18.

———. "Mired in Debt, a Boston Suburb Is Taken Over by Massachusetts." *New York Times* (September 13, 1991): A-21.

Buzbee, William W. "Urban Sprawl, Federalism, and the Problem of Institutional Complexity." *Fordham Law Review* 68 (October 1999): 57–136.

Cabana, Andrew S. "Missing the Target Municipal Litigation Against Handgun Manufacturers: Abuse of the Tort System." *George Mason Law Review* 9 (Summer 2001): 1127–1175.

Cahill, Anthony G., and Joseph A. James. "Responding to Municipal Fiscal Distress: An Emerging Issue for State Governments in the 1990s." *Public Administration Review* 52 (January/February 1992): 88–94.

———. "State Responses to Local Government Fiscal Stress," in *Municipal Year Book*. Washington, DC: International City/County Management Association, 1996, 59–70.

Cahill, Anthony G., Joseph A. James, Jean E. Lavigne, and Ann Stacey. "State Government Responses to Municipal Fiscal Distress: A Brave New World for State-Local Intergovernmental Relations." *Public Productivity and Management Review* 17 (Spring 1994): 253–264.

Cammisa, Anne Marie. *Governments As Interest Groups: Intergovernmental Lobbying and the Federal System*. Westport, CT: Praeger, 1995.

Campbell, Alan K. "States at the Crossroads." *National Civic Review* 55 (November 1966): 559.

Celis, William, III. "Michigan Votes for Revolution in Financing Its Public Schools." *New York Times* (March 17, 1994) A-1.

Childs, Richard S. *Civic Victories: The Story of an Unfinished Revolution*. New York: Harper and Brothers, 1952.

Cigler, Beverly A. "State-Local Relations: A Need for Reinvention?" *Intergovernmental Perspective* 19 (1993): 15–18 .

Cisneros, Henry. "Mayor Cisneros Comments on State of U.S. Cities" in extension of remarks of Hon. James J. Florio, *Congressional Record* (March 25, 1986): E961.

City Fiscal Conditions in 1998. Washington, DC: National League of Cities, 1998.

City of Clinton v. Cedar Rapids and Missouri River Railroad, 24 Iowa (1868): 455, at 475.

Clark, Gordon L. *Judges and the Cities: Interpreting Local Autonomy*. Chicago: University of Chicago Press, 1985.

Cleveland, Harland. "The Municipal Balance Sheet: Balancing Urban Needs and Financial Resources." *Proceedings of the American Municipal Congress, 1960*. Washington, DC: American Municipal Association, 1961, 9–15.

Coalition to Improve Management in State and Local Government. *Improving Local Services Through Intergovernmental and Intersectional Cooperation*. School of Urban and Public Affairs, Carnegie Mellon University, Pittsburgh, 1992.

Cohen, David. Philadelphia Mayor's Office, testimony before U.S. House Government Reform and Oversight Committee, District of Columbia Subcommittee, March 8, 1995, televised on C-Span2.

Cole, Richard L., Rodney V. Hissong, and Enid Arvidson. "Devolution: Where's the Revolution?" *Publius: The Journal of Federalism* 29 (Fall 1999): 99–112.

Cole, Richard L., and John Kincaid. "Public Opinion and American Federalism: Perspectives on Taxes, Spending, and Trust—An ACIR Update." *Publius: The Journal of Federalism* 30 (Winter/Spring 2000): 189–201.

Cole, Stephanie. "Home Rule in Illinois." *Illinois Issues* (August 1975): 243–246.

"Comments About Tuesday's Vote to Override Engler's Veto," Associated Press (August 13, 2002), n.p.

Congressional Budget Office. "An Assessment of the Unfunded Mandates Reform Act in 1997." Washington, DC: G.P.O., February 1998.

Congressional Quarterly. *Governing State and Local Source Book 2001.* Washington, DC: Congressional Quarterly, 2001.

Conlan, Timothy J., James D. Riggle, and Donna E. Schwartz. "Deregulating Federalism? The Politics of Mandate Reform in the 104th Congress." *Publius: The Journal of Federalism* 25 (Summer 1995): 23–39.

Connecticut Advisory Commission on Intergovernmental Relations. *Local Government Cooperative Ventures in Connecticut: Executive Summary.* Hartford: Connecticut Advisory Commission on Intergovernmental Relations, June 1996.

Connecticut Conference of Municipalities. *The State of Municipalities in Connecticut: A Public Policy Report.* New Haven: Connecticut Conference of Municipalities, February 1995.

Cooke, Jeremy R. "Bill Lets City Teachers Live Outside City." *Pittsburgh Post-Gazette* (July 22, 2001): C-3.

Cooper, Claire. "State High Court OKs Tax Challenges," *The Sacramento Bee* (June 5, 2001): A-3.

Cooper, Jamie, and Linda Tarr-Whelan. "Turning Urban Nightmares to Dreams." *State Government News* (October 1991): 14–15.

Cooperman, Saul. "View from the State." *American School Board Journal* 175 (November 1988): 24–25, 50.

Council of State Governments. *State Planning: New Roles in Hard Times.* Lexington, KY: Council of State Governments, 1976.

"Counties Are Out of Date in California." *State Legislatures* (March 1991): 9.

Cox, William. "Lessons of Receivership: The Legacy of Chelsea." *Government Finance Review* 9 (August 1993): 21–22, 24.

Creating Excellence in Education: The Role of Phoenix City Government. Morrison Institute for Public Policy, School of Public Affairs, Arizona State University. Robert Melnick Project Director; Linda Sandler, Principal Author. December 1988.

Curry, Leonard P. *The Corporate City: The American City As a Political Entity, 1800–1850.* Westport, CT: Greenwood Press, 1997.

Cyr, Ed. "Thoughts on the Chelsea Receivership." *Government Finance Review* 9 (August 1993): 23–24.

Dalton, Linda C., and Raymond J. Burby. "Mandates, Plans, and Planners." *Journal of the American Planning Association* 60 (Autumn 1994): 444–461.

Danielson, Michael, and Paul G. Lewis. "City Bound: Political Science and the American Metropolis." *Political Research Quarterly* 49 (March 1996): 203–220.

Dearborn, Phillip M. "Local Property Taxes: Emerging Trends." *Intergovernmental Perspective* (Summer 1993): 10–12.

Decker, Jane Elizabeth. "Management and Organizational Capacities for Responding to Growth in Florida's Nonmetropolitan Counties." *Journal of Urban Affairs* 9 (1987): 47–61.

DeSantis, Victor S. "State, Local, and Council Relations: Managers' Perceptions." *Baseline Data Report* 23 (March-April 1991).

Desmond, Thomas C. "States Eclipse the Cities." *National Municipal Review* 44 (June 1955): 296–300.

De Soto, William. "Cities in State Politics: Views of Mayors and Managers." *State and Local Government Review* 27 (Fall 1995): 188–194.

DeWitt, Benjamin Parke. *The Progressive Movement: A Nonpartisan Comprehensive Discussion of Current Tendencies in American Politics.* Seattle: University of Washington Press, 1915.

Deyle, Robert E., and Richard A. Smith. "Local Government Compliance with State Planning Mandates: Effect of State Implementation in Florida." *Journal of the American Planning Association* 64 (Autumn 1998): 457–469.

Diegmueller, Karen, and Drew Lindsay. "NJ Moves Toward Takeover of Newark Schools." *Education Week* (August 3, 1994): 20, 25

Dillon, John Forrest. *Commentaries on the Law of Municipal Corporations.* Boston: Little, Brown, 1911.

Dodge, William R. "Regional Problem Solving in the 1990s: Experimentation with Local Governance for the 21st Century." *National Civic Review* 79 (July–August 1990): 354–366.

Downs, Anthony. *New Visions for Metropolitan America.* Washington, DC: Brookings Institution and Cambridge, MA: Lincoln Institute of Land Policy, 1994.

Durant v. State of Michigan 566 N.W.2nd 272 (Mich.1997).

Dye, Thomas R., and Thomas L. Hurley. "The Responsiveness of Federal and State Governments to Urban Problems." *Journal of Politics* 40 (February 1978): 196–207.

Economies and New Ideas for Cities: Proceedings, American Municipal Congress, 1963. Washington, DC: American Municipal Association, 1963.

Educational Commission of the States. *Fiscally Dependent/Independent School Districts.* Denver, CO: February 18, 1997.

———. *State Takeovers and Reconstructions.* Denver, CO: August 2000, with updated information as of January 2001.

Ehrenhalt, Alan. "As Interest in its Agenda Wanes, a Shrinking Urban Bloc in Congress Plays Defense." *Governing* (June 1991): 33–37.

———. "Powerless Pipsqueaks and the Myth of Local Control." *Governing* (June 1999): 7–9.

———. "The Czar of Gridlock." *Governing* (May 1999): 20–27.

Eigerman, Jared. "California Counties: Second-Rate Localities or Ready-Made Regional Governments?" *Hastings Constitutional Law Quarterly* 26 (Spring 1999): 621–709.

Elazar, Daniel J. "Local Government in Intergovernmental Perspective," in *Cooperation and Conflict: Readings in American Federalism,* Daniel J. Elazar et al. eds. Itasca, IL: F.E. Peacock, 1969, 416–423

———. *The American Partnership: Intergovernmental Cooperation in the Nineteenth-Century United States.* Chicago: University of Chicago Press, 1972.

Emerson, Kirk, and Charles R. Wise. "Statutory Approaches to Regulatory Takings: State Property Rights Legislation Issues and Implications for Public Administration." *Public Administration Review* (September/October 1997): 411–422.

Erie, Steven P. *Rainbow's End: Irish-Americans and the Dilemmas of Urban Machine Politics, 1840–1985.* Berkeley: University of California Press, 1988.

Ewing, Reid. "Transportation Utility Fees." *Government Finance Review* (June 1994): 13–17.

Fain, Howie. "Rent Control in Massachusetts: Notes on the Cambridge Electorate." *National Civic Review* 84 (Spring 1995): 161–163.

Farkas, Suzanne. *Urban Lobbying: Mayors in the Federal Arena.* New York: New York University Press, 1971.

Fesler, James W., ed. *The 50 States and Their Local Governments.* New York: Knopf, 1967.

Finke, Doug. "Edgar Nixes Bill Banning Pay Raises." *State Journal-Register* (Springfield, IL, April 29, 1965): 1.

Fiscal Planning Services, Inc. *Dedicated State Tax Revenues: A Fifty-State Report,* June 2000.

Fisher, Glenn W. *The Worst Tax? A History of the Property Tax in America.* Lawrence: University of Kansas Press, 1996.

Fisher, Michael. "Cities' Voice at the State Level Reaches Out LOBBY: The Effort Seeks to Rally Local Groups and Push for Action in Sacramento." *Sacramento Press-Enterprise* (August 13, 2001): B-01.

Fix, Michael, and Daphne A. Kenyon, eds. *Coping with Mandates: What Are the Alternatives?* Washington, DC: Urban Institute Press, 1990.

Flentje, Edward. "State Mandates As Family Values?" *Current Municipal Problems* 22 (1996): 510–512.

Florestano, Patrica S., and Vincent L. Marando. *The States and the Metropolis.* New York: Marcel Dekker, 1981.

Flowers, Paul, and John T. Torbert. *Mandate Costs: A Kansas Case Study.* Topeka: Kansas Association of Counties, 1993.

Fordham, Jefferson B. "Home Rule—AMA Model." *National Municipal Review* 44 (March 1955): 137–142.

Fossett, James W., and J. Fred Giertz. "Money, Politics, and Regionalism: Allocating State Funds in Illinois," in *Diversity, Conflict, and State Politics: Regionalism in Illinois,* Peter Nardulli, ed. Urbana and Chicago: University of Illinois Press, 1989, 222–246.

Fox, Kenneth. *Better City Government: Innovation in American Politics, 1850–1937.* Philadelphia: Temple University Press, 1977.

Frisken, Frances. "The Toronto Story: Sober Reflections on Fifty Years of Experiments with Regional Governance." *Journal of Urban Affairs* 23 (2001): 513–541.

Frug, Gerald E. "The City as a Legal Concept." *Harvard Law Review* 93 (April 1980): 1059–1174.

Fuchs, Ester R. *Mayors and Money.* Chicago: University of Chicago Press, 1992.

Fuhrman, Susan H., and Richard F. Elmore. "Understanding Local Control in the Wake of State Educational Reforms." *Educational Evaluation and Policy Analysis* 12 (Spring 1990): 82–96.

Gainsborough, Juliet F. "Bridging the City-Suburb Divide: States and the Politics of Regional Cooperation." *Journal of Urban Affairs* 23 (2001): 497–512.

Gannon, Drew Patrick. "An Analysis of Pennsylvania's Legislative Program for Financially Distressed Municipalities and the Reaction of Municipal Labor Unions." *Dickinson Law Review* 28 (Winter 1994): 281–305.

Gardner, Michael. "Payback Time for Cities and Counties? Copley News Service, May 28, 1999, n.p.

Georgia Municipal Association. *Calculating the Cost of State and Federal Mandates: Getting Started.* Atlanta: Georgia Municipal Association, March 1993.

Gewertz, Catherine. "California Superintendent Leaves Second District in Disarray." *Education Week* 20 (January 10, 2001): 5.

Glaab, Charles N., ed. *The American City: A Documentary History.* Homewood, IL: Dorsey Press, 1963.

Glendening, Parris N., and Mavis Mann Reeves. *Pragmatic Federalism.* Pacific Palisades, CA: Palisades, 1977.

Gold, Steven D. "A Better Scoreboard: States Are Helping Local Governments." *State Legislatures* (April 1990): 27–28.

———. "Local Taxes Outpace State Taxes." *PA Times* (July 1993): 15, 17.

———. "Passing the Buck." *State Legislatures* (January 1993): 36–38.

———. "State Aid to Localities Fares Poorly in 1990s," in *State Fiscal Brief.* New York: Rockefeller Institute of Government, Center for the Study of the States, June 1994, 1–5.

———. "The State of State-Local Relations." *State Legislatures* (August 1988): 17–20.

———. "Time for Change in State-Local Relations." *Journal of Policy Analysis and Management* 6 (Fall 1986): 101–106.

Gold, Steven D., and Sarah Ritchie. "State Policies Affecting Cities and Counties in 1991: Shifting Federalism." *Public Budgeting & Finance* (Spring 1992): 23–46.

Goodnow, Frank J. *Municipal Home Rule: A Study in Administration.* New York: Columbia University Press, 1916.

Government in Metropolitan Areas: Commentaries on a Report by the Advisory Commission on Intergovernmental Relations. Washington, DC: G.P.O., 1962.

Grattet, Paul M. "TABOR Too Broad a Brush." *Denver Post* (March 29, 1998): J-2.

Graves, W. Brooke. *American Intergovernmental Relations.* New York: Charles Scribner's Sons, 1964.

Green, Harry A. "State Mandates to Local Governments." Memorandum to Tennessee Advisory Commission on Intergovernmental Relations Commissioners, August 28, 1995.

Green, Paul M. "Legislative Redistricting in Illinois: A Historical Analysis," *Comparative State Politics* 9 (October 1988): 39–75.

Green, Robert L., and Bradley R. Carl. "A Reform for Troubled Times: Takeovers of Urban Schools." *The Annals of the American Academy of Political and Social Science* (2000): 56–68.

Greene, Barbara P. "Counties and the Fiscal Challenges of the 1980s." *Intergovernmental Perspective* 13 (Winter 1987): 14–18.

Greene, Lee S., and Jack E. Holmes. "Tennessee: A Politics of Peaceful Change," in *The Changing Politics of the South,* William C. Havard, ed. Baton Rouge: Louisiana State University Press, 1972, 165–200.

Griffith, Ernest S. *A History of American City Government, The Conspicuous Failure, 1870–1900.* New York, Praeger, 1974.

———. *A History of American City Government, The Progressive Years and Their Aftermath, 1900–1920.* New York: Praeger, 1974.

Grodzins, Morton. *The American System: A New View of Government in the United States.* Chicago: Rand McNally, 1966.

Gullo, Theresa A., and Janet M. Kelly. "Federal Unfunded Mandate Reform: A First-Year Retrospective." *Public Administration Review* 58 (September/October 1998): 379–387.

Gunther, John J. *Federal-City Relations in the United States: The Role of the Mayors in Federal Aid to Cities.* Newark: University of Delaware Press, 1990.

Haider, Donald. *When Governments Come to Washington: Governors, Mayors and Intergovernmental Lobbying.* New York: Free Press, 1974.

Hammersley, Margaret. "Masiello, in Swipe at State Mandates, Envisions Unions, Firms Bidding on Services." *Buffalo News* (February 17, 2000): B-5.

Hamilton, Christopher, and Donald T. Wells. *Federalism, Power, and Political Economy: A New Theory of Federalism's Impact on American Life.* Englewood Cliffs, NJ: Prentice-Hall, 1990.

Hannah, Susan B. "Writing Home-Rule Charters in Michigan: Current Practices in Constitution Making." *National Civic Review* 84 (Spring 1995): 140–148.

Hanson, Russell L. *Governing Partners: State-Local Relations in the U.S.* Boulder, CO: Westview, 1998.

Harmon, Brian, and Mark Hornbeck. "Fight Builds over Schools: Detroit Board Battles Back with Reform Plan, Engler Takeover Moves Forward in Lansing." *Detroit News* (February 10, 1999) A-1.

"Has Michigan Gone Crazy: Killing School Tax, It Stages a Great Experiment." *Buffalo News* (July 31, 1993): 2.

Hays, R. Allen. "Intergovernmental Lobbying: Toward an Understanding of Priorities." *Western Political Quarterly* 44 (December 1991): 1081–1098.

———. "State-Local Relations in Policy Implementation: The Case of Highway Transportation in Iowa." *Publius: The Journal of Federalism* 18 (Winter 1988): 79–95.

Healy, Patrick. "Looking Back: How the NLC Was Born." *Nation's Cities* (November 1974): 14–18.

Hefner, Paul. "Valley Cityhood: Voters to Decide." *Daily News of Los Angeles* (October 13, 1997), news section.

Henderson, Lenneal J. "Metropolitan Governance: Citizen Participation in the Urban Federation." *National Civic Review* 79 (March/April 1990): 105–117.

Herdt, Timm. "County, Cities Pay Big Bucks to Lobby." *Ventura County Star,* Ventura County, California (December 29, 1997): A-1.

Higgins, Randall. "Rowland Discusses Municipal League," *Chattanooga Times/ Chattanooga Free Press* (June 12, 2002): B-3.

Hill-Holtzman, Nancy. "Cities' PAC Gets More Flak Than Influence in State Capitol." *Los Angeles Times* (June 1, 1999): Metro, B-1.

Hills, Roderick M., Jr. "Dissecting the State: The Use of Federal Law to Free State and Local Officials from State Legislative Control." *Michigan Law Review* 97 (March 1999): 1201–1286.

Hoene, Christopher. "History Voters Not Kind to Property Tax," *Nation's Cities Weekly* (May 14, 2001): 35.

Hoene, Christopher, Michael W. Baldassare, and Michael Shires. "The Development of Counties As Municipal Governments: A Case Study of Los Angeles County in the Twenty-First Century." *Urban Affairs Review* 37 (March 2002): 575–591.

Holden, Matthew. "The Governance of the Metropolis As a Problem in Diplomacy." *Journal of Politics* 26 (1964): 627–647.

Hoppe, Christy. "More Cities Turning to Lobbyists: High Stakes, Short Session Force Move, Officials Say." *Dallas Morning News* (December 26, 1998): A-1.

Horte, Richard H. "State Expenditures with Mandate Reimbursement," in *Coping with Mandates: What Are the Alternatives?* Michael Fix and Daphne Kenyon, eds. Washington, DC: Urban Institute Press, 1990.

Hovey, Harold A. "Analytic Approaches to State-Local Relations," in *A Decade of Devolution: Perspectives on State-Local Relations,* E. Blaine Liner, ed. Washington, DC: Urban Institute Press, 1989, 163–182.

———. "State and Local Tax Policy: Looking Ahead." *Intergovernmental Perspective* 16 (Fall 1990): 5–8.

Hughes, Mark Alan, and Peter M. Vandoren. "Social Policy Through Land Reform: New Jersey's Mount Laurel Controversy." *Political Science Quarterly* 105 (1990) 97–111.

Hunt, Kathy. *Wyoming Home Rule: A Current Status Report.* Cheyenne: Wyoming Association of Municipalities, 1994.

Hunter v. City of Pittsburgh, 207 U.S. (1907) 161, at 178.

Illinois Municipal League Committee on Home Rule, "The Home Rule Experience" in *Illinois Local Government,* Lois M. Pelekoudas, ed. Institute of Government and Public Affairs, University of Illinois, May 1961, 54–59.

Jackson, Peter D., Jeffrey Wasserman, and Kristiana Raube. "The Politics of Anti-smoking Legislation," *Journal of Health Politics, Policy, and Law* 18 (Winter 1993): 787–819.

Jacobs, James. "Taxpayers Bill of Rights or Wrongs?" *Denver Post* (March 29, 1998): J-1.

Jacobson, Peter D., Jeffrey Wasserman, and Kristiana Raube. "The Politics of Anti-smoking Legislation." *Journal of Health Politics, Policy and Law* 18 (Winter 1993): 787–819.

Jefferson, Thomas. Letter to Benjamin Rush, September 23, 1800, reprinted in *The American City: A Documentary History,* Charles N. Glaab, ed. Homewood, IL: Dorsey Press, 1963, 52.

Jeffrey, Blake R, Tanis J. Salant, and Alan L. Boroshok. *County Government Structure: A State-by-State Report.* Washington, DC: National Association of Counties, 1989.

Jenks, Stephen. "County Compliance with North Carolina's Solid-Waste Mandate: A Conflict-Based Model." *Publius: The Journal of Federalism* 24 (Spring 1994): 17–36.

Jennings, John F. "Advice from a Friendly Insider." *The School Administrator* (August 1996): 10.

Johnson, Lyndon B. "Partnership in Public Service," in *Economies and New Ideas for Cities: Proceedings, American Municipal Congress, 1963*. Washington, DC: American Municipal Association, 1963, 19–22.

Johnson, Robert C. "NJ Takeover of Newark Found to Yield Gains, but Lacks Clear Goals." *Education Week* 19 (May 31, 2000): 17.

Johnson, Robert C., and Jessica L. Sandham. "States Increasingly Flexing Their Policy Muscle." *Education Week on the Web* (April 14, 1999).

Johnson, Walter, and Carol Evans, eds. *The Papers of Adlai E. Stevenson*. Boston: Little, Brown, 1973.

Jones, Donald L. *State Municipal Leagues: The First Hundred Years*. Washington, DC: National League of Cities, 1999.

Jones, Victor. "The Organization of a Metropolitan Region." *University of Pennsylvania Law Review* 105 (February 1957): 538–552.

Jones, Victor, David Magleby, and Stanley Scott. "State-Local Relations in California." Working Paper Number 16, Institute of Governmental Studies, University of California, Berkeley, 1975.

Joyce, Phillip G., and Daniel R. Mullins. "The Changing Fiscal Structure of the State and Local Public Sector: The Impact of Tax and Expenditure Limitations." *Public Administration Review* 51 (May/June 1991): 240–253.

Kantor, Paul. *The Dependent City Revisited: The Political Economy of Urban Development and Social Policy*. Boulder, CO: Westview Press, 1995.

Kaplan, Marshall, and Sue O'Brien. *The Governors and the New Federalism*. Boulder, CO: Westview Press, 1991.

Kelly, Janet M. "A New Approach to an Old Problem: State Mandates." *Government Finance Review* 9 (December 1993): 27–29.

———. "Institutional Solutions to Political Problems: The Federal and State Mandate Cost Estimation Process." *State and Local Government Review* 29 (Spring 1997): 90–97.

———."Lessons from the States on Unfunded Mandates." *National Civic Review* 84 (Spring 1995): 133–139.

———. "Mandate Reimbursement Measures in the States." *American Review of Public Administration* 24 (December 1994): 351–376.

———. *State Mandates: Fiscal Notes, Reimbursement, and Anti-Mandate Strategies*. Washington, DC: National League of Cities, 1992.

———. "Unfunded Mandates: The View from the States." *Public Administration Review* 54 (July/August 1994): 405–408.

Kincaid, John. "Metropolitan Governance: Reviving International and Market Analogies." *Intergovernmental Perspective* (Spring 1989): 23–27.

Kirby, Andrew. "A Smoking Gun: Relations Between the State and Local State in the Case of Fire Arms Control." *Policy Studies Journal* 18 (Spring 1990): 739–754.

Kolesar, John N. "The States and Urban Planning and Development," in *The States and the Urban Crisis,* Alan K. Campbell, ed. Englewood Cliffs, NJ: Prentice-Hall, 1970, 114–138.

Kotler, Milton. *Neighborhood Government: The Local Foundations of Political Life*. Indianapolis, IN: Bobbs-Merrill, 1969.

Krane, Dale et al., eds. *Home Rule in America: A Fifty-State Handbook*. Washington, DC: CQ Press, 2001.

Ladd, Helen F. "Big-City Finances," in *Big-City Politics, Governance, and Fiscal Constraints,* George E. Peterson, ed. Washington, DC: Urban Institute Press, 1994, 201–269.

―――. "The State Aid Decision: Changes in State Aid to Local Governments, 1982–1987." *National Tax Journal* (December 1991): 477–496.

Ladd, Helen F., and John Yinger. *America's Ailing Cities.* Baltimore: John Hopkins University Press, 1989.

Landau, Brent W. "Recent Legislation: State Bans on City Gun Lawsuits." *Harvard Journal on Legislation* 37 (Summer 2000): 623–638.

Lawrence, Michael A. "Do 'Creatures of the State' Have Constitutional Rights? Standing for Municipalities to Assert Procedural Due Process Claims Against the State." *Villanova Law Review* 47 (2002): 93–116.

Leach, Richard H. *The Federal Government and Metropolitan Areas.* Cambridge, MA: Harvard University Press, 1960.

Leonard, Lee. "Big-City Democrats; Mayors Demand a Little Respect from Legislature," *Columbus Dispatch* (October 5, 2002): B-6.

Levine, Charles H., and James A. Thurber. "Reagan and the Intergovernmental Lobby: Iron Triangles, Cozy Subsystems and Political Conflict," in *Interest Group Politics,* Allan J. Cigler and Burdett A. Loomis, eds. Washington, DC: Congressional Quarterly Press, 1986, 202–220.

Loftus, Tom. *The Art of Legislative Politics.* Washington, DC: CQ Press, 1994.

Logan, Wayne A. "The Shadow Criminal Law of Municipal Governance." *Ohio State Law Journal* 62 (2001): 1409.

Long, Betty, Deputy Director, Virginia Municipal League. "2002 General Assembly Proved Costly for Local Government." *Virginia Town & City* 37 (May 2002), n.p.

Lorelli, Michael Fitzpatrick. *Special Report: State and Local Property Taxes.* Washington, DC: Tax Foundation, August 2001.

Low, Seth. "An American View of Municipal Government in the United States," in *The American Commonwealth,* James Bryce, ed. New York: Macmillan, 1906, 650–666.

Lyons, W. E., and David Lowery. "Governmental Fragmentation Versus Consolidation: Five Public-Choice Myths About How to Create Informed, Involved, and Happy Citizens." *Public Administration Review* 49 (November–December 1989): 533–543.

Macchiarola, Frank J. "The State and the City," in *Governing New York State: The Rockefeller Years,* Robert H. Connery and Gerald Benjamin, eds. New York: The Academy of Political Science, 1974, 104–118.

Macdonald, Austin F. *American State Government and Administration.* New York: Crowell, 1934.

MacFarquhar, Neil. "Judge Orders a State Takeover of the Newark School District." *New York Times* (April 14, 1995): A-1, B-6.

Mackey, Scott. "Keeping a Lid on Property Taxes." *State Legislatures* (March 1997): 10–11.

―――. *State Programs to Assist Distressed Local Governments.* Denver, CO: National Conference of State Legislators, March 1993.

―――. "Telecommunications and the Tangle of Taxes." *State Legislatures* (February 2000): 22–25.

MacManus, Susan A. "Enough Is Enough: Floridians' Support for Proposition Three Limiting Mandates on Local Government." *State and Local Government Review* 24 (Fall 1992): 103–112.

————. "Mad About Mandates: The Issue of Who Should Pay for What Resurfaces in the 1990s." *Publius: The Journal of Federalism* 21 (Summer 1991): 59–75.

MacVicar, John. "League of American Municipalities." *Annals of the American Academy* 25 (1905): 165–167.

Magleby, David B. "Ballot Initiatives and Intergovernmental Relations in the United States."*Publius: The Journal of Federalism* 28 (Winter 1998): 147–163.

Mahtesian, Charles. "Semi-Vendetta, Cities and the New Republican Order." *Governing* (June 1996): 30–33.

————. "The Endless Struggle Over Open Meetings." *Governing* (December 1997): 48–51.

————. "Whose Schools?" *Governing* (September 1997): 34–38.

Mamet, Sam. *Mandates: Controlling Your Municipality's Destiny.* Denver: Colorado Municipal League, n.d.

Mansfield, Harvey C. "Functions of State and Local Governments," in *The 50 States and Their Local Governments,* James W. Fesler, ed. New York: Knopf, 1967: 104–157.

Marando, Vincent L., and Mavis Mann Reeves. "Counties as Local Governments: Research Issues and Questions." *Journal of Urban Affairs* 13 (1991): 45–53.

————. "Counties: Evolving Local Governments, Reform and Responsiveness." *National Civic Review* 80 (Spring 1991): 222–226.

————. "State Responsiveness and Local Government Reorganization." *Social Science Quarterly* 61 (December 1988): 996–1004.

Martin, Lawrence L., and Ronald C. Nyhan. "Determinants of County Charter Home Rule." *International Journal of Public Administration* 17 (1994): 955–970.

McBain, Howard Lee. *The Law and the Practice of Municipal Home Rule.* New York: Columbia University Press, 1016.

McDermott, Kevin, and Patrick J. Powers. "Illinois Cities Protest Plan to Cut Revenue Sharing." *St. Louis Post-Dispatch* (May 11, 2002) news section, 12.

McDowell, Bruce D. "Advisory Commission on Intergovernmental Relations in 1996: The End of an Era." *Publius: The Journal of Federalism* 27 (Spring 1997): 111–127.

McGoldrick, Joseph D. *Law and Practice of Municipal Home Rule.* New York: AMS Press, 1967.

McLarin, Kimberly J. "Newark School Officials Pitch a Plan for System." *New York Times* (July 26, 1994): B-5.

————. "Schools in Paterson Lagging on Standards, Report Says." *New York Times* (November 4, 1994): B-6.

Melvin, Don. "Who Needs a Charter?" *Atlanta Journal and Constitution* (July 1, 1995): C-2.

Mields, Hugh Jr. "The Property Tax: Local Revenue Mainstay." *Intergovernmental Perspective* (Summer 1993): 16–18.

Mikesell, John L. "Lotteries in State Revenue Systems: Gauging a Popular Revenue Source After 35 Years." *State and Local Review* 33 (Spring 2001): 86–100.

Miles, Rufus E. "The Origin and Meaning of Miles' Law." *Public Administration Review* 38 (September/October 1978): 399–403.

Miller, Donald E., and Patrick A. Pierce. "Lotteries for Education: Windfall or Hoax? *State and Local Government Review* 29 (Winter 1997): 34–42.

Miller, Jim. "The Legislative Process: What We Must Do." *Minnesota Cities* (February 1994): 5.

Missouri v. Jenkins, 495 U.S. 33 (1990).

Mitchell, Allison. "Giuliani Urges New Agenda for Cities: Self-Reliance." *New York Times* (January 12, 1995): B-1.

Mohr, James C. *The Radical Republicans and Reform in New York During Reconstruction*. Ithaca, NY: Cornell University Press, 1973.

Molotch, Harry. "The City As a Growth Machine: Toward a Political Economy of Place." *American Journal of Sociology* 82 (1976): 309–330.

Moore, Paul D. "General-Purpose Aid in New York State: Targeting Issues and Measures." *Publius: The Journal of Federalism* 19 (Spring 1989): 17–31.

Morgan, David. "The Use of Public Funds for Legislative Lobbying and Electoral Campaigning." *Vanderbilt Law Review* 37 (March 1984): 433–472.

Morgan, David R., and Michael W. Hirlinger. "Intergovernmental Service Contracts: A Multivariate Explanation." *Urban Affairs Quarterly* 27 (September 1991): 128–144.

Morgan, David R., and Robert E. England. "State Aid to Cities: A Causal Inquiry." *Publius: The Journal of Federalism* 15 (Spring 1984): 67–82.

Morgan, David R., and Mei-Chiang Shih. "Targeting State and Federal Aid to City Needs." *State and Local Government Review* 23 (Spring 1991): 60–67.

Morial v. Smith & Wesson Corp., 785 So.2d 1 (La. 2001).

Morlan, Robert L., ed. *Capital, Courthouse, and City Hall*. 5th ed. Boston: Houghton Mifflin, 1977.

———. "Local Governments: An Embarrassment of Riches," in *The Fifty States and Their Local Governments,* James W. Fesler, ed. New York: Knopf, 1967, 505–549.

Mott, Rodney L. *Home Rule for America's Cities*. Chicago: American Municipal Association, 1949.

Mueller, Keith J. "Explaining Variation in State Assistance Programs to Local Communities: What to Expect and Why." *State and Local Review* 19 (Fall 1987): 101–107.

"Municipal Annexation Authority Faces Renewed Attacks," TML Online (1998): 10.

Natale, Jo Anna. "Documenting the State's Case Against Paterson." *The American School Board Journal* 181 (December 1994): 26.

———. "In 20 States a Takeover is 'The Ultimate Audit.'" *American School Board Journal* 181 (December 1994): 24–25.

Nathan, Richard P. "State and Local Governments Under Federal Grants: Toward a Predictive Theory." *Political Science Quarterly* 98 (Spring 1983): 47–57.

National Governors' Association. *Reflections on Being Governor.* Washington, DC: National Governors' Association, 1981.

National League of Cities. *Annual Survey of City Fiscal Conditions.* Washington, DC: National League of Cities, 1999.

Neiman, Max, and Catherine Lovell. "Federal and State Mandating: A First Look at the Mandate Terrain." *Administration and Society* 14 (November 1982): 343–372.

———. "Mandating as a Policy Issue—The Definitional Problem." *Policy Studies Journal* (Spring 1981): 667–680.

Newman, Meredith, and Nicholas Lovrich. "The Hearing of Local Government Interests in State Legislatures: The Effects of Prior Service in City or County Government; a Research Note on Preliminary Findings." Paper prepared for delivery at the 1995 annual meeting of the Pacific Northwest Political Science Association, Bellingham, WA, October 1995.

"News from the Nation's Counties," *County News* (March 27, 1995): 22.

Nice, David C. *Federalism: The Politics of Intergovernmental Relations.* New York: St. Martin's Press, 1987.

Norris, Donald F. "Prospects for Regional Governance Under the New Regionalism: Economic Imperatives Versus Political Impediments." *Journal of Urban Affairs* 23 (2001): 575–591.

"Note: Missed Opportunity: Urban Fiscal Crises and Financial Control Boards." *Harvard Law Review* 110 (January 1997): 733–750.

"Notes: City Government in the State Courts," *Harvard Law Review* 78 (1965): 1596–1616.

Novak, Christopher A. "Agriculture's New Environmental Battleground: The Preemption of County Livestock Regulations." *Drake Journal of Agricultural Law* 5 (Winter 2000): 429–469.

Novinson, John. "Unfunded Mandates: A Closed Chapter?" *Public Management* 77 (July 1995): 17–19.

Oakerson, Ronald J., and Roger B. Parks. "Metropolitan Organization: St. Louis and Allegheny County," *Intergovernmental Perspective* 17 (Summer 1991): 27–30, 34.

Oates, Wallace E. "Local Property Taxation: An Assessment." *Land Lines* (May 1999). Published online by Lincoln Institute of Land Policy, www.lincolnist.edu.

Orum, Anthony. *City Building in America.* Boulder, CO: Westview Press, 1995.

Ostrom, Vincent, Charles Tiebout, and Robert Warren. "The Organization of Government in Metropolitan Areas: A Theoretical Inquiry." *American Political Science Review* 55 (December 1961): 831–842.

O'Toole, Daniel E., and Brian Stipak. "Coping with State Tax and Expenditure Limitations: The Oregon Experience." *State and Local Government Review* 30 (Winter 1998): 9–16.

Owens, David W. "Local Government Authority to Implement Smart Growth Programs: Dillon's Rule, Legislative Reform, and the Current State of Affairs in North Carolina." *Wake Forest Law Review* 35 (Fall 2000): 671–705.

Pagano, M. A. "State-Local Relations in the 1990s." *Annals American Academy of Political Science* 509 (May 1990): 94–105.

Palmer, Jamie L., and Greg Lindsey. "Classifying State Approaches to Annexation." *State and Local Government Review* 33 (Winter 2001): 60–73.

Parks, Roger B. "Counties in the Federal System: The Interlocal Connection." *Intergovernmental Perspective* 17 (Winter 1991): 29–32.

Paul, Amy Cohen. *Future Challenges, Future Opportunities: The Final Report of the ICMA Future Visions Consortium.* Washington, DC: International City/County Management Association, 1991.

Peirce, Neal. "Angry States Left with Tab for Social Services." *Washington Post* syndication, August 1989.

———. "Maryland's 'Smart Growth' Law: A National Model?" *Nation's Cities Weekly* (April 28, 1997): 5.

Pelissero, John P. "State Aid and City Needs: An Examination of Residual State Aid to Large Cities." *Journal of Politics* 46 (August 1984): 916–935.

People ex rel. LeRoy v. Hurlbut (24 Mich. 44, 1871).

Pertman, Adam. "Bridgeport Mayor Files for City's Bankruptcy." *Boston Globe* (June 8, 1991): Metro section, 25.

Peterson, Paul E. *City Limits.* Chicago: University of Chicago Press, 1981.

Pettinari, David G. "Michigan's Latest Tax Limitation Battle: A Tale of Environmental Regulation, Capital Infrastructure, and the 'Will of the People.'" *University of Detroit Mercy Law Review* 77 (Fall 1999): 83–154.

Plunkitt, George Washington. "New York Is Pie for the Hayseeds," in *Plunkitt of Tammany Hall.* William L. Riordon, ed. New York: E. P. Dutton, 1963, 21–24.

Porter, Douglas R. "Reinventing Growth Management for the 21st Century." *William and Mary Environmental Law and Policy Review* 23 (Fall 1999): 705–738.

———. "State Growth Management: The Intergovernmental Experiment." *Pace Law Review* 13 (Fall 1993): 481–503.

Portner, Jessica. "State Takeover of Troubled Schools Debated." *Mercury News* (November 24, 2001) A-1.

Posner, Paul L. *The Politics of Unfunded Mandates: Whither Federalism?* Washington, DC: Georgetown University Press, 1998.

Press, Charles. "State Governments in Urban Areas: Petty Tyrants, Meddlers, or Something Else?" *Urban Interest* 2 (1980): 12–21.

Proceeding of the American Municipal Congress, 1962. Washington, DC: American Municipal Association, n.d.

Property Tax Commission, "Report of Recommendations to Governor Christine Todd Whitman," September 1998.

Public Opinion Online. Roper Center at University of Connecticut.

Rankin, Bill. "Fate of Atlanta Gun Suit Up to High Court." *Atlanta Constitution* (September 20, 2000): B-1.

Reagan, Michael D., and John G. Sanzone. *The New Federalism.* New York: Oxford University Press, 1981.

Reecer, Marcia. "Battling State Takeover." *American School Board Journal* 175 (November 1988): 21–25.

Reed, B. J. "The Changing Role of Local Advocacy in National Politics. *Journal of Urban Affairs* 5 (Fall 1983): 287–298.

Reed, Thomas H. "Comments on the Advisory Commission Report As a Whole," in *Government in Metropolitan Areas: Commentaries on a Report by the Advisory Commission on Intergovernmental Relations.* Washington, DC: U.S. Government Printing Office, 1962, 1–5.

Reeves, Mavis Mann. "Galloping Intergovernmentalization As a Factor in State Management," *State Government* 54 (1981): 102–108.

Reichley, A. James. "The Political Containment of the Cities," in *The States and the Urban Crisis,* Alan K. Campbell, ed. Englewood Cliffs, NJ: Prentice-Hall, 1970, 169–195.

Reid, Karla. "'Comeback' from State Control Means Solvency for Compton." *Education Week* 20 (January 31, 2001): 1, 14, 15.

Reuss, Henry S. *Revenue-Sharing: Crutch or Catalyst for State and Local Governments?* New York: Praeger, 1970.

Reynolds v. Sims, 377 US.S. 533 (1964).

Rich, Michael J. "Distributive Politics and the Allocation of Federal Grants," *American Political Science Review* 83 (March 1989): 198–213.

Richmond, Todd. "Shared Revenue Hot Button for Budget Repair Lobbyists." Associated Press State and Local Wire (August 21, 2002), n.p.

Rimbach, Jean. "Paterson Schools Now in State Hands."*Record* (Hackensack, NJ, August 8, 1991): D-9.

Rinard, Amy. "State Lawmakers Cool to More Local Funding." *Milwaukee Journal Sentinel* (April 9, 1999): 1.

———. "Kettl Panel Work All for Naught," *Milwaukee Journal Sentinel* (May 20, 2001): 02Z.

Rosenthal, Alan. *The Third House: Lobbyists and Lobbying in the States.* Washington, DC: CQ Press, 1993.

Rusk, David. *Cities Without Suburbs.* Washington, DC: Woodrow Wilson Center Press, 1995.

Saiger, Aaron. "Note: Disestablishing Local School Districts as a Remedy for Educational Inadequacy." *Columbia Law Review* 99 (November 1999): 1830–1870.

Salant, Tanis J. "Shifting Roles in County-State Relations," in *County Governments in an Era of Change,* David R. Berman, ed. Westport, CT: Greenwood Press, 1993, 107–122.

Salmore, Barbara G., and Stephen A. Salmore. *New Jersey Politics and Government.* 2d ed. Lincoln: University of Nebraska Press, 1998.

Sayre, Wallace S., and Herbert Kaufman. *Governing New York City.* New York: Russell Sage Foundation, 1960.

Sbragia, Alberta M. *Death Wish: Entrepreneurial Cities, U.S. Federalism, and Economic Development.* Pittsburgh: University of Pittsburgh Press, 1996.

Schaller, Lyle E. "Home Rule—A Critical Appraisal." *Political Science Quarterly* 76 (September 1961): 402–415.

Schatt, Paul. "The Bottom Line." *Phoenix Gazette* (January 10, 1993): G-2.

Schneider, Craig. "Regional Solutions Gaining." *Atlanta Journal and the Atlanta Constitution* (January 30, 2000): A-1.

Schneider, Mark. "Intermunicipal Competition, Budget-Maximizing Bureaucrats, and Levels of Suburban Competition." *American Journal of Political Science* 33 (August 1989): 612–628.

———. *The Competitive City: The Political Economy of Suburbia.* Pittsburgh, PA: University of Pittsburgh Press, 1989.

Schragger, Richard C., "The Limits of Localism." *Michigan Law Review* 100 (November, 2001): 371–472.

Shaffer, Robert M. "Comment: Unfunded State Mandates and Local Governments." *University of Cincinnati Law Review* 64 (Spring 1996): 1057–1088.

Shepardson, David, and Brian Harmon. "Rehire Board, Suit Demands: Coalition Attempts to Reinstate Elected School Trustees." *Detroit News* (September 14, 1999): D-1.

Short, Raymond S. "Municipalities and the Federal Government." *Annals of the American Academy of Political and Social Science* 207 (January 1940): 44–53.

Shultz, William J. "Limitations on State and Local Borrowing Powers." *Annals* 181 (September 1935): 118–124.

Smith, Harold B. "Associations of Cities and Municipal Officials." *Urban Government,* vol. 1, Part IV of the Report of the Urbanism Committee to the National Resources Committee, Washington, DC: G.P.O., 1939, 181–211.

Sokolow, Alvin D. "State-Rules and the County-City Arena: Competition for Land and Taxes in California's Central Valley." *Publius: The Journal of Federalism* 23 (Winter 1993): 53–69.

———. "The Changing Property Tax and State-Local Relations." *Publius: The Journal of Federalism* 28 (Winter 1998): 165–188.

Southern Burlington County NAACP v. Township of Mount Laurel, 336 A2d 713, (NJ 1975).

Spindler, Charles. "Alabama," in *Home Rule in America: A Fifty-State Handbook,* Dale Krane, Platon N. Rigos and Melvin B. Hill, Jr., eds. Washington, DC: CQ Press, 2001: 23–32.

Stabrowski, Donald J. "Oregon's Increasing Use of the Initiative and Its Effect on Budgeting." *Comparative State Politics* 20 (February 1999): 31–45.

———. "Oregon and Measure Five: One Year Later." *Comparative State Politics* (October 8, 1993): 32.

Starkey, Danielle. "Stung by a Grab of Property Taxes by the State, County Governments Are Fighting Back." *California Journal* (August 1993): 21–23.

Starn, Michael L. "Tax Limitation in Various States." *Current Municipal Problems* 23 (1997): 523–528.

State and Local Government Commission of Ohio. *Unfunded Mandates: Regaining Control at the Local Level.* Columbus: State and Local Government Commission of Ohio, December 8, 1994.

State and Local Source Book 2000. Supplement to *Governing Magazine.*

"States Take Lead in Mandate Relief." *State Trends Bulletin* (February/March 1996): 8.

"State of the Cities: 1999, Special Report." *Nation's Cities Weekly* (January 25, 1999): 5–9.

Stein, Robert M. "The Allocation of State Aid to Local Governments: An Examination of Interstate Variation," in U.S. Advisory Commission on Intergovernmental Relations, *State and Local Roles in the Federal System.* Washington, DC: G.P.O., 1982, 203–226.

———. "The Targeting of State Aid: A Comparison of Grant Delivery Mechanisms." *Urban Interest* 2 (1981): 47–60.

Stein, Robert M., and Keith E. Hamm. "A Comparative Analysis of the Targeting Capacity of State and Federal Intergovernmental Aid Allocations: 1977, 1982." *Social Science Quarterly* 68 (September 1987): 447–477.

———. "Explaining State Aid Allocations: Targeting Within Universalism." *Social Science Quarterly* 75 (September 1994): 524–540.

Stephens, G. Ross, and Nelson Wikstrom. *Metropolitan Government and Governance: Theoretical Perspectives, Empirical Analysis, and the Future.* New York: Oxford University Press, 1999.

Stewart, D. Michael. "Counties in the Federal System: The Washington Connection." *Intergovernmental Perspective* 17 (Winter 1991): 18–20.

Stewart, Michael J. "Growth and Its Implications: An Evaluation of Tennessee's Growth Management Plan." *Tennessee Law Review* 67 (Summer 2000): 983–1017.

Straayer, John A. "Direct Democracy and Fiscal Mayhem." *Comparative State Politics* (February 1993): 6–12.

Strawley, George. "Politicians in Philadelphia, Pittsburgh Hit a Rough Spot in Harrisburg." The Associated Press State and Local Wire, June 27, 2001, n.p.

"Strengthening Public Schools." *Nation's Cities Weekly* (July 1, 1996): 4.

Stutz, John C. *Proceedings, First and Second Conferences: The American Municipal Association and the Municipal League Compendium.* Lawrence, KS: The American Municipal Association, 1926.

Swarthout, John M., and Ernest R. Bartley. *Principles and Problems of State and Local Government.* New York: Oxford University Press, 1958.

Swope, Christopher. "Fighting the Wage War on Local Turf." *Governing* (June 1996): 35–37.

————. "Power to the People?" *Governing* (January 2001): 36–39.

————. "Rent Control: Invisible No More." *Governing* (January 1998): 28–29.

Syed, Anwar Hussain. *The Political Theory of American Local Government.* New York: Random House, 1966.

Tabb, William K. *The Long Default: New York City and the Urban Fiscal Crisis.* New York: Monthly Review Press, 1982.

Taft, Charles P. "The Challenge of City-State Relations," in *Proceedings, American Municipal Congress, 1962.* Washington, DC: American Municipal Association, n.d., 20–26.

Teaford, Jon C. *The Municipal Revolution in America: Origins of Modern Urban Government, 1650–1825.* Chicago: University of Chicago Press, 1973.

Telford v. Thurston 95 Wn. App. 149, 974 P.2d 886 (Wash. App. 1999).

Tewel, Kenneth J. "The New Jersey Takeover Legislation: Help or Hindrance to Improvement in Troubled School Districts?" *Urban Review* 23 (December 1991): 217–229.

"Text of Judge Robert B. Krupansky's Order for State Takeover," *The Cleveland Plain Dealer* (March 9, 1995) 4B–5B.

Thomas, Clive S., and Ronald J. Hrebenar. "Interest Group Power in the Fifty States: Trends Since the Late 1970s." *Comparative State Politics* 20 (August 1999): 3–16.

Thomas, James D., and William H. Stewart, eds. *Alabama Government and Politics.* Lincoln: University of Nebraska Press, 1988.

Thomas, John P. "Financing County Government: An Overview." *Intergovernmental Perspective* 17 (Winter 1991): 10–13.

Thompson, Joel A., and G. Larry Mays. "The Impact of State Standards and Enforcement Procedures on Local Jail Performance." *Policy Studies Review* (Autumn 1988): 55–71.

Tiebout, Charles. "A Pure Theory of Local Expenditure." *Journal of Political Economy* 64 (October 1956): 416–435.

Tocqueville, Alexis de. *Democracy in America,* trans., Henry Reeve. New York: D. Appleton, 1899.

Todd, Barbara. "Counties in the Federal System: The State Connection." *Intergovernmental Perspective* 17 (Winter 1991): 21–25.

Turner, Robyne S. "Intergovernmental Growth Management: A Partnership Framework for State-Local Relations." *Publius: The Journal of Federalism* 20 (Summer 1990): 79–95.

"Unfunded Mandates Rank as Highest Priority Concern of Local Officials." *Nation's Cities Weekly* (January 10, 1994): 8.

U.S. Advisory Commission on Intergovernmental Relations. *Changing Public Attitudes on Government and Taxes.* Washington, DC: G.P.O., various years.

———. *City Financial Emergencies: The Intergovernmental Dimension.* Washington, DC: G.P.O., July 1973.

———. *Local Government Autonomy: Needs for State Constitutional, Statutory, and Judicial Clarification.* Washington, DC: G.P.O., October 1993.

———. *Mandates: Cases in State-Local Relations.* Washington, DC: G.P.O., September 1990.

———. *Metropolitan Organization: The Allegheny County Case.* Washington, DC: G.P.O., February 1992.

———. *State and Local Roles in the Federal System.* Washington, DC: G.P.O., 1982.

———. *State Laws Governing Local Government Structure and Administration.* Washington, DC: G.P.O., March 1993.

———. *State Mandating of Local Expenditures.* Washington, DC: G.P.O., 1978.

———. *Tax and Expenditure Limits on Local Governments.* Washington, DC: G.P.O., March 1995.

———. *The Organization of Local Public Economies.* Washington, DC: G.P.O., December 1987.

———. *The State of State-Local Revenue Sharing.* Washington, D.C: G.P.O., 1980.

U.S. Census Bureau, Federal Aid to States for Fiscal Year 2001. Washington, DC: G.P.O., April 2002.

U.S. General Accounting Office. *Legislative Mandates: State Experiences Offer Insights for Federal Action.* Washington, DC: G.P.O., 1988.

Urban Land Institute. "The Effect of the Collapse of Commercial Property Values on Local Government Revenues and Tax Burdens," n.d.

Vanlandingham, Kenneth E. "Municipal Home Rule in the United States." *William and Mary Law Review* 10 (Winter 1968): 269–314.

Virginia Legislature, Joint Legislative Audit and Review Commission. *Intergovernmental Mandates and Financial Aid to Local Governments.* House Document no. 56. Richmond, VA, 1992.

Von Kampen, Todd. "State Controls Few Assessors." *Omaha World-Herald* (October 25, 1999): 9.

Walker, David B. "Intergovernmental Relations and the Well-Governed City: Cooperation, Confrontation, Clarification." *National Civic Review* 75 (March/April 1986): 65–87.

———. "Snow White and the 17 Dwarfs: From Metro Cooperation to Governance." *National Civic Review* 76 (January/February 1987): 14–28.

———. *The Rebirth of Federalism: Slouching Toward Washington.* Chatham, NJ: Chatham House, 1995, 250.

Wallace, Allan D. "Governance and the Civic Infrastructure of Metropolitan Regions." *National Civic Review* (Spring 1993): 125–139.

Wallace, S. C. *State Administrative Supervision over Cities in the United States.* New York: Columbia University Press, 1928.

Walters, Jonathan. "Lobbying for the Good Old Days." *Governing* (June 1991): 33–37.

————. "The Property Rights Bust." *Governing* (June 1999): 38–41.

————. "Reinventing the Federal System." *Governing* (January 1994): 49–53.

Walters, Lawrence C., and Gary C. Cornia. "The Implications of Utilities and Tele-communications for Local Finance." *State and Local Government Review* 29 (Fall 1997): 172–187.

Walters, Steven. "Kettl Plan a Victim of Budget Wars; Lauded Program for Re-form Has No Political Constituency." *Milwaukee Journal Sentinel* (May 16, 2001): B-1.

Walton, Judy. "Cities Join Push for Tax Reform." *Chattanooga Times/Chattanooga Free Press* (October 10, 1999): C-1.

Ward, D. Michael, and Lewis L. House. "A Theory of Behavioral Power." *Journal of Conflict Resolution* 32 (1988): 3–36.

Wasson, David. "House Growth Management Plan Too Radical for Governor, Oth-ers." *Tampa Tribune* (March 24, 2000): Metro section, 6.

Watts, Vivian E. "Federal Anti-Crime Efforts: The Fallout on State and Local Gov-ernments." *Intergovernmental Perspective* (Winter 1992): 35–38.

Waugh, William L. Jr. "States, Counties, and the Questions of Trust and Capacity." *Publius: The Journal of Federalism* 18 (1988): 189–198.

Waugh, William L. Jr., and Gregory Streib. "County Officials' Perceptions of Local Capacity and State Responsiveness After the First Reagan Term." *Southeastern Political Review* 18 (Spring 1990): 27–50.

Weiland, Paul S. "Preemption of Local Efforts to Protect the Environment: Implica-tions for Local Government Officials." *Virginia Environmental Law Journal* 18 (1999): 467–506.

Weissmann, Dan. "State Takeovers, Painful but Productive." *Catalyst* (March 1993): 7–8.

Wennberg, Jeffrey. "Cooperation, Not Coercion, Will Solve Drinking Water Cri-sis." *Nation's Cities Weekly* (April 18, 1994): 2.

West, Ben. "The Effect of Reapportionment on State Actions," in *Proceedings, American Municipal Congress, 1962*. Washington, DC: American Municipal Association, n.d., 48–53.

"Why County Revenues Vary: State Laws and Local Conditions Affecting County Finance." Report prepared by Legislative Analyst's Office, State of California, May 7, 1999, 1.

Williams, Joan C. "The Constitutional Vulnerability of American Local Govern-ment: The Politics of City Status in American Law." *Wisconsin Law Review* (1986): 83–153.

Wilson, Laval S. "Takeover: The Paterson Story." *American School Board Journal* 181 (December 1994): 22–26.

Wolman, Harold, and Michael Goldsmith. "Local Authority As a Meaningful Ana-lytic Concept." *Urban Affairs Quarterly* 26 (September 1990): 3–27.

Wong, Kenneth K. "Fiscal Support for Education in the American States: The Parity-to-Dominance View Examined." *American Journal of Education* 97 (Au-gust 1989): 329–357.

Woodwell, Jamie. *The State of America's Cities*. Washington, DC: National League of Cities, 1998.

Wright, Deil S. *Understanding Intergovernmental Relations*. Pacific Grove, CA: Brooks/Cole, 1982, 1988.

Yates, Douglas. *The Ungovernable City: The Politics of Urban Problems and Policymaking.* Cambridge, MA: MIT Press, 1977.

Young, Charles. "How States' Mandates Make Local Taxes Go Up." *Sunday Record* (June 19, 1994): NJ-1, NJ-2.

Zelinsky, Edward A. "The Unsolved Problem of the Unfunded Mandate." *Ohio Northern University Law Review* 23 (1997): 741–781.

————. "Unfunded Mandates, Hidden Taxation, and the Tenth Amendment: On Public Choice, Public Interest, and Public Services." *Vanderbilt Law Review* 46 (November 1993): 1355–1415.

Zimmerman, Joseph F. "Some Remedies Suggested for State Mandated Expenditure Distortions." *Current Municipal Problems* 21 (1994): 93–110.

————. *State-Local Relations: A Partnership Approach.* 2d ed. New York: Praeger, 1995.

Zumwalt, James W. "The Local Government Role: Home Rule and Short Ballots," in *Proceedings: A Symposium on the Alabama Constitution.* Center for Governmental Services, Auburn University, February 15, 1996, n.p.

Index

About the Author

David R. Berman is a professor of political science, Arizona State University. He has written extensively in the area of state and local politics. This book represents a blending and extension of numerous book chapters and articles he has written over the last several years plus some new research activity, particularly of a theoretical, legal, and historical nature.